Thank you for buying this book. For each copy sold £2 will go to support the work of The Princes Trust.
To find out more about the work of The Princes Trust, go to www.princes-trust.org.uk
If you like this book, please tell others!

Thank you for buying this book. For each copy sold £2 will go to support the work of

# WILL

## ANDREW RIGBY

Copyright © 2012 Andrew Rigby
All rights reserved.

Copyright © 2012 ANDREW RIGBY
All rights reserved.

ISBN: 1468171984
ISBN 13: 9781468171983

*This book is dedicated to my beautiful wife, Helen, without whose encouragement it would never have been written, and to our two children, Hannah and Thomas.*

*Thanks also to Neville Cardus, Patrick Collins and John Cooper Clarke, all of whose work encouraged me to have a go.*

# Prologue

"How much?"
"For one egg?"
"How many million?"

"Quick, someone lend me a pen so I can put two more noughts on these arse wipes they call money. Arse wipes, that's all they're fit for. Actually, cheaper than buying some. Now then ladies and gentlemen, what am I bid for three arse wipes? Do I hear ten million? Buy now while stocks last. In ten minutes you know you'll only be able to afford one!"

As Helmut Sandler launched into his extravagant cameo, the frown on Hilda Morten's brow deepened. Peter Jurgensen grasped the hand of his wife more tightly. Michael Schwartz nudged his former comrade from the trenches, Rudi Hensmann, in the ribs. He pointed to his mouth, bereft of all but two teeth.

"Two pickle stabbers. All I'm left with now. Barbed wire soup. That's what caused these. Remember Rudi? Month old horse meat. Rock hard vegetables? Remember how the fat used to float on the top? What would you give now for a bowl of gorgeous, succulent, nutritious, barbed wire soup?"

"Well, old friend, maybe you buy the vegetables and I'll provide the horsemeat."

"I remember when I could afford one box of matches."

"A surgeon, that's what I should be. I can slice these cement block loaves they call bread as thin as writing paper."

"Writing paper? No point- guess how much I paid for a stamp the other day? Fifteen million? Nowhere near."

As Freuntz guarded the entrance to The Hoffmann Emporium, he lowered one arm to allow nineteen year old mother to be, Christe Pries, to squeeze past. Immediately the anecdotes ceased and Christe was besieged by questions.

"Christe, Christe- any cooking oil left?"
"How much for onions?"

"Onions? How many millions do you think you'll need for them? Tell you what; I'll go halves with you."

Christe finally managed to escape from the jostling crowd. Her non-committal shrug, and slightly shifty smile, indicated both the guilt and relief she felt that she had actually been able to buy something. Immediately, the calculations began. Huge wads of notes were removed from dolls' prams, ancient shopping bags and the depths of threadbare jackets. Frau Gafner, a broad shouldered, heavy browed divorcee, had made full use of her voluminous underwear. A rough and ready calculation informed the decision as to whether it was worth queuing any longer. It was already six p.m..

"Only three allowed in at once. Christ, at this rate that's another hour at the earliest." Shoulders sagged.

"And then they might not have what you want." Frowns deepened.

"And even if they do, I bet we can't afford it. The price of anything they might have will have gone up since this morning." Peter led his wife away.

"Never mind this morning. It doesn't matter when you start. By the time you get in you can bet things will be way more expensive than when you began."

"This morning, that's when I did start queuing. Like every morning." Heads nodded in agreement.

"One thing, though. This money really burns well. I managed to make some stew. Twelve bundles, or so. The fire was really roaring. Didn't have any meat, though. More like soup, really. Well, it would have been soup- with some more vegetables in." Four more detached themselves from the queue, and drifted away in despair.

By eight, it was time for the last customer to leave. Frau Seeke had waited patiently since noon. However, once inside, the Hoffmann shelves were bare, other than for things which were too expensive, or she couldn't possibly use. She refused, as a matter of pride, to barter on the black market like so many.

On each occasion she seemed more wizened, shrunken and defeated by the daily grind of simply surviving. But something kept her coming. Hunger was the obvious answer, but Freuntz felt it was something inside her, a stubborn conviction that things would sort themselves out, if only she could endure.

Her arthritic gait caused her clogs to scrape on the cobbles and dusk was falling. At least it was September and no one had frozen to death whilst waiting, as had happened in Stellgahle in February. On that occasion a newly widowed mother of three had simply given up the ghost, curled up in the snow, and it had been half an hour before anyone noticed.

Freuntz could watch her as she shuffled down the long, straight street leading away from the medieval quarter. The streets were virtually deserted by now as there was so little to spend money on. Two figures emerged from the shadows and quickened their stride. Within moments they were behind her.

He yelled a warning to Frau Seeke. He set off. It was already too late. Before Freuntz could intervene, Frau Seeke was bundled over, and, after a manic flurry of whirling activity, the eruption of paper slowly began fluttering back to earth, covering the cobbles. The two figures darted down a side street.

As Freuntz finally reached the diminutive figure, it was clear to him what had happened. The old woman was in tears as she sobbed,

"My bag, my purse, gone. Gone. They've taken my …" before another wave of sobs engulfed her. Freuntz cradled her in his arms and surveyed the scene. Banknotes lay in bundles everywhere. Others were still being carried on the breeze, their denominations a mocking indictment of those who put their faith in paper money. Millions? Billions? of marks lay strewn across the street. The two thieves had worked out that that they were worthless. They were correct. A real item could at least be bartered.

Democracy for you, thought Freuntz, ruefully. Something has got to be done. It was September 25th, 1923 and the exchange rate for one dollar was now 98,860,000 marks.

# PART ONE

Northern France and Germany,
1918-1923

# CHAPTER ONE

Only the discipline instilled by hours of training kept his eyes fixed on the distant horizon. This was different, though. This was retreat, the latest one. Had the previous four years of sacrifice been in vain?

Amidst a cacophony of tramping feet, barked orders and barely subdued oaths, Freuntz was determined to focus on the lights of St Valery, winking seductively on the horizon as dusk fell. It would offer balm for his aching feet, relief from the pain in his shoulders, rapidly reddening from the weight of his equipment, and a chance to remove his saturated greatcoat.

"Sod it and keep marching" was the philosophy which had sustained armies down the ages. The low drone alerted him. Just as he turned to encourage his rawest recruits, a thunderous rush of air was followed by the high pitched shriek of engines. Machine gun bullets splattered the gravel. Ricochets clanged against the wall amidst the frenzied shrieks to "Get in the fucking ditch now!" The raid was over in an instant, the fleeting image of the roundels of the French planes seared in his memory forever.

The French, the fucking French, thought Freuntz, as his frightened men began to regain their composure. Instinct told him to remain still until the danger had passed, but the weight pressing down on him was leaving him little option. He was struggling to breathe as he tried to lever himself free, refusing to accept that it could be fatigue. The warm liquid trickling down his face alarmed him. Was he being pissed on? The salty taste told him otherwise. With a grunting, upward heave, the shattering realisation dawned.

There, eyes lolling and breath rasping, was Meinke, Oswald Meinke, boyhood friend, team mate, and comrade in arms since 1914.The same Meinke whose carotid artery was gushing, his life blood draining away with each second of inaction. Freuntz felt his hands turn to putty, the sodden gauze of the field dressing unyielding, despite his frantic efforts.

"You can't die now, you stupid bastard!" shrieked Freuntz. Finally the dressing was thrust into the breach. It was the lips which told him it was over, the final guttural grunt no longer answered by the reflex rise and fall of the rib cage. Freuntz thrust the dressing even more forcefully into the wound, as if the effort itself would reverse the sequence of events. He had become familiar with the lottery of life during the previous four years, and rarely gave it a second thought. But now he was staring, transfixed. Harsh reality quickly intruded.

Meinke was just one of five who bled to death on the road to St Valery as the light began to fade. Freuntz knew all eyes were on him. He straightened up and began to bark out the orders. The corpses were heaved onto a waiting wagon and covered with potato sacks which were then, in turn, sat upon by the wounded.

Once the march resumed, the conviction that he had let Meinke bleed to death added an edge of shame to the cocktail of emotions which were beginning to corrode even his martial spirit. Retreat, retreat, and all at the hands of the fucking French.

As a good corporal should, Friedrich Schleime knew when to take the reins of command. He marched backwards and forwards along the column, cursing and cajoling. The briefest of discussions decided that it would be Groener and Mandel who would be responsible for the crates.

They were approaching St Valery, and soon it would be dark.

✲ ✲ ✲

Blonde made them think of home, made them remember, made them forget, meant that they paid more, thought Sophie. As she finished applying the last of her depleted make up collection, the realisation gnawed at her as she examined herself in the mirror. Things were changing and about to change even faster. For the last week the clattering looms in the machine room had been accompanied by a more sinister percussion, the sounds of muffled explosions.

At first, she and Natalie had exchanged a series of quizzical glances, but the explanation did not require any grasp of military strategy. Equipment was being destroyed. The Germans were leaving, the Germans were retreating, the Germans were beaten. The quiet of the supply base was gone for ever, as the field grey columns moved through the village, only this time they were going east.

For Sophie life was going to become more complex. Her meagre wages at the mill had been supplemented by her activities at La Pigalle, the biggest estaminet in the village. The last twelve months had meant that for three nights a week she was on offer, doe eyed and available. She knew the sentimental songs, she had learnt to tolerate the aroma of overcooked offal which passed for food, but above all she knew how the boys, as she called them, yearned for affection and longed for home. Blonde made it easier.

But blonde might not be the asset it had once been. The hissing of "Boche bitch" was an everyday occurrence as the inhabitants of St Valery prepared themselves for retribution and the dispensing of arbitrary justice. It was coming to all who had embraced occupation rather too enthusiastically, as opposed to the ox like acceptance of the vagaries of life which was a feature of so many rural communities.

How to respond? For Sophie there was only one answer.

"Never take a backward step," had been drummed into her for as long as she could remember. It accounted for the countless arguments about the injustices meted out to her at school. It helped her confront the constant sniping of her parents, whose creed, ironically, this was.

She would be there tonight. After all, how many more nights might there be? This was a night for the last of the rouge, the remnants of the lipstick and her special underwear.

## Chapter Two

Left behind in the gathering gloom, Groener and Mandel, two of the Three Musketeers, both farm boys, grimaced as they realised they had drawn the short straw. They not only had to locate the eight special crates from the dozens scattered all over the road, but get them to the branch line at Chemeny before seven. They had far more pressing arrangements.

Orders were orders though. Eventually the crates were located and loaded.

"What do you reckon?"

"I'm fucked if I know. Farm chemicals, maybe? Who can read words that long any way, even in broad daylight? There's a clanging inside, so something is metal." Dusk was falling and time was short.

Their eyes met, their shoulders shrugged. With a couple of tugs on the reins they were under way. In no time they were overtaking their comrades, who launched a volley of abuse at the smirking pair. Groener simply extended his arm, and languidly raised two fingers. Heller pointed at an imaginary watch, and gave a knowing wink.

✭ ✭ ✭

St Valery had been by passed by Von Moltke's sweeping assault in 1914 and had escaped many of the ravages of war. Once through the centre of the town, the road was relatively free of traffic.

"Can't be far now, there's a bridge that's the half-way point," said Groener, as Mandel attempted to slow the galloping mare, once the gradient became less pronounced. "There it is. Give the nag some lash, you woman, or we'll never be back in time for you know what," he added, with a throaty chuckle.

No sooner had the words been uttered than a shriek of pain, accompanied by a sickening crack, saw the wagon judder to a halt as the mare collapsed and the pair were pitched headlong. Luckily for Groener he was thrown forward onto the shoulders of the writhing animal, whilst Mandel was thrown into a pothole even deeper than the one which had brought the mare, and hence their mission, to grief.

Once they had regained their breath, their feet and their sense of urgency, the first decision was a simple one. With his pistol pressed against its temple, Mandel blasted the gallant creature out of its misery.

"Now what? There was no way we can get to fucking Chemeny, or wherever he said. Can't just leave them either."

"You're right for once," said Mandel, replacing his gun in its holster. "We are sure to be marching this way tomorrow, and even if a thousand crates were by the road you can bet the 'old man' will spot ours."

The moon emerged from behind the clouds and the temperature began to drop.

"What do we do now then? Which crate is which?"

"Just fucking find those eight. One crate looks just like another so let's find the eight and leave the rest. And who can identify one more dead horse?"

The moon emerged, and below the huge rock they could see that the sloping sides of the valley gradually flattened. By the side of the river itself, a mixture of scrub foliage and low rocks fringed the river bank. Sweating and cursing, they negotiated the steep bank twice, and placed each of the crates carefully in the undergrowth. But time was slipping by.

"This fucking wood makes them twice as heavy as the others!" spat Groener, as they covered the crate with branches. "This is going to take for ever. Listen, I've got it."

They scrambled back up the bank, and after pausing with hands on knees to regain their breath, Groener outlined his plan. "Get hold of that corner. Then on three, let's just launch them."

"I'm fucked. Can't we take a breather?" Mandel gasped.

"No time, no time. Bend your back, or we'll still be here in the morning."

Rolling his eyes, Mandel did as he was told.

"One, two, three heave!" The first of the remaining crates disappeared into the murk below. Once the last crate was disposed of, Groener lent against the bridge to regain his breath, and draped an arm around the shoulders of the speechless Mandel.

"See, you are good for something after all!"

Invisible from view, the crates began to settle, only two of the cases splitting on impact. The delighted conspirators shook hands vigorously, and began to jog back towards the village. The moon disappeared behind the clouds.

✭ ✭ ✭

Freuntz was an infrequent drinker, but the events of the day needed to be put in to some kind of perspective.

"Just leave the bottle," he grunted to the waiter, and downed the first glass in two gulps.

Heller was the most vocal of the raw troops Freuntz regarded as his 'kinder'. He watched Freuntz, his unchanging countenance, and the newly opened bottle. His plan began to take shape.

Heller knew that despite everything, Freuntz still had their respect. On more than one occasion, the collection of farm hands, office clerks and shop assistants had owed their lives to his steadfast courage under fire. Their respect verged on admiration, although one point perplexed them. His complete refusal to join in the sexual banter which permeated their every conversation, had led to the speculation, at first in ones and twos, at first behind cupped hands, but with increasing frequency, about him. Had he? Was he? Why not?

Nobody dared to say anything to his face, but the topic dominated conversation, as the new boys to the company who, whilst still respecting him, eschewed the awe and reverence of the more experienced soldiers. They found it difficult to comprehend how the iron grip he kept on his emotions made any sense when death might come at any moment.

They all knew better than to challenge him openly, though. Pohler was still in hospital, after all. Heller remembered how some apparently innocent remarks from the callow recruit had convulsed Freuntz.

"Turnips, that's all they have to eat now. Turnips. Is that what it has all been about? Still better than here though. It will all be over soon and then we can sum up, sum up whether it was worth it. My dad has had enough -and he's not the only one. Says we should do what the Russians did. Throw it in. Socialism is the way ahead, he says. You can shove that Empire stuff, all that 'Place in the Sun' right up your…"

Freuntz had been engrossed in the latest series of caricatures on the top bunk. In the half light, he launched himself at the unsuspecting Pohler. In an instant, Pohler felt the grip tightening around his throat, the weight of his assailant forcing his chest against the wooden boards which supported the dugout. Two sickening sounds indicated the ferocity with which Pohler's head was rammed against the framework of the doorway which led to the trench line. It took Schleime, and two others, to drag Freuntz away. They had saved Pohler's life.

"You red, bolshy, bastard! Defeat? Give up? Four years? Four years and you want to give up?" he aimed a flailing boot at the stricken Pohler, who slumped to the floor, whimpering. Schleime tightened his grip on Freuntz. Eventually, the wave of aggression ebbed, and his body relaxed. Without a second glance, he clambered back up to his bunk and resumed drawing.

✯ ✯ ✯

Instinct told Freuntz that one more glass would finish him off, and then, what fun the boys would have at his expense? His vulnerability would be there for all to see. That was what he secretly feared, and what fuelled his iron resolve. The fear that he wasn't in control and could be manipulated for their pleasure set the alarm bells ringing, but for some reason more faintly than normal. He was glad to see his boys enjoying themselves. But as melancholy began to reassert its supremacy, it was the face of his mother which emerged, then receded, through the haze.

Why had he never been good enough, worthy of her praise, or merely an acknowledgement that his efforts to please her did indeed meet with her approval, no matter how grudging? What had happened to render her almost mute, when a few words would have sufficed; so blank, when a warm glance would have meant everything?

The constant yearning for approval had had a corrosive effect on his attitude towards women. He had come to see them as all powerful, capable of demanding affection yet equally capable of rejecting it, regardless of how ardently it was offered.

He turned to survey the scene behind him, in preparation for as dignified an exit as possible. He was relieved to see two of his 'chicks'. Groener and Mandel, order two beers with a marked sense of urgency. They gave him a thumbs up, despite their flushed complexions, but then engrossed themselves in earnest but covert conversations, as if fearing they might be overheard. The rising crescendo of yells, whoops and the low moan of the accordion made it unlikely. The moan was accompanied by the touching, but tuneless, rendition of one of those sentimental songs which could only be rendered by the homesick, the lovelorn and the scared.

Freuntz was tempted to join them, but decided not to. As he swirled the remaining wine, he was back in Verdun. The memory of the searing pain, as his thigh was split from top to bottom by shrapnel, was usurped by the memory of his panic as he suffocated in the rubble of the brickworks.

The vice like grip on his chest was weakening, his efforts to force a hand through the debris becoming more feeble by the minute, as he slipped in and out of consciousness. The glimmer of light had appeared just as he was about to accept the inevitable. Meinke had thrust his hand through the rubble. Freuntz had grasped it with all that remained of his dwindling strength, desperate to convince his would be rescuer-and himself-that he was alive.

How could Meinke be dead?

✳ ✳ ✳

Well, that was easy enough, thought Sophie, as she descended the staircase. The money, little as it was, had been carefully concealed in the dresser. There was still time for one more. A portly sergeant from Westphalia had proved to be the wheezing test of endurance she had anticipated, as soon as his garlic drenched breath first played upon her cheek. But the older ones had their compensations-they were grateful for a start- and anything longer than ten minutes meant an enhanced status with their smirking comrades. She could play them like a violin.

By contrast, the shaven headed private from Koblenz had approached the whole experience as a re-run of the Schlieffen Plan, urgent, aggressive, thrusting, but ultimately unsuccessful. She knew how to console them though, how to reassure them and send them back with warm words and assurances that next time they would be better. How else would she get an opportunity to better herself, to leave the stifling social milieu of St Valery for ever? The sneers and abuse served only to harden her sense of purpose.

Madame Bonnard, the chain smoking proprietor of La Pigalle, had excited her sense of adventure with tales of her exploits in Montmartre in her youth. Could they possibly have been true? Is that what men are really like? Is that what men wanted done to them? With a warm smile which revealed her tobacco stained teeth, a plump arm which embraced Sophie's slender waist with ease, and a resigned tone in her voice, she nodded ruefully that "Yes," was the answer to all these questions.

As she handed over Madame Bonnard's percentage for the evening, she was already surveying the seething mass below. The atmosphere could almost be tasted. Was there a sense amongst the crowd that this might be the last time? And if you loved life, this was the place to live it, just in case it was.

The previous two had been erased from her memory. Hair combed, lips moistened, blouse unbuttoned, there was time for a third.

✫ ✫ ✫

"You ask her."
"No you ask her."
"It was your idea. Get her asked."
"You tart! Same as always. The Italians have more go in them than you. This is a job for men, not boys," interrupted Heller, the eldest of the three slurring privates.
"Well, thank fuck the war's as good as over and we can fuck off home. Get in there. I'm going for a piss"

Heller's sense of importance amongst the "Three Musketeers", a self awarded sense of seniority based solely on his alleged prowess with women, had grown as the night progressed. The more lurid suggestions were considered, leered over and then rejected. Now, however, there was what he enjoyed, and had hoped to find in the army, a mission, a plan, a sense of purpose.

He rose to his feet. The copious amount of alcohol took its inevitable toll. The room spun, and he yearned for his mouth to function. He grasped desperately for something to steady himself. Missing the chair completely, he lurched forward, to be submerged by the ample bosom of Madame Bonnard, as she collected the glasses.

"Once we have closed, mon cher, once we have closed!" she chuckled, before extricating Heller from her cleavage, and pointing him in the direction of the bar.

The cackling of his so called comrades had a salutary effect on Heller's self image as a ladies man. He turned to mouth a final, abusive comment to his helpless audience, before trying to focus on the scheme they had hatched, to remember the script, and to remember what his opening line would be. With some difficulty, he veered towards the target.

Sophie had barely assumed the alluring demeanour she had found guaranteed success. She sipped her wine, and awaited the inevitable. He collapsed onto the chair beside her. He ransacked the recesses of his memory, and managed to blurt out his opening conversational gambit.

"How much do you charge to break someone in, then?"

Savoir-faire was one of those typical French phrases Heller resented for their sophistication. But, he had been sensible enough to realise, in his sober moments at least, that it could prove invaluable in his womanising career. He had also recognised that it was a career which was, for now, definitely a work in progress.

She smiled at his attempts at sophistication, arched her eyebrows, and prepared the response given to so many over the last twelve months, the massage which Heller's faltering self confidence required.

"The women must fight amongst themselves for a piece of you. You can pay if you want, but I'd save your money," she responded, as she assessed him quickly.

Empty flattery from a real woman, whose aroma, lustre and availability were here and now, instead of in his fevered imagination, had the desired effect. As the adrenalin surge fought with the depressant effect of the alcohol, he did his best to outline the plan, to risk some slightly risqué comments of his own, and even to make eye contact on a couple of occasions, before shattering the illusion he yearned to cultivate,

"How much for us to watch?"

# Chapter Three

It was now almost five months since the hated Armistice. But even the dappled sunshine of a perfect spring morning couldn't persuade Freuntz that post war Stanheim was still home. He pushed his food half heartedly round his plate, and hoped that the café in the corner of the square would be a good vantage point. The first of the shambling column appeared. The bravado with which the red flags were held aloft cut Freuntz to the quick. He felt his pulse begin to race and fists clench.

Was this the new post war world the last of his recruits had spoken about? Workers paradise-what about duty? Strikes in munitions factories of all places-what about loyalty? Brother workers-what about country? "Peace now" had seduced so many, ground down by the depredations of hunger, cold and a casualty list which just kept growing. No wonder they had lost. But for Freuntz it wasn't an anonymous 'them' who had lost, it was him. It hurt.

More of the column were visible in the square now. His eyes were beginning to moisten. He forced himself to get a grip. Astonished, he realised that beneath the bandoliers of bullets, the red arm bands and the fluttering banners, at least half a dozen of the marchers were wearing field grey uniforms. He attempted to comprehend this betrayal of all he had believed in. He felt overwhelmed by their apparent ownership of the square. The leaflets were foisted upon unwilling bystanders, the chants became more vociferous, the beating drums more compelling. Suddenly, the tumult was dramatically amplified.

In an instant, a second group had emerged from a nearby side street. Their shambolic nature rendered them little more than a mob. In what seemed to be a blink of an eye they had launched themselves at the rear of the column, as if by instinct they had detected that this is where the least committed would be. What staggered Freuntz further was that the majority of this column also wore the field grey, but without a semblance of the hated red. Their tattered home made flag was that of the Second Empire.

Freuntz needed little invitation to join the heaving throng. In a split second he had selected his target. The fury and frenzy of close quarter fighting had always had a calming effect on him, as if his demons were under control; banished, however temporarily, until the surge of aggression was spent.

His elbow to the jaw flattened the spindly youth to his left. To the right he blocked the punch which was about to be administered to a prostrate, grey clad figure. A well aimed boot sent its proponent sprawling backwards. Experience always seemed to slow down events, no matter how frenetic. It was this quality which alerted him to the raised rifle of the column leader.

Clearly unused to using a weapon, his hesitancy gave Freuntz his chance. He launched into a headlong lunge which sent the corpulent figure flying backwards, jolting the rifle from his hands. Detached from the grappling frenzy around him, his focus was now on one task, and one task only, to finish off this embodiment of the Asiatic virus which had infected his Germany, and ultimately helped to defeat it.

Astride the dazed figure, Freuntz raised one fist high, about to squeeze the life from his hapless victim with the other. Suddenly, his grip was prised loose. From behind him, a muscular arm dragged him away from the ashen figure. The sound of police whistles, and a sixth sense which told him other groups were joining the fray, confirmed that it was time to disappear. He was heaved half way to his feet, and propelled towards the side street from which the mob had first emerged.

By now the combatants were scattering. The police and regular army units administered their own summary justice to the straggling remnants, right in front of the dumbstruck bystanders. The unseen arm thrust Freuntz forward down a maze of side streets. He gradually straightened up from his crouch. The tension began to evaporate. His heart still pounding, the arm propelled him against, and then through, a half open door, down some damp steps to a dimly lit cellar.

"Welcome brother. You're obviously one of us. We can use good men like you."

✯ ✯ ✯

As he picked at a plate of watery potatoes and translucent cabbage, his new comrade Kaltz wasted little time.

"Strength, that's what we had, strength, even right up to the end. We could have gone on. You know that and I know that." Freuntz felt Kaltz grip his forearm more tightly. "Of course we could. Armistice? We were conned.Cheated. Let down by spineless bastards here at home. Stirred up by those Red bastards. Socialism? Communism? The nation, that's what it's all about. Do we survive as nation? Not only survive, though. No, no. More than that. Rise again. Rise again. Get back our place, our rightful place."

Kaltz was almost screaming. Freuntz was flecked with spittle. Kaltz drew nearer. He was now only inches away, eyes blazing.

"Democracy? You must be fucking kidding! Strength, that's what counts. Win the battle. Just like today. Just like up at the Dorfell plant. Plenty of redundancies coming up there. Plenty of people with grievances, looking to make a stand, wondering which side to be on. We're going to show them. Just like today. That's why we need good men, men who went through it."

Freuntz couldn't help but admire the vehemence with which Kaltz put forward his views, and as the afternoon progressed, Freuntz realised that there was much they had in common.

"Amiens, Freuntz, Amiens. Were you there?" Freuntz nodded. "One more heave, one more push. We could have done it. We could."

"You're right," said Kaltz. "The spire, the cathedral spire. You know, it used to appear through the mist, every morning. It was like it was taunting us, teasing us. This far, and no further. The high point. And then, all the way back to Germany. All that, all that, and for what? To be told we were giving up? It was here we lost it, here. Right here in Stanheim- and a thousand other places. Let's get back to normal. Let's get comfortable. Let's get back to stuffing our fat faces. No honour! No pride! Lost it here. Not in France. No, undefeated, that was us." Eventually the stridency of his tone abated, and Kaltz appeared to relax.

The afternoon slipped by as the reminiscences became more maudlin, the recriminations more venomous. Kaltz eventually produced a crudely drawn card, the red, white and black colours predominant, with the number six on the back.

"The next meeting is tomorrow. You'll need this to get in."

"Six? Don't need a ticket if there are only six of you."

"No this is a card to say I've verified you, you're chosen by me, and we can use you. See you there."

# Chapter Four

*If this is what winning is like, God help us if we lose next time* was a thought Sophie was unable to ignore. Neither could she suppress the mantra, constantly reiterated by her friend Natalie; never be off, never be ill, never tell them you can't work. These three commandments gave a semblance of purpose, but no sense of joy, to the daily, two mile trudge to the mill.

At least, now it was July, she no longer needed the layers of threadbare cotton and tattered woollens with which she had tried to keep the March winds at bay. Rising before dawn each day, the relentless pattern had repeated itself as the stark landscape, with its bare trees and furrowed fields, depressed her on the way there, and lengthened the journey home.

But easy choices were no longer available. Life in St Valery only involved hard choices now. She had feared victory, especially a victory which left a void where authority was absent, law and order in retreat and retribution arbitrarily dispensed. But, perplexingly, this hadn't happened. The Germans hadn't continued to retreat, but had simply stopped where they were, like so many grey-clad sheep. They had waited, with their customary sense of obedience, until the first French units had arrived to disarm them.

Events had polarised opinion in the village. The sense of elation which should have been overwhelming was somehow muted, communicating the undeniable impression of people performing a script written by someone else, going through the motions in the most desultory manner. For after all, what was there to celebrate?

Sophie knew better than to try to join in conversation on the rare occasions she visited the village shops, but the debate which swirled around her had constant themes. Saturday morning at the bakery had been no different

"Smash them. Smash them now. We'll never have a better chance."

"1870, 1914, how many times? How many more times?"

"Make them pay, pay for what they have done to us. Half a chance, not even half a chance, and they will be back."

As Sophie constantly replayed the debates in her mind, she realised that not everyone felt the same. They just didn't express it openly. The subdued majority feared the future, feared for France, and found it impossible to comprehend how conflict of any kind might ever be contemplated. Ever.

The news from Versailles had failed to stifle the debate. Was it too harsh or not harsh enough? Who would get the money paid in reparations-not the likes of us was the one point of consensus. Occupy the whole fucking place was a point passionately put, but passively received, with a shrug of the shoulders and a desire to talk about something else, anything else.

Even more than the eloquent silence of the recently bereaved, the hospitalisation of Madame Bonnard, hip broken and jaw wired, and the blackened frontage of La Pigalle, encouraged her silence. Sophie had escaped the rough and ready settling of scores so far, but not the simmering resentment of whispered oaths and caustic asides. The image of Madame Bonnard emphasised that silence was the judicious course of action. After all, she still had her looks.

Head down, eyes averted, her daily return to the one room above the butchers left her breathless as she accelerated the last part of the journey, regardless of how weary she felt. The adrenalin spurred, then drained her. More often than not, once her pulse rate returned to normal and the wine took its effect, she fell asleep in her work clothes, resigned to repeating the process tomorrow.

This was the last of the journeys, a journey which had had to start progressively earlier, as the vomiting increased and the wincing intensified. One of the few school lessons she had enjoyed was a rudimentary science course whose broad brush title was 'nature study'.

To ease the journey, she quickly recapped her own favourite recollections of the changing seasons. The dog tooth violets and the eruption of the yellow forsythia had been bettered only by the speckling of the fields with the azure blue of the cornflowers. The pink fingers of sunrise were today a thing of beauty and placed Dreamers Rock in sharp relief, whilst the river, now a trickle, told her she was more than half way there.

The day ahead would be a hot one. The prospect of another stint in the ill-ventilated machine room, last day or not, filled her with foreboding. But the lush greenery of the lime trees was no compensation for hard cash. She quickened her step, and ignored, as best she could, the stabbing pain. She was grateful that it would be a while before she had to climb the hill again.

A month off without pay could be granted in exceptional circumstances, although two weeks was more usual, she had learnt. Her vomiting and fainting made her a liability which could no longer be ignored, even by the handful of her work mates she regarded as sympathetic. The rest, older mainly, and with the sly but vitriolic relish peculiar to women, had instigated a long running campaign of attrition which focused on her lack of morals, patriotism, and common sense. On one point she almost agreed with them. How had she fallen for the plans Heller had slurred in her ear? Only oral, he had said. Now, her baby was due any day.

She entered the mill yard, the sweat already visible on her forehead. She was ready to answer the barrage with a last one of her own. But, to her astonishment, she was confronted by the rotund figure of the owner, Monsieur Lafarge, whose handlebar moustache emphasised the monosyllabic nature of any conversation which wasn't about business.

"Not today, mademoiselle. No more. Not for a while."

Sophie was unsure what he meant. He clicked his fingers and a horse drawn wagon clattered into the yard. He patted the rump of the horse. "The mighty Eugene. He has been here as long as I have. I am sorry that is all I can offer, at the moment. Our lorry, our one lorry. Requisitioned for the big push, last August. I have the receipt." He tapped his top pocket. "I read it often. I am not optimistic, though." He smiled briefly. "Today is the day for the food parcels, though."

Her expression told him that food was the last thing on her mind. "For your aunt, perhaps?"

The dutiful demeanour of the chestnut mare would stay with Sophie for ever. Monsieur Lafarge nodded knowingly. He fixed Sophie with a stern, yet caring, look. With a whispered command to the driver, a flick of the whip to the hindquarters set the hooves clattering across the courtyard. For Sophie, the rough hewn planks of the wagon could have been Cinderella's carriage.

✯ ✯ ✯

The journey to Chemeny, home of her maternal Aunt Francoise, had passed quickly, but was a distance she could never have walked. Aunt Francoise knew about childbirth, having gone through the process six times herself, with four of her children surviving. She had a special affection for Sophie, having brought her up as her own after Sophie's mother had died. Her supposed expertise conferred a sense of authority upon her within the village, where she frequently acted as midwife and childminder, sometimes both at the same time.

The daily hubbub of Francoise's kitchen, often overrun with assorted progeny of all shapes and sizes, barely penetrated the overwhelming sense of relief Sophie felt, as she contemplated the challenge ahead. No more old cows giving her 'the evils', as Natalie called it, no clattering looms, and no more bleeding fingers. No backward steps either, even though the ordeal ahead did scare her a little.

On her birthday, on that very kitchen table, Sophie gave birth. The shock of her broken waters seemed, at first, to set in train a series of rhythmic contractions. Slowly, the pain intensified. The frequency increased. Sophie screamed. Aunt Francoise soothed. Sophie grimaced. Aunt Francoise soothed. Sophie cursed. Sophie felt faint. Aunt Francoise mopped her brow. A second cigarette was needed. Sophie cursed. Aunt Francoise cooed. Sophie screeched. Aunt Francoise encouraged. She knew there was not long to go. It had already been over two hours. The moment approached. Aunt Francoise watched Sophie closely, as she writhed and gasped. If she was to light her fifth cigarette, she would have to be quick. She was. She rolled back her sleeves, and delved deep. Aunt Francoise soon located the head. One turn of her whipcord wrists, one final push, and it was over.

"A girl, Sophie, you have a girl! You have your Nicole." She snipped the chord, wiped away the blood and mucus, and took another drag. She placed Nicole next to her mother.

"Oh Aunty, Oh Aunty. My language. How can I apologise? I don't even say such things to the old cows." Aunt Francoise mopped her brow and chuckled,

"It's always the same, mon cher, If men had to give birth there wouldn't be any born. Not any."

✯ ✯ ✯

The fortnight passed all too quickly. The clamp on her nipple had caused her to wince, as Francoise had predicted, but it was more than compensated by the cooing, the gazing and the dribbling. As the memory of the pain was gently erased, the miracle that was a new life worked its magic.

Her return was by wagon once again, paid for by her aunt as a regular part of her aftercare. This time, her thoughts were of the future. Was there one? One child, one job and no father. The odds weren't in her favour. With a sense of foreboding, she climbed the stairs, with Nicole resting against her neck.

Madame Chalroix fixed her with her customary look of contempt, for it had been her husband's idea to let the room to her in the first place. The effort of conversation for her was always a painful one, and, with a grunted "For you", she thrust the letter into Sophie's hand.

Perplexed by the fact that she had probably received no more than six letters in her life, she attempted to unlock the door, keep Nicole secure, and wondered. The address was scrawled, but there was no mistaking the stamp.

It was German.

# Chapter Five

The cellar of the Prinz-Eugen reminded him of his time on the Western Front, more starkly than he would have preferred. The dimly lit interior, with its low ceilings and foetid atmosphere, took him back momentarily to the bombardments which had driven some men mad. Even the rats, it was alleged. A quiet smile spread across his lips. He reflected that the earth shattering mayhem, far above, had had little physical effect on them, due in no small measure to the excellence of German engineering, German construction skills, German discipline, Ger…

"Card!Card!"

The speaker, barely visible in the gloom, possessed only half of what would be regarded as a face. The scar tissue on the remainder stretched painfully, allowing words to be formed in a hissing whisper. Freuntz produced his card. A shaft of light, from the door behind, illuminated a row of clinking medals.

Nodding, he entered the half lit cellar. Freuntz was unfamiliar with the aroma, imbued with stale sweat, spilt beer and strong tobacco, typical of so many such establishments in the working class districts of so many German towns. The foaming beer arrived without prompting. It placed Freuntz in a predicament. Still unemployed, he had planned to observe, listen, and contribute only if pressed, but not drink if he could avoid it. Fumbling for change, he was relieved that he thought he had enough, but could not be sure.

"Save it. First time. And the last."

The huge figure retreated towards the bar. Freuntz was aware that another had slipped into the space beside him. As he became more accustomed to the murk, he could make out his new companion.

"Bandell, Hessian Guards", he barked. "Kaltz was impressed yesterday. Takes a lot to impress him."

"Well, it had to be done," Freuntz began. "Those swaggering red bastards. It's as if they own the fucking place."

Bandell, who always equated incoherence with passion, nodded approvingly, and ordered another brimming glass. The new comrades began to compare the histories, memories and experiences, unique to the crucible of war. The conversation continued. Freuntz was forced to ask why it was so gloomy.

"He thinks it adds to the atmosphere, builds up the tension. It's easier to play with peoples minds when it's dark. Never read a ghost story? See you after." Bandell disappeared, leaving Freuntz alone with his thoughts, sipping his beer with an evident distaste which the gloom concealed perfectly.

After about five minutes, Freuntz sensed a change in the atmosphere. He was aware of a lull in the conversation of the dozen or so fellow drinkers, of benches being shuffled into place, and a heightened sense of tension. Nothing happened for a further five minutes. It was evident that no one was prepared to break the spell.

Just as the mystifying experience was about to prove too much for Freuntz, the doors burst open. The lights dimmed further, applause rippled in the dark. He was aware of a squat shape, marching briskly to the far end of the cellar. In perfect synchronization, light suddenly flooded a rudimentary stage. Four grey clad figures could be seen, flanking the squat figure. They partially obscured a red, white, and black banner, with what he surmised were the words "Fatherland Front" emblazoned across the middle. To the right of the speaker, jaw jutting, arms folded, was Kaltz.

Freuntz had only been to a theatre once, and he had hated the experience intensely. The one thing he remembered was how the voices of the actors rose and fell to create the spell which enchanted the audience. There was to be no such subtlety tonight.

A torrent of pseudo economic jargon, interspersed with blinkered military analysis, was unleashed on the audience, all of whom, apart from Freuntz, seemed to know what to expect. They broke into bouts of self-conscious applause, as they had their hatreds rationalised and their prejudices reinforced. Freuntz struggled with much of the terminology, especially the assault on big business, which confusingly was meshed with a litany of the evils of Communism. Freuntz was baffled. Weren't they opposites? How could they both be enemies? He was struggling to keep up.

However, as the high water mark of the rhetorical tide approached, the thread which linked the reasons for Germany's demise was revealed in the most inflammatory of terms. The lurid descriptions shocked even Freuntz, who assumed he had heard it all. At last it was over; the secret was out, the cause revealed, and the culprits condemned. The Jews. As the speaker soaked up the applause, Freuntz had little time for reflection before Kaltz was beside him.

"What do you think, then? Good, isn't he?"

Freuntz was unsure how to respond, but assumed the required reaction was to concur.

"Good, I'll introduce you."

After about five minutes of back slapping and animated conversation, the speaker approached. Freuntz immediately noticed that his right ear was missing, as was his right eye. Heinrich Moeller had been decorated five times in total. He not only wore the medals with pride, but used them as the framework of his story. It was only when the last of his exploits was recounted, that Freuntz began to take more than a cursory interest.

Moeller had been at Belleau Wood in 1918. He told the story of how the raw American units learnt, in the most brutal of fashions, the lessons all armies had learnt from 1914 onwards. Frontal assaults on machine gun positions were suicide.

"Just aim. Didn't even need to aim, really. Just point, point and spray. But, you know what, they just kept coming. Can't lose men at that rate unless you've got millions. And they had. But you know what was best? You couldn't miss those black bastards…those buck niggers. Just imagine, a country that needs to use those monkeys. If they ever come to …" But Freuntz had had enough,

He had drained his beer at last. The intensity of the oratorical onslaught, coupled with the lack of oxygen, meant that he yearned for fresh air. Momentarily, he was back beneath the rubble of Verdun, the crushing weight and the scrabbling of the ever loyal Meinke. The prickle of panic spurred him up the stairs. The evening air quickly restored a sense of equilibrium.

As he climbed the hill away from the centre of town, he couldn't grasp two ideas which had been half explained. Black soldiers. In Germany? Never. But what really set him thinking was the death of his mother. Just how good, how caring, how committed had Doctor Jakobs been?

He hadn't thought about it before, but now he couldn't think of anything else.

✣ ✣ ✣

As usual it was Madame Poiller who got the news first. Madame Poiller was part of a double act with Madame Chalroix, typical of so many small communities. They were the source of gossip, the dispensers of folk wisdom. Their withering opinions on the assorted inadequacies of the male species imbued their pronouncements with an authority which brooked no challenge.

The devastating news of the death of Monsieur Lafarge spurred Sophie on, despite the swirling conflict of emotions, and the warm, early morning drizzle which ran down her back. A fear for the immediate future, and the prospect of more verbal attrition from the old cows, could not detract from her overriding sentiment - one of sadness at the demise of Monsieur Lafarge. His lingering look in the factory yard, that morning-was it only a month ago? - was an image she couldn't shift.

"Died quick, he did, lot of pain so they say. They've sent for Lionel and Olivier already," Madame Poiller had added with the relish of one determined to make the most of her latest stint as the font of all knowledge. Sophie felt she knew all she wanted to about pain, and quickened her stride.

✵ ✵ ✵

The scene in the yard was one of low key chaos. Bedraggled workers conversed in small groups, some animated, some listless, all bemused. The hastily produced leaflets were already turning to pulp on the cobbles. Sophie felt she needed an ally. Where was Natalie?

Instead it was Agnes, the most venomous of the old cows, who suddenly made a bee line for her. Flanked by two of her retinue she hissed,

"Bad news for you dear. Sounds like it's last in first out. You'll need to get your knickers off even quicker now." Encouraged at the opening of verbal hostilities by her leader, Monique was emboldened to add,

"Yes. And get a revolving door for your bedroom, you little whore." The three cackled, staring at Sophie, awaiting her reaction. She brought the cackling to a halt immediately. She began an exaggerated mime of wiping her eyes, retching violently, and staggering as if drunk. It reminded her tormentor of how her only son, Pascal, had met his end in the first gas attack at Ypres, in 1915.

It seemed that Monique was about to release four years of pent up anguish. She visibly blanched, her shoulders tensed. In the nick of time, Natalie appeared, and dragged Sophie forcibly away.

"You silly bitch. It's allies you need, not enemies. You've enough of those already."

The choice of these military terms diffused her desire to settle with Agnes and her herd, there and then. The edge to Natalie's comments, and the teeming drizzle, combined to force Sophie to focus on her predicament. She was brought up to date with recent developments, and who the key players were likely to be. Prospects would be bleak indeed, if she was one who had to go. She was certain of that.

"They're closing for a week. They're trying to get Lionel in. He's meant to be the business brains of the two sons. The other's just a waster from what I can tell. Everyone is going to get the chance to speak. It's about what tactics we should use. If it's the usual loud mouths, we're finished. Come on." Sophie needed little encouragement to follow Natalie up the stairs.

Typically for such occasions, it was the most passionate and incoherent who seized the floor. As the ill thought out suggestions poured forth, there was a palpable sense of frustration. The steam from their sodden clothes intensified the humidity, the temperature rose, tempers shortened.

"The war was good for us, but now it's over. Who needs German uniforms? Not even the Germans."

"Blankets? Anyone can make them. Where's the margin?"

"No margin, no future."

"The stuff we used to make, the lace wear, the bedspreads, we can't produce enough to make a profit."

"We all know Monsiuer Lafarge wasn't one for modernising."

"Craftsmanship. Fine in its own right, but it can only get you so far."

"Problems. We all know what the problems are. It's solutions we're after."

Sophie desperately tried to follow the ebb and flow of debate, whilst gleaning some comfort from the distress she had caused. Monique was still dabbing her reddened eyes. Conscious that her case was in danger of going by default, she seized the moment.

One of the clients of whom she was fondest had been a captain from Mainz. He had astonished her by explaining that, in contrast to Germany, British women were doing so many jobs, previously done by men. Leaping onto the low bench, amidst derisory snorts from the cows, Sophie had read the situation perfectly. She began her argument with the words

"Sisters."

The meeting had been monopolised by the men, although they were a minority of the workforce, and the shock effect worked to her advantage, which she capitalised upon quickly. She launched into a series of arguments which were ill formed when taken on their own, but which had a common thread. They were living in new times, women had shown they could match men and were being rewarded for their efforts in England. They were gaining a limited right to vote.

Now, before the new owner arrived, was the opportunity to make things more equal and more fair, not only in France, but right here in the factory. Her final plea, which was put as the efforts of her rallying cry were taking their toll, and her voice was becoming a croak, was to live up to the standards of the Revolution

"After all, egalité is what France is meant to be about. What we stand for. What defines us. Let us demonstrate it right here. We will never get a better chance."

As she finished, the unfamiliarity of public speaking, the confusion of her arguments, and the passion with which she had put them, made her feel dizzy. She buckled at the knees. Instinct told her not to weaken, and as Natalie helped her down, she became aware of a smattering of applause.

The men in the audience were trying to come to terms with the implications for them, when Henri Chalmy, who until now had kept his own counsel, mounted the bench.

Chalmy was the only one in the factory who hadn't cared who won the war, "The bosses war," were words he spat out with a depressing regularity. An injury at the factory had rendered him unfit for military service, and his truculent views had done him few favours with Monsieur Lafarge. But his knowledge of machinery made him indispensable. His knowledge also extended to a wide ranging, but shallow, familiarity with socialist ideas. He peppered his conversations with references to Proudhon, Syndicalism and Rousseau. This left his listeners bemused, but burnished his image as a self- taught intellectual.

He resolved to use the appeal Sophie had made to the emotions of the crowd, to provide his own analysis, however flawed. He knew better than to ram the Russian Revolution down the throats of his conservative, ill-educated workmates. But he was determined to employ the gestures and phrasing no self- respecting orator would be without. Above all, though, he knew he had to keep it short.

"We are truly living in momentous times," he began in a whisper. "The hand of history is upon us. We must grasp it." Only a few of the audience heard this. None of those who did, knew what it meant. Undaunted, he pressed on.

"The days of the bosses are coming to an end. All the worth of this factory is here in this room. Look around. Can we not decide what to make, how to make it? How much to charge?" He paused. "How much we should earn?" Now he had their attention. He grasped both straps of his overalls for dramatic effect.

"These machines we see around us. They are but assembled metal. If not for us-for you"- at which he fixed the front row with a glazed stare- "they would rust and eventually crumble. The worth,"- he was desperate to avoid the word capital-"the value, the only value of this factory is you! you! you!" He jabbed a finger at half a dozen of the audience, one by one, each of whom felt obliged to nod in agreement. Throwing back his head, he rammed home his point.

"There will be no redundancies, not a single one. We are not men and women. We are human beings. We are workers, and we will not be divided, categorised or driven apart. We will stand together, share the sacrifices," at which point he nodded slowly, "For sacrifices there will be. But we will stand together next week, united not divided, and the future can be ours."

The temptation to use the word "Comrades" was narrowly avoided. As the workers tried to digest his ideas, he turned to Sophie, and gave her a look which indicated that he saw her as a worthy ally in the hard bargaining which lay ahead. She was almost his equal. Almost, but not quite, he reflected, his sense of superiority over his fellow man-and woman-suitably reinforced.

✷ ✷ ✷

The journey home was a slow one. Despite her desire to see Nicole, she had been drained by her outburst, perplexed at its origins, but satisfied with the grudging respect shown by some of her workmates. Many had never shown the slightest interest in her. The joint plan which she had brokered- as an equal with Chalmy- was to share the short time over a fortnightly period, two days one week, three the second.

"Well, how did it go?" Madame Chalroix asked her, as soon as she got through the door. Sophie grinned wryly, as she appreciated this doomed attempt to reinforce her grip on the village bush telegraph. Sophie shrugged her shoulders. Once inside the sparsely furnished room, she needed all her powers of concentration to feed, change and play with Nicole.

She woke two hours later and it was still there. The handwriting had the most slanted style she had ever seen. The home made birthday card showed a landscape which was undeniably St Valery, and was perfectly shaded in a range of pastel crayons. Also included was a broad ribbon of a most lustrous jade, a colour she had never seen, even at the factory. But who was the message from? And who was it for?

She needed a drink.

✲ ✲ ✲

"Blame? Blame? How the fuck are we the only ones to be blamed?" roared Freuntz. "Those gutless bastards. Social fucking Democrats. Fucking useless the lot of them." Freuntz screwed the newspaper into a ball, and began to jump up and down on it. His neighbour, Heinrich Greintz, had been unemployed for three months and, whilst embarrassed by such public fury, felt obliged to sympathise.

"Versailles.Versailles. They want to finish us. No question about it. How are we expected to get off our knees?"

"Knees? Knees? We're flat on our backs with their foot on our throat! They've robbed us of The Saar. And look at this." He pointed to the remnants of the headline, barely visible on the shredded front page. "Look-fifty to go, fifty! And you get to know from the paper. Can't make coke without coal. Can't make steel without coke."

Unnoticed, Greintz slipped away. The news from Versailles made Freuntz wince, and not for the first time he realised that once again Moeller had been proved right by events. If this is what the so called democrats were prepared to stomach then, yes, Germany was finished unless something was done.

One thing upset Freuntz. He had been brought up never to swear, and he was aware of how coarse his language had become. He resolved that there would be no more. Never swear, never cry.

Freuntz had attended the Fatherland Front meetings only sporadically since April, and the message had been constant. It was only the bit about the Jews he couldn't accept. It wasn't a lack of revolutionary zeal which had prevented him from attending however. His long hours as a labourer at the Gehfarn coke plant meant that he was ready to sleep as soon as he got home. That wouldn't be a problem any longer.

✸ ✸ ✸

Stanheim was suffering far more serious economic turmoil, however, as the Dorfell dispute threatened to flare up again. It had been 'settled' in the most acrimonious terms, with forty redundancies, all issued to those who just happened to have Communist sympathies. The sacked workers had maintained a picket which was generally peaceful, apart from the shift changeover. Then the agitation increased, and the poison in the atmosphere could be tasted.

A police presence barely managed to contain the vehement recriminations which thankfully, to date, had seen comparatively few injuries from the flying stones and gravel. The rumours were that another forty at least were to be sacked immediately, and even more alarmingly there were also rumours that allied troops would be deployed in the town for the first time, should the situation deteriorate.

News was expected by noon, and Freuntz felt the urge to demonstrate solidarity, although he was not sure who with. As he climbed the hill, the clamour could be heard several streets away. The police were barely managing to keep the swaying mob from the factory gates. The mob was not only far more animated than on previous occasions, but also three or four times larger. It seemed that a significant proportion of Stanheim's workforce was being drawn towards the plant, as if sensing that the coming news would have seismic implications for the town. Freuntz realised he was no longer at the back of the crowd, but at its seething centre.

Disjointed chanting was beginning to cohere into something more unified. The gates were forced open by another body of police, who appeared from inside the factory. A podium, which was no more than two wooden crates, was hastily erected inside the yard. Four more policemen escorted a gaunt figure towards it. Freuntz guessed this was the chief shop steward, Jurgen Pollmann.

Never a great orator, Pollmann's voice barely carried beyond ten metres, and the occasion was clearly beyond him. At first, the mob fell silent in an attempt to hear the grim news. The barely decipherable news from Pollmann was misheard, misunderstood and then distorted further, as the rapidly evolving version spread like wildfire.

Advance news about the numbers of redundancies had been conveyed to the authorities. The contingency plans included a desire to see the allied troops blooded. Taking advantage of the focus on events in the square, they had formed up in the cramped side streets. Their moment had almost arrived.

Instinct told Freuntz to duck. As the first half brick whistled past his ear, he was already in a half crouch. The missile would have flattened the scrawny figure in front of him, had the crowd not been so dense as to prevent it. Initially held upright by the crowd, the hail of missiles intensified. As fear took hold, the first to flee forced the dazed youth backwards before trampling him underfoot. The pandemonium, caused by the first volley of shots, now placed a premium on clear thinking.

The mob began to scatter. From his prone position, he was able to gain a partial picture of events through the gaps in the crowd. He sensed that the action was nearer to the gates, which were being forced shut. As he straightened up, the view, though fragmented, was unmistakeable. Kaltz, and about twenty others, he quickly estimated, had donned black cloth forage caps as a means of identification. They were already embroiled in a series of brawls, despite being vastly outnumbered by their left wing opponents.

Freuntz instinctively recognised that the shots had been aimed high, deliberately. He struggled to get to Kaltz, reeling under a concerted assault of boots and fists. He was almost there when, to his astonishment, he was overtaken by two figures in the iconic blue of the French army. In an instant, Freuntz came face to face with an unpalatable reality-they were black. A sideways glance quickly absorbed two other pairs. Sent in as a snatch squad, to isolate and remove the perceived catalysts, it was an admission that the situation was rapidly slipping out of control.

With a clubbing action of immense force, their rifle butts laid Kaltz's assailants out cold. But now the semi-conscious Kaltz was being dragged towards the watching troops, all with rifles raised. All, bar their captain, were black. Those Fatherland Front combatants near to Kaltz, as if by telepathy, now detached themselves from their battle with the Communists and, in a swarming assault, overwhelmed his would be captors.

Now, aggression, loyalty, but above all a primeval racism, combined to lend a deadly edge to the massed assault on the blue clad figures. Freuntz had a sense of a pack of ravening wolves, tearing a wounded animal to pieces, as his stamping action made contact with bone at least twice, before more shots rang out. This time, they were not aimed high.

What was fortunate for Freuntz was the exact opposite for others in the murderous mob. With their backs to the French troops, they were easy targets. Karl Lindemann, barman at the Prinz Eugen, was dead before he hit the ground, as a single bullet smashed into his temple. A volley of shots slammed into the muscular back of his brother, Horst. As the figures crumpled, Freuntz prostrated himself besides the groaning Kaltz, and waited for the firing to stop.

# Chapter Six

It was a commonly accepted truth, within the village, that Monsieur Chalroix had enjoyed a 'good war'. Commonly accepted most definitely, but accepted also with the underlying layer of resentment typical of the deprived and the exploited. Monsieur Chalroix, on the other hand, had long held the view that life owed him more. Its offerings had been inferior fare for a man of his pretensions. The war had offered him his chance.

Meat quickly became scarce once the frontlines solidified in the Autumn of 1914. Scarcity now equalled power and patronage. The prices were high and the quality low, all proof to Monsieur Chalroix that mighty providence was at last looking favourably upon him. If the Feudal System were to be brought back, he was confident he would be amongst the upper echelons.

Those he saw as social equals, for none were betters, were rewarded with extra rations or better cuts. Underpinning his apparent generosity was the hope that his munificence would be rewarded. His ambition to roar around the country lanes in one of the high powered saloons, which he had seen on a rare visit to Paris, would be rapidly fulfilled.

Social standing was not the only area in which he felt he had been dealt an inferior hand. His waxy moustache, and immaculate centre parting, had been maintained since his teens. He was convinced that his looks were sufficiently smouldering to render any women who entered his orbit incapable of resisting his charms.

Sadly, a harsh reality had intruded, and he was trapped in a marriage which had been loveless from the start. Only the stifling Catholic morality of rural life kept them together, in a state best described as hostile indifference.

The shrewish demeanour of Madame Chalroix was sufficient to stifle the ardour of all but the terminally desperate. Indeed, the alternative rumour mill, centred on the regulars at Le Café d' Orleans, had long hinted that the village spinster, Madame Defuy, was getting rations of something other than brisket. The sniggering speculation enlivened many an evening, providing the oppressed males of St Valery with a way to stop Madame Chalroix, when in full flow. An enquiry, with exaggerated politeness, as to how MonsieurChalroix was keeping, and whether he was at home, usually did the trick.

However, apart from small victories at the expense of Madame Chalroix, the real bone of contention was the stranglehold her husband held. Offal was in plentiful supply, and was staple fare at La Pigalle. But they were convinced that Monsieur Chalroix had access to secret supplies - and they were right. Two German cooks had been able to operate a black market until 1917, when the British naval blockade began to bite with a vengeance.

Ever enterprising, Monsieur Chalroix had realised that all over Northern France were dead horses. These were the key to riches, as far as he was concerned. Eventually his accomplices were discovered, but not before he had amassed and sold vast amounts. Its origins were of little interest to Monsieur Chalroix, and neither was its age. He had continued the practice in peacetime, and was keen to gain favour with Monsieur Lafarge, now normality had started to return.

The news of the death of Monsieur Lafarge therefore offered a challenge, and an opportunity. His last supplies had had the date of slaughter crudely indicated in rough crayon, and it took little ingenuity to change the 3 to an 8, before offering it to Monsieur Lafarge. His demise, and the prospect of short time at the mill, conveniently brought the second part of his plan into play-Sophie.

It was he who had argued forcefully that she should be offered the room on her arrival in the village, a week before the war had started. He had harboured his lustful intentions for long enough. Now he had to make the most of these propitious circumstances. Reduced wages, and an extra mouth to feed, were two of the three aces he held. The third, an unavoidable increase in rent, he would play at the earliest opportunity. With Madame Chalroix on her weekly visit to her elderly aunt, it would be tomorrow.

✼ ✼ ✼

Two consecutive days of drenching drizzle had confined Sophie to the cramped apartment, but the reappearance of late summer sunshine meant she could finally escape. Her post war drive to self improvement was already threatening to lose its impetus. Banging away on the ancient Remington typewriter had temporarily lost its appeal. She thrust the teaching manual to one side.

Strapping Nicole into the sling she had fashioned herself, she escaped the early morning activity associated with the half day market. She was immune to the good natured banter of the stallholders, busily engaged in setting out their produce. However, she could not resist the peaches, offered with a twinkle in his eye by a wizened character she guessed must be at least seventy. She was headed for Dreamers Rock, trying to convince herself that she needed time to think. In reality, she preferred to put off any hard decisions for as long as possible.

Having passed the morning in idle but enjoyable daydreaming, she returned, just as the last of the stallholders were saying their goodbyes. Watching from the bay window of the newly refurbished La Pigalle, Monsieur Chalroix had a perfect view of the main street. He allowed her to pass, then emerged, blinking in the sunshine, and quickened his pace.

Once level, he apologised for not seeing Sophie immediately on her return, complimented her on her radiant good health, and scrutinised her closely. He was eager to see what effect, if any, his opening gambit had had. Sophie was uncertain how she should respond to this unexpected development, given that their communication rarely consisted of more than a nod, although she had noticed some of his looks. This was one which suggested purpose.

"Such a shock about Michel, I knew him so well. And the mill, not good news, unfortunately. Neither of the sons are businessmen." He nodded sagely, as would any man of the world in these circumstances.

Sophie responded, "Yes, yes. Indeed it was a shock. Even though he was old." Her emphasis on the last word was ignored by Monsieur Chalroix. "What a lovely man he was, yes, those are the two words you would use to describe him. Lovely. And old." She looked again at Monsieur Chalroix, but he was oblivious to her hints, his gaze fixed firmly on her bosom. Sophie pressed on. "People are still coming to terms with events." She awaited his next move.

"Money will be tight, no doubt. It is not easy, it is never easy. No, short time, and you with a little one to feed. No, it will be difficult for many to make ends meet. Credit is such an unpleasant business, and even for me, fewer customers with less money affects me just as badly." He was relishing his role as the world weary entrepreneur.

"Each and every one of us will be forced to make the most of our assets." Sophie was shrewd enough to realise that she was being set up, but was unsure what for. She had realised, long ago, that quizzically raised eyebrows ensured that the preceding sentence would be elaborated upon, and it duly was. They entered the shop. Sophie's heart began to pound. He was climbing the stairs, behind her.

"You see, mademoiselle, when times are hard everyone has to work harder, maybe differently, or even…" and with what he imagined was the coup de grace, "make greater use of the skills one already has."

As she turned the key, to her relief, Nicole began to cry. Some brief respite was bought, during which time she tried to work out what he meant. But there was no let up. Although she missed some of his closing sentence, there was no disguising the reptilian relish with which he informed her,

"I'll be up at four"

✣ ✣ ✣

Thankfully, Nicole was asleep when the knock came, but Sophie was alarmed at his appearance at close quarters. He had obviously been drinking, and his leathery skin was flushed, but at least the alcohol helped conceal the bad breath.

Her heart had begun to race once more at his appearance, and definitely not from desire. By now it was thumping, as the implications of his rambling monologue became clear.

"We all have needs, mademoiselle, needs. And if our needs are not met, why who is to say we are wrong to have them met in other ways? It is only natural; yes it is the way things should be." His slurring meant that she could only pick out fragments, as the monologue continued. "No understanding … not that kind of woman … the last time was before the war…needs … rent…ends meet … could do her a favour … needs…"

Nicole was now beginning to stir. Sophie's head began to clear. She grimly realised that the alternatives were stark, the choices dismal, and the course of action clear. It wasn't business, it certainly wouldn't be pleasure, but her predicament was dire. A rapid assessment was needed. His wide eyed, knowing look left few doubts that he expected his needs, indeed, to be met. This would be just the first instalment.

For Sophie, her time at La Pigalle had been largely on her terms. She quickly resolved that, no matter how unpalatable things might become in many ways, this was no different, and it was up to her to turn the situation to her advantage. With a firm glance of her own, she indicated that the sparring was over.

He lunged towards her, to try to kiss her, always a promising first move he had convinced himself, but she tilted her head away, leaving Monsieur Chalroix with the blurred impression that she was teasing him. This would be a more prolonged encounter, a challenge worthy of his self awarded status as a Lothario. His next fumbling move towards her blouse was quickly parried by an upward flick of her wrist. She led him towards the sofa, and immediately seized the initiative.

She pushed his shoulders down and fixed him with a firm stare, one which he mistook for lust, but she intended as contempt. She placed both arms above his head, and kept them there. She pressed her hand down firmly on his wrists. This was nothing like Madame Defuy, where he did all the work and it was over in seconds. He couldn't bear to even think of Madame Chalroix, as it would ruin the moment completely.

His prone position, the rush of alcohol to his head, and the proximity of the nubile figure he had long lusted after, brought a beatific smile to his face. A feeling that it was all too much welled up inside him. And, as Sophie went rhythmically and systematically to work, it very quickly was.

She gazed intently at him, so as to avert her eyes from the main action, as her other hand demonstrated its intimate familiarity with the contours of the male anatomy. Sighing in the rehearsed, pseudo appreciative manner which had always stood her in good stead on such occasions, she synchronised her actions with his groaning. The result was all too predictable. Her hand was sticky, but she resisted the temptation to wipe it on her dress, or on the sofa. Monsieur Chalroix was left to groan like a beached whale, for whom the tide, both physically and metaphorically, had ebbed.

Sophie forced herself to be busy, as the prospect of further encounters, more intimate, more prolonged even, began to depress her. Nicole was now stirring. She quickly placed her over her shoulder, anything to avoid Monsieur Chalroix, and his comically serene expression.

He dressed slowly, so as to savour the moment, but hadn't the grace to acknowledge her presence. Inwardly, he was elated at the prospect of who knew how many such encounters in the future. For after all, he was without question her social superior. He looked in the mirror, straightened his parting, gave his moustache a rakish twirl, and booked his next appointment

"Friday at four, then".

# Chapter Seven

The decision not to press charges had been taken at the highest level. The cathartic events at the Dorfell plant had forced all sides to pull back, to allow temperatures to cool, options to be considered, and the chances of social schism, feared openly by so many, to recede. The Senegalese troops had been withdrawn in haste, although their replacement by regular French troops was only marginally less humiliating. The chance of finding any reliable witnesses was deemed to be both impossible and counterproductive in the drive to restore calm.

Freuntz was usually glad of the chance to reflect, but the proximity of his erstwhile colleagues made concentration a difficult process, interspersed as it was by grunting, groaning, and intermittent farting. The scars of battle were all too evident. The teeth marks on Moeller's cheek were a bright red. What had he been doing in the middle of all that, with only one eye? Couldn't let his boys down, I suppose, reflected Freuntz. Friedrich shifted constantly, in a forlorn attempt to get comfortable on the bare boards, whilst the purple and yellow bruising, beneath both eyes, merely hinted at the severity of the beating Graumann had taken.

Freuntz silently feared that their forced confinement would offer Moeller the opportunity to launch into one of his blistering monologues at the slightest opportunity. However, to his surprise, Moeller proved to be a reflective, taciturn figure who spent most of his time staring at the ceiling, when he wasn't asleep. An audience to galvanise was what got Moeller going.

Occasionally Moeller would use his captive audience to rehearse his arguments.

"The battle in the square wasn't a defeat, boys. Oh no, no, no. It was a victory, boys, a victory. A chance to plant our flag, an opportunity to let them know we are here, and we won't be backing down. No armistice here, or anywhwere." Moeller was gradually becoming more animated. "All over Germany boys, ALL over Germany, there are groups like ours. Small groups I grant you, small groups, but feeling resentful, feeling hurt, feeling humiliated."

"But where had they been at the decisive moment, taking the fight to the enemy, taking the blows and shedding the blood? Nowhere." he spat. "But it's not courage they lacked, no, not courage. Just leadership, that's all they need." He let the sentence hang in the air before swinging his legs back onto his bunk, closing his eyes, and ignoring his cell mates for the rest of the afternoon.

He had grown up in Hanover where his father owned the first cinema in the town, quickly grasping the value of showmanship and a sense of theatre. He had already realised that a captive audience in a darkened hall, all there for one purpose, were ripe for manipulation, providing that the message was simple. And he could do simple.

He was already planning his lead role. Two dead brothers were propaganda gold dust, but two dead martyrs were the mother lode. He could see the flag draped gun carriage, the silent streets, and the stirring graveside oration he would deliver. He couldn't help drooling at the prospect. The afternoon passed quickly.

For Freuntz, retrospection continued to focus on one topic. How could they have lost the war? He and his comrades had suffered and bled and endured. Why could the people back home not have endured, not have bled, not have hung on just a while longer when victory had been within their grasp? What had undermined them? But, even as he mulled it over for the hundredth time, he winced at the results of his one foray into this area.

✯ ✯ ✯

The long hours at the Gehfarn coke plant merged into days of shovelling and sweating, with little in the way of conversation. Most of his workmates were older, had been excused military service, and put his reserved manner down to the war. Freuntz welcomed the physical effort, which he believed had a scourging effect on his guilt, imagined or otherwise. They preferred to slack on the job whenever they got the chance.

The only light relief, amidst the belching fumes, was when Eva sashayed across the yard, on any and every pretext. Divorced from her husband, a miner, Eva knew she still had it, knew they lusted after it, and was prepared to let them have it. But on a strictly look, and don't even think about touching, basis.

She worked hard on her spontaneous retorts, although their lumpen wit rarely advanced beyond a request to 'set her puppies free', a regret that they didn't have two such billowing pillows on which to rest their heads or, more prosaically, a query as to whether she was still 'going short'.

Graphic suggestions as to how the situation could be remedied were readily forthcoming. The finale was always the same; a synchronised display of crotch grabbing, which reminded her of the baboons she had once seen at the Cologne Zoo.

These humorous entreaties invariably lost their thrust when their cackling dissolved into a chorus of hacking and wheezing, as they dredged up the dust flecked mucus from the depth of their lungs. She could never resist a smile, for at least they were still in the game, still trying. But Freuntz was a puzzle. Why was he immune to her charms, blind to her availability? Why did he not make a move, any kind of move?

When the elderly foreman, Haubrich, dropped dead by the ovens, his funeral offered her the opportunity to assess his potential. Once Haubrich had been laid to rest, the workforce descended on 'The Konigsberg' to pay their informal respects.

Freuntz was still a reluctant drinker, but on occasions had stopped on the way home to replace some of the fluid, lost amidst the fumes. As he waited for his colleague, Jurgens, to return from the bar, he reflected that this was unknown territory. They hadn't been there ten minutes, and it would be his second glass. There was definitely a need to slow down.

Eva realised that to approach him alone might scare him off altogether. She took Helga for company, beginning with some simple enquiries, to which her diligent research had already provided the answers. The foaming beer gave him the excuse to avoid eye contact. He was aware that Helga had led Jurgens away, leaving him as the tethered prey.

She relished the fact that she was making most of the running. She opened up the debate by reminding him that her mother had always warned her about the quiet ones, and how marvellous it must have been in France "…with all those Mademoiselles, and their boyfriends away fighting". He pretended not to notice the twinkle in her eye, and committed himself to no more than a few brusque responses. After a while, she began to wonder whether this might be a challenge even beyond her, and the conversation was in danger of petering out altogether.

Freuntz was unable to conjure up the witty repartee on which she thrived. He squirmed inwardly as he desperately sought a line of response which would buy him time to plan his escape. As his brain fogged, and his mind went blank, he used his failsafe conversational standby. Or at least he thought he had, for almost perceptibly the atmosphere changed. The enquiry,

"And your parents, are they still in Sta …?" remained unanswered, as the significance of his conversational faux pas began to sink in. Only someone as clumsy as Freuntz could have blundered in so gauche a manner. The effect was immediate. Eva's parents had been but two of the elderly residents of Stanheim who died in the deadly flu epidemic which had cut a swathe through Germany, and many other parts of Europe. Her tone changed immediately. Her expression darkened.

"No, dead the pair of them, within two days of each other. Flu– I ask you– flu. What a way to go. Scrabbling for coal on the slagheaps, turnips they had to dig out with a pickaxe. No wonder they are dead. And then, and then, once they got them home, and they thawed out, mush, black mush." She shook her head before continuing.

"Fighting over cinders on the railway tracks, with people half their age, bread made with sawdust. Was it any wonder? Look at the trees, even now, not a branch- and no point going to the park, they chopped up all the benches."

Warming to her theme she continued. "Why did we put up with it? Why? They had the right idea in Russia. What was he called- Lenin was it? He had the right idea, shot the Tsar and all the rest of them. Should have done that here. He'd have been a hero. That posturing clown -The Kaiser- he soon got out, didn't he?"

Freuntz needed to relieve the emotional turmoil he had stirred up, but before he could speak, she was off again. "War? War? Who asked us? No one, that's who, and all for what? We've no land, no coal, and how much do we owe? How are we going to pay? You know what it said in the papers? That with any luck we'll have paid it back by 1988, yes 1988. We'll all be long gone, and so will Germany. All those mothers, all those widows, all those daughters with no fath…"

Freuntz had been ready to sympathise with her plight. But this assault on the sacrifices he and his comrades had made, in conditions no one at home could imagine, saw him launch into a passionate defence of their efforts, before turning to the weak willed and spineless efforts of so many on the home front. He ought to have realised that her eyes by now were watering. As the bull headed condemnation reached a crescendo, she tipped her glass over his head, turned on her heels, and stormed out.

✣ ✣ ✣

Disappointingly for Moeller, the opportunity to produce, direct, and star in a propaganda show piece had been well anticipated by the authorities. A staged series of low key releases was instigated, in the hope that the trickle would not resonate in the minds of a population eager to move on, and above all, avoid the social fracture many were predicting. The authorities were proved right.

By isolating the members of the Fatherland Front within the prison, a coordinated demonstration of defiance was prevented. Even more galling for Moeller, it had been prevented until the funeral of the Lindemann brothers had taken place, in the sombre fashion demanded by their grieving mother. Like so many, she was appalled by what was happening to Germany.

Attempts to reduce the antagonism of the inmates had been made by extending meal times, and the provision of a limited amount of constructive activity. Only Freuntz took the opportunity so provided, and began to reacquaint himself with a skill he had long neglected, calligraphy.

As day broke, with the first sulphurous fumes already rising from the coke plant, the four were released. As predicted, there were few members of the Union who still thirsted for confrontation. 5-30 was too early, even for the most zealous. With firm handshakes, but only tentative back slapping, the four melted into the mist, after brief assertions of loyalty and a determination to meet again, soon.

Freuntz was glad to take some prolonged exercise, and the opportunity it afforded to put things into perspective. Was Eva right? Were his expectations, so narrowly focused by his experiences in France, completely unrealistic? Hunger, cold and disillusion were a potent combination. But he had tolerated it, as had so many of his comrades. Even as he was about to justify his jaundiced viewpoint once more, he was already compromising. An image of beloved parents, dying in the dark and cold, began to temper his anger.

He was in no doubt that he would be one of the first to be sacked, as the post Versailles realities began to take effect. That was a wound which would take time to heal, on top of another unsuccessful encounter with a woman.

One thing she was right about was the state of the remaining trees, which, as they emerged from the spectral gloom, reminded him so much of the shattered stumps of the Western Front. By now, he was by the river and the familiar tenements of Stellgahle were showing signs of life. The mist ensured that the smoke produced by the cheap, brown coal was trapped close to ground level, rendering it even more pungent than normal. For Freuntz, it was the sweet smell of freedom. As the change jangled in his pocket, the immediate plan was clear; a coffee, then on to see 'Old Man' Hoffmann. He would know where to get what he needed.

✲ ✲ ✲

What was that noise? Sophie yearned to bury her head beneath the blankets, but her curiosity got the better of her. Her eyes half open, she stumbled to the window as Nicole was beginning to stir.

In peacetime, cars were still a rare sight in St Valery. Two arriving at once was almost unheard of. But these were police cars. Like iron filings to a magnet, a crowd of twenty villagers was gathered below. Others were joining them.

Madame Poiller was already there. Sophie shook her head. She could imagine her drooling at the manna from heaven presented by a visit from the police. Guilt or innocence played no part in their considerations. Hector Brulet, owner of the rival butchers shop was especially animated.

"Not before time if you ask me. The pair of them. Him, thinks he's Lord of the Manor. Always has done. Too smart, too smart. Too smart for his own good. As for her…"

Richard Lemeny was nodding furiously. "Must be something juicy, I reckon. Serious. I mean. Two cars. When was the last time that happened? Deserve what's coming to them. The pair of them. You're exactly right. Too many fancy ideas, him. And it's not before time that she had her wings clipped. And her mouth." Madame Poiller smiled.

The percussion inside Sophie's skull meant that she could not be sure where the policemen were. Her suspicions were confirmed. A loud rap on the door was answered by a bellowing Mr Chalroix, directing his wife to see what was going on. Her reply was muffled. Sophie grinned at what it was likely to have been.

She was unable to resist the chance to eavesdrop from the top of the stairs. Through the half opened living room door, she struggled to make sense of the fragments of conversation she was able to hear. Monsieur Lafarge. Two others. Poisoned meat. Further investigations. Knowingly sold. Charged with murder! Sophie couldn't keep up.

She could hear sobbing. She tried to make sense of what she had just heard. They were male tears. She heard the door slam below. A distraught Monsieur Chalroix, head bowed, shoulders heaving, his arms handcuffed behind him, was being steered through the stunned onlookers. The crowd appeared to fall silent. The doors were opened, he was bundled in, and the two cars pulled quietly away.

Perplexed by this astonishing development, Sophie returned to the window to observe the aftermath. Heads were being shaken, arms were being folded meaningfully across chests, and tongues were beginning to clack. The speculation was wild, the condemnation rife. The serene figure of Madame Poiller was the orchestrator, gleefully relishing the demise of her erstwhile colleague- and despised rival.

Sophie knew this was an opportunity to grasp, but, infuriatingly, she couldn't work out how. Harsh experience had taught her the folly of failing to follow her instincts in the past, but on this occasion she was prepared to wait.

An afternoon of blissful sunshine, with Nicole gargling happily on her knee, was spent in the shadow of Dreamers Rock. By contrast, she returned to a darkened house which seemed to have had all life sucked out of it. As she climbed the stairs, the living room door was shut, the hallway dark. Sophie paused briefly to listen to the heaving sobs.

Religion, of all things, was to provide the chance she needed, next day. Attendance at church was compulsory, in as much as only the sturdiest souls could tolerate the social ostracism which befell anyone with an independent frame of mind. Resident for almost five years, Sophie was still viewed as a newcomer. She knew she revelled in the role of social outcast. 'God botherers', and 'po faced papist poison', were two of the more repeatable retorts Natalie had helped her construct. Sophie was unbending in her view. She had enough guilt of her own, without having more heaped on her on a weekly basis.

The smell of warm bread from the bakery was one she always found difficult to resist. She purchased two croissants, in absolute silence, and made her way back towards the butchers. To her amazement, the figure of Madame Chalroix emerged. But this was a completely different Madame Chalroix, transformed from the broken, guilt racked, creature she had expected.

Her auburn hair was swept back from her face, her clothing was immaculate, and her broad brimmed hat was both elegant and stylish. But it was her posture which struck Sophie most. Her shoulders were back, her chin tilted upwards, and her eyes, reddened though they were, sent out a defiant message. She was ready to run the gauntlet, and face her accusers head on. Sophie immediately recognised a kindred spirit, and as the sunlight briefly illuminated her half concealed profile, she could see, at last, why Monsieur Chalroix might once have found her attractive.

Sophie quickly worked out her next move. Observing the congregation emerge an hour later, the speed with which Madame Chalroix scuttled across the cobbles decided it. Sophie knew what Madame Chalroix was going through. She contrived to meet her, as she fumbled for her key. Sophie was correct. The ordeal had shaken her, her complexion was ashen, and she was on the brink of tears. Before any words of condolence could be offered, she was convulsed by a series of howls. She slid slowly down the wall, and sat slumped against the counter.

Never comfortable with genuine emotion, as her time at La Pigalle had involved so much which was false, Sophie calculated that waiting would pay dividends, and she was correct. Putting an arm around the distraught figure, she slid down next to Madame Chalroix. With a firm push, the door was closed, the world would be kept at bay, and eventually the sobbing would cease.

It did, and after a brief period of silence Madame Chalroix seemed to undergo a remarkable transformation. She levered herself up the counter, smoothed down her crumpled skirt, and for some reason rearranged, rather than removed, her hat. It seemed to Sophie as if these simple actions were the start of the rest of her life, and a new chapter was to begin, especially as Sophie then heard the magic words,

"Thank you mademoiselle, thank you, thank you, thank you. You will share a glass with me, no?"

✲ ✲ ✲

It quickly became apparent that Madame Chalroix was a drinker of heroic proportions, with a capacity which dwarfed anything Sophie had encountered- and that included her own redoubtable capabilities.

The story of the poisoned meat and the resulting fatalities were described in detail, before the depressant effects began to take over. Soon, Madame Chalroix was telling her life story. The most poignant part, the one which explained so much for Sophie, was of her exile from her home village as a result of a miscarriage, the result of an illicit affair with a farm labourer. She had been fourteen. Ostracised by her family, grateful for the compassion of the local nuns, she had effectively withdrawn from society for much of her youth.

She explained how she had met Monsieur Chalroix, and how handsome he had seemed. But her revelation, on their wedding night, had effectively killed the marriage stone dead. And yet, and this was what made most impression on Sophie, despite everything, she had stood by him.

As the afternoon faded into a purple and golden haze, the sun set and dusk fell, the two outsiders realised they only had each other. Just before Madame Chalroix finally passed out, Sophie had enough presence of mind to realise the end was nigh. She led her carefully upstairs, and having loosened her beautiful silk blouse, removed her crumpled hat and stroked her face tenderly. She stole quietly out of the room. The snoring began.

Sophie had learnt a lot, not least how Madame Chalroix managed to make it through each day, why her attitude to men was so venomous, but above all, how their alliance was likely to proceed.

The news about the factory was the icing on the cake.

# Chapter Eight

The Hoffmann Emporium was a brand name in search of premises more prestigious than their current location. However, given Stanheim's topography, it was as good as it was likely to get, and in many ways was perfect. Property in the old, medieval heart of the town was scarce, expensive, and somehow, never available to Jews.

Hence its location on the periphery emphasised the relentless urge to move up the social and economic ladder. This was what had driven Jacob Hoffmann for so long. He could see what he wanted, but was denied. He was as good, as successful, and as enterprising as them. Here was the evidence, right on their doorstep. However, the flame was dimming, the urge less strong. As with so many other things, it was all down to the war.

Like all immigrants, the urge to prove themselves more patriotic than the host community had fuelled his drive for acceptance, since arriving from Hungary in 1895. He was one of many, forced to emigrate by the fear of the pogroms which flared up across Eastern Europe at the slightest provocation. His younger brother, Ezra, had not stayed for long, enthralled by the opportunities available in America. A trivial argument over advertising meant that he had not seen his brother Moshe for twelve years, even though his pawn brokers shop was only two miles away.

But it was through his sons that he had hoped to gain real acceptance. He had been part of the cheering throng who marched down from Stellgahle to celebrate the declaration of war in 1914. Not only that, he encouraged them to sign up at the first opportunity. He had written off Jacob, a thirty year old, wheezing asthmatic. But Michael and David, separated by eighteen months, offered far more promise.

Their photographs, stiff backed and resolute, were the first thing customers noticed as they approached the counter. They had adopted the expression of synthetic invulnerability, which all soldiers summoned up for the cameras. But the photographs now told a more sombre tale. Draped across each of their photographs was an Iron Cross, each accompanied by the commendation of their commanding officer.

Mister Hoffmann had been proud to relate their exploits at first. It helped him to cope. When the British tanks had effected their breakthrough at Cambrai, in November 1917, it had seemed that a decisive blow was about to be struck. However, indecision, surprise at their own success, and desperate courage on behalf of the Germans first slowed, and then halted, the advance. The Hoffmann boys had not run, like so many, but instead had lain in their shell holes, let the tanks run above them, and then engaged them from behind. They had accounted for three between them, before both were cut down in a hail of machine gun bullets.

They were not the only casualties however. Already weakened by hunger, the biting cold, and the devastating news in early December, had broken Mrs Hoffmann's heart. She had died on Christmas Eve. Mr Hoffmann would not last long either, if Freuntz was any judge. He had seen so many men lose it, the desire to carry on simply evaporating. From then on, it usually happened sooner than later.

Prior to his imprisonment, Freuntz had been spending more time there. His empathy with the father of two war heroes had offered Mister Hoffmann some solace, and lubricated the conversations between them. It gave Mister Hoffmann an excuse not to talk to Jacob- how he regretted giving him that name. His very existence now set his teeth grinding, and the tears welling.

Freuntz had had such a spartan upbringing that the variety of produce Mister Hoffmann somehow managed to source, the lustre of the textiles in the drapery section, and the range of literature in the book section, had meant that an hour could pass without him looking at the same thing twice.

He opened the door, as Mister Hoffmann was placing the last of his produce outside. It was reduced in both quality and quantity from pre-war days, but still an impressive display. The mist still clung close. Freuntz could not be sure if this was why his complexion was more pallid than normal. Even more puzzling was the question of why he was manhandling the stuff in the first place.

"What a weasel, he's f...cleared off to Berlin. Now, of all times. Wants to play the clarinet he says, Berlin is where the future is, and Jews can merge into the background a lot easier there. He's been yapping about it for so long I didn't pay him any attention any more. He couldn't be more in the background than he was here. Woke up this morning and he's finally done it. I didn't think he had it in him. Now of all f... times." Mister Hoffmann wheezed, as the effort of conversation took second place to the effort of stacking. Freuntz admired how, despite his anguish and near exhaustion, he refrained from actually swearing.

"Upstairs was his idea, the only decent one he had in all his time, and now, how am I meant to keep that going, as well as all this?"

The place upstairs was a new development. The Emporium was really three shops knocked into one, and upstairs had remained undeveloped, apart from a basic office. Jacob's idea had been that as people faced hard times, the loss of the main wage earner, and a need for ready cash, they could buy the pick of the treasured possessions at rock bottom prices. He was already being proved correct.

Freuntz, unusually for him, decided to risk rejection without first calculating the odds.

"I could give you a hand. I spend half my time here anyway. That is, until you can get somebody permanent in. Your sons were two good Germans. They would weep at how things are now, but they will change, believe me."

For both men, this was the first time in a while that things had fallen into place to their benefit. As if in recognition, the first shaft of sunlight pierced, then quickly dispersed, the mist. Even better, the material he needed would be here by Friday.

※ ※ ※

Sophie couldn't remember much about the details of their pact. Last night, at least, they had both seemed committed. Hadn't they? She gave thanks for the extra day of respite, provided by a Tuesday start at the mill. The shorter hours would be equal in the first week. This had saved Sophie. She was in no fit state to exhibit her newly discovered powers of leadership.

Deaf to the increasingly agitated Nicole, she dreaded having to get upright. Sophie buried her head under the pillow; anywhere would do to avoid the sunshine, already flooding the room. She was unsure how long she slept for, but guilt about her negligence towards Nicole would not allow her to put the moment off any longer.

Her gastric juices fought an unequal struggle with the alcoholic residue she had not vomited away last night. She stumbled towards Nicole's cot. Aghast, she found Nicole was gone. She stood bolt upright, pain jabbing her chest. Running anywhere was not an idea she could begin to contemplate in her current state. Clinging for grim death to the bannister, she inched her way down stairs.

To her astonishment, she entered the immaculate living room to see Madame Chalroix rocking a clearly contented Nicole. Sophie could not help but notice the radiance of her expression, the bloom of her complexion, and the serenity of her manner. This was a moment she could never have dreamt of, thought Sophie, just before the room began to revolve.

The effort Sophie had expended now exacted its toll. Her skin was clammy, and her cheeks flushed. She dashed for the back door where, despite her best intentions, she threw up all over the nasturtiums. Always a good colour match, she reflected wryly. She went back inside to confront the chuckling Madame Chalroix.

Madame Chalroix was turning out to be a formidable woman, the more Sophie discovered about her. She had clearly been up early, as several half finished cups of coffee had yet to be cleared away. The table was covered with ledgers, bank books, and what looked like graph paper. There was a definite spring in her step, and Sophie couldn't help thinking that the post-Monsieur Chalroix era was already off to a flying start. Elements of their conversation- those that she could recall- began to make sense.

She had been the business brain of the two, and had hoarded considerable sums to ease the hurt of her husbands public philandering. Her plan was to close for the week to allow the gossip to abate, and the shock to recede. She would source the beef from only two of the local farmers, both keen to restore their business and willing to negotiate on price, whilst she would supplement her stock with fresh caught chicken and rabbit. This was where Sophie came in.

She had been brought up in Veziers, a town which owed its existence and subsequent growth to its position as a junction of four railway lines. The early inhabitants were country people who were desperate to maintain their connections with the land, its traditions and habits, fearful that urbanisation would devour their individuality, and they would be absorbed within an amorphous suburban mass.

Her father had been a hard drinking railwayman. She was the son he cursed his wife for not providing, Undeterred by such niceties, he raised Sophie as a country girl, with whom he would have to make the best of a bad job. She trapped her first rabbit at seven, skinned her first one at eight, and shot her first pigeon at ten. She could neck a chicken blindfold, and felt a special pride in eating whatever she caught.

Sophie would catch the rabbits, Madame Chalroix would look after Nicole, and between them they would dig up the prize vegetables Monsieur Chalroix cultivated, when he wasn't fornicating. In addition, they would raise their own chickens. It seemed a perfect partnership of two strong minded personalities.

Madame Chalroix was energised. She skipped back from the kitchen, determined to toast the future. Sophie's digestive tract was already in a state of nervous trepidation. As the jaunty proposition was put, "It's past noon, definitely time for a starter." Sophie was already half way to the back door. In almost perfect symmetry, the sunflowers were pebbledashed, and she slumped against the whitewashed wall. The last sound she heard was Madame Chalroix, in a mockingly regretful voice, "Ah well, all the more for me. Sure I can't tempt you Sophie? Sophie?"

But Sophie was already asleep.

✧ ✧ ✧

Constant recalibration of the odds had preceded virtually all the decisions Freuntz had ever made, other than in battle. But his spontaneous suggestion to Mister Hoffman, on top of his performance at La Pigalle-well it was almost becoming a habit, he thought, almost permitting himself a grin. But now the doubts began to crowd out the lightened mood he had felt on leaving his new employer.

The sun was bathing the town in a gentle autumnal glow and Freuntz had half a day to pass, plenty of time for those doubts to take root. Reflection was a process which suited his reserved personality. Prison had provided the opportunity to reach a number of decisions.

Fresh air was always preferable to the clinging damp of his fourth floor apartment in Stellgahle. He headed for the benches by the riverside, to weigh up, once more, the pros and cons. After all, mustn't rush into anything.

Violence was acceptable to achieve the restoration of Germany's prestige, and according to Moeller, it could only be led by a warrior elite. This was where Moeller had confused him, once again. For was it not a well organised elite who had brought revolution and ruin to Russia? He could accept the coruscating venom with which Moeller had lambasted the politicians- they had accepted the Versailles settlement, without a whimper. But part of him wondered what they could have done differently. The simmering tension and sporadic violence of the last ten months would be but a foretaste, if the Allies, as they had threatened, occupied the whole of Germany.

He had been right about the blacks though, that was the ultimate insult, and a physical embodiment of Germany's prostrate position. Some things were too much to bear. That was definitely one of them. But the Jews. Where did they fit in?

Mister Hoffmann had shown him consideration and understanding from the first. After all, where would his new found vegetarianism be, without the special produce available there? His rudimentary dishes were both colourful, and actually tasted of something. Paprika seemed to have limitless applications.

But more than that, how much more German could he be, if not by sacrificing his sons in the hour of national need? And they weren't the only ones. The Spengler twins, eviscerated by the same shell, during the desperate, but doomed push to The Marne last summer. Ariel Liebowitz, killed in the same raid, on the road to St Valery. No, Moeller was definitely wrong there.

But where he was right was in the weakness of the new politicians. After the battle at the Dorfell plant, a tap on the wrist was all they had received. Weak! Weak! Weak! A machine gun and a factory wall would have delivered the sentence they deserved, had the roles been reversed.

The attempts to balance the conflicting arguments were starting to make his head ache. The ducks were now waddling towards him. As they raced for the stale bread, which he had almost forgotten to spread, he stood up and recapped the decisions which his time in prison had helped him arrive at.

He would give Germany five years. Surely the country would be heading back to the top by then? If not, he would go to America. Thirty two wouldn't be too old and still give him plenty of time to start afresh. He would continue with his vegetarianism, and he would read. He had to be able to match Moeller's powers of reasoning to make sense of current events. He would call at the library on his way home. But above all he would save.

And tomorrow he would meet Moeller and the others at the Prinz Eugen.

✲ ✲ ✲

His previous visits had been characterised by a nervous anticipation, which had rarely been in vain, as Moeller fulminated against the myriad injustices which had befallen Germany. This time it was different, other than showing his tattered membership card. There was no one on the door and, on entering, the frisson of danger, so tangible on other occasions, was replaced by the cowed resignation of the leaderless.

The dozen or so regulars welcomed Freuntz, as if he was a conquering hero. He was the only one of his cellmates to make an appearance.

"Where is everyone?" Freuntz asked. He sat down opposite Hubert, in one of the booths.

"Friedrich, back in hospital. Breathing difficulties. Coughing blood as well so they say. Graumann, doesn't leave the house now." The circling gestures by his temple, which Hubert enacted with a smirk, suggested that there were mental problems. "Moeller, long gone. We won't see him for a while, if ever. Sure to be in Munich, for my money. That's where Kaltz went. Things are really bubbling down there."

Once the pleasantries were over, the beer was ordered and the reminiscing began, but then faded within minutes. Democracy and all its ills received the customary verbal battering, but in a more muted fashion than before. The talk of revolution smacked of nothing better to do, rather than suggesting any serious purpose.

Freuntz was conscious of the fact that the alternative was likely to be a prolonged drinking session, with more war stories, followed by tuneless renditions of songs, rendered unrecognisable from the original. Drinking slightly quicker than was good for him, Freuntz realised that he needed not only to make his excuses and leave. He had to explain why.

"I started with old man Hoffmann today. You know, lost both sons at Cambrai. Only part time to begin with," he added quickly before adding even more defensively, "Jobs… jobs, no jobs for the likes of us, eh boys? Got to get them when you can," in a desperate attempt to curry favour.

The sentence trailed away as the prospect of exclusion from the band of brothers lay in the balance. After a short silence, it was Hubert who led the grunts of acquiescence. The rest nodded dutifully.

As he drained the beer, the relief that the hurdle had been overcome led to a feeling of exhilaration that he was still one of them. They shook hands, and swore undying allegiance to Germany. But as he climbed the stairs, he couldn't help but feel pity for them, as well. Without Moeller to tell them what to think, they were like so many sheep awaiting the return of their shepherd, their anti Semitism not even skin deep.

He raised his collar as the evening chill made his cheeks tingle. The mist began to roll off the river. The twenty minute walk would take only ten as the beer went straight to his bladder. Urinating in the trenches was fine, but in a German back street? Out of the question. However, cold and alcohol complemented each other perfectly. When he finally found the entrance to a darkened back alley, propriety came a poor second to need.

The sense of blessed relief was delicious, and he was content to let the foaming, steaming cascade run its course. He was briefly back in junior school, where he and Meinke had had regular competitions in who could piss furthest, highest, longest and yellowest. But as the image faded, it was Moeller who reclaimed his attention. His boys were leaderless, Kaltz was gone, and others had melted away. The prospect of a full day at work, coupled with an empty bladder, put the spring in his step, only to have the difficulty he might encounter spelled out in crude whitewash on the gable end,

"Jews out"

# Chapter Nine

The clock showed ten past four, and she had been awake for over an hour. It was an unusual feeling to be anxious. Normally, she reacted instinctively, leaving no time for second thoughts, doubts, or the feelings of others to impinge. This was different.

The feelings of melancholy since the birth had not been erased, despite the events of the last week. Her new alliance with Madame Chalroix, conceived amidst a haze of vin ordinaire and grief, would be put to the test straight away. And then there was work. They would look at her in a different light now. Could she match up to their expectations? What of her new boss, and how to compete with Chalmy, his long words and pince-nez spectacles?

Nothing for it. Doing something is always better than doing nothing was but one of the homilies she had learnt from her father. Within minutes, her cotton dress was flung on, her shawl was round her shoulders, and with Nicole sighing contentedly she tiptoed down the stairs.

She grabbed the simple, home-made traps she had fashioned between the final bouts of vomiting-was it only twelve hours ago? She set off into the gloom. God, how the cobbles cut through the soles of her boots, so thin you could read the newspaper through, she had joked with Natalie. A brief tinge of regret that her career at La Pigalle had at least enabled her to purchase a few extras, even at black market prices, was now the least of her considerations. It was time to move on.

The first, violet tinges of dawn were already in evidence, and with the ancient rock as her benevolent sentry, she quickly went to work. She had noticed the first burrows appear in the undergrowth, whilst playing with Nicole. The feelings flooded back. This was her land, her domain, and here she was in total control. Not the mill, not La Pigalle, not St Valery, with its shifting undercurrents of disdain and disapproval.

Her father hadn't taught her a lot, but what he had taught, he had taught well. She knew the patterns of the burrows, as if by instinct. In no time at all, the rabbits responded as rabbits had always responded, meeting the end they always met. Six in ten minutes, she reflected, her knapsack heavy with plunder, a smile of satisfaction on her lips. How could they be so dumb? Only good at one thing, rabbits. Just like people, really. She winced, as the gravel of the country lane was replaced by the cobbles of the main street.

✫ ✫ ✫

Her approach to the mill was more measured than it had been eight days previously. Tremors of uncertainty were balanced by the still lingering remorse at the way Monsieur Lafarge had met his end. His determination to help his employees in times of difficulty had literally been the death of him. Had he been able to distribute the last parcel to Jeanne as intended, that would have been the end of her as well, instead of him.

Absence makes the heart grow fonder, she had once read. Although it was true in the case of Monsieur Lafarge she hoped that her two tormentors had died in agony. Accordingly, it was not fondness, but malice, which suffused her thoughts as she passed her loom, watched by her colleagues, most of whom were smoking, some even nodding respectfully, whilst awaiting the next move. Jeanne would be easy meat without malevolent influence of her now former allies. A half salut! to Monsieur Chalroix and his corner cutting ways -two out of three was not bad.

She had realised that being first to greet the new owner could be of pivotal importance. But as she entered the office, Chalmy was already poring over what looked like a balance sheet, the prolonged pushing of his spectacles to the end of his nose radiating disdain.

To the left, a mouse like figure was forcing a battered hat onto her head, as if heading out into a force ten gale. Madeleine Graffny had been with Monsieur Lafarge for forty two years, and his death, with the new era it would undoubtedly usher in, was her cue to leave the new world to others. She had been the glue which had held the whole enterprise together through thick and thin- and there had been plenty of thin. Never without a handbag, a solution or an opinion, the latter was being offered for the last time, in her customary trenchant manner.

"Be careful Monsieur, be careful, he will be the end of this place. Lower than a snake's arse, that one. Brother or not, just be careful." She sucked on her teeth, straightened her hat, and with her coat buttoned up to her neck, headed out of the factory for the last time. So much venom in one so small, thought Sophie. I like that!

With the door closed, Sophie turned to introduce herself to Lionel Lafarge. Thin was the first impression he made, not helped by being hunched at the table, as Chalmy loomed over him. Thin lapels, thin tie, thin shoulders, and a thin smile which was half-heartedly offered, as he invited her to sit down. His sickly pallor seemed drained of life, and Sophie wondered how long he might have left. Not long was the answer. As any consideration of the retching attempts to remove the phlegm from his lungs could have told her, Lionel Lafarge was dying.

His bookish manner, coupled with a zealous avoidance of any physical exertion when young, had meant that his call up papers had left him a shuddering wreck. His physical attributes meant he was unsuited to front line combat, but his mental capacities meant he was invaluable to the artillery. He had an instinctive grasp of geometry, muzzle velocity, patterns of fire, and the science of logistics. He had been promoted to captain, decorated twice, but hadn't been able to stop shaking since. He had never been a smoker prior to the war, but the cigarettes, given freely to help calm shattered nerves, had had their predictable effect. He couldn't survive without the tar laden succour they offered. He was now getting through two packs a day.

Chalmy had spent much of the previous week getting to grips with 'Das Kapital', but still couldn't get past page four, despite several attempts. His jargon laden interjections had already caused Lionel to smoke even more rapidly than normal. He was ready for a different voice.

Lionel quickly summed up his appreciation of the situation, and Sophie realised he was thinking along the same lines as she and Natalie had discussed so often.

"You were absolutely right mademoiselle, of course you were. My father was many things, but an eye for art was one thing he never had. Even I thought the things were fine, in their own way, but difficult to make enough for us to survive. No, mademoiselle, astute, very astute. A new era does-as you so rightly say-require new thinking."

Chalmy squirmed in his seat.

"The designs were, well, dowdy I would describe them. Fine for the last century, I suppose. We need a complete re-launch, new markets have to be found and an advertising campaign of some kind has to be developed, although I must confess, I have no idea where to start."

Chalmy struggled to contain a welling sense of frustration. Nodding more furiously than was probably necessary, Sophie seized the moment.

"Yes, yes, Monsieur. I couldn't agree more." She resisted the temptation to flutter her eyelashes. "Play to our strengths, concentrate on what we know, can produce, and base it on what is around us. The whole world wants a fresh start. Leave the last five years behind, clean fresh, colours, simple designs and use nature. That's what is needed. A time to heal, and nature will do it to the land. Some brightness and simplicity can help us do it for people."

Sophie realised that her thought processes were operating on a different time scale to her vocal chords, and decided to quit while she was ahead. Nevertheless, the jumbled oration had the effect of brightening the contorted expression Lionel had worn, ever since Chalmy had started to lecture him on the evils of the bourgeoisie.

Chalmy, on the other hand, knew enough about tennis, a game he associated with louche aristocrats and oppressors of the masses, to know he was forty love down. He was pinned even more firmly at the back of the court when Monsieur Lafarge, who had had enough of decision making for one day, sought to round off the meeting.

"And of course, we will need to replace Madame Graffny."

Why not? thought Sophie. This time, there was a flutter of the eyelashes, patented at La Pigalle. She lowered her voice, and replied,

"Monsieur, I can type."

Game, set and match.

✡ ✡ ✡

Her return home passed in a blur, as she yearned to tell Madame Chalroix about the developments. She was breathless, as she entered the living room. A picture of contented bliss awaited her. Madame Chalroix was pulling faces and hiding her face behind her hands, as a giggling Nicole wriggled with glee on the striped eiderdown, spread across the floor. She had had a marvellous day; deals had been done, discounts agreed, and lines of credit negotiated.

Yes, the bottle was open, but virtually full, and the glass by her side had hardly been touched. The last of the sun was just discernible, as the curtains were half closed. Its soft light seemed to ooze contentment.

Sophie tried hard, but couldn't suppress the idea that things might be picking up at last.

# Chapter Ten

All things considered, Metternich had made the best of a difficult situation at The Congress of Vienna. Or so it had seemed, on first reading, but now Freuntz was unclear. However, what he was clear about was that history was a lot more complex than he had ever imagined, and that was just from the German viewpoint. He was also clear that his appetite for knowledge was being whetted, with every night he spent in the reading room of the Workmans Academy. The last fourteen months had been an intellectual journey which he was eager to continue.

He had begun with a random sample from the second hand books which were starting to accumulate, upstairs at The Emporium. Three editions aimed at school students-'Frederick the Great: Warrior and Statesman', 'A Beginners Guide to the Teutonic Knights', and 'Romans on the Rhine' – had encouraged him to fill in the gaps between these separate eras. It seemed there was no end to it.

He slumped further in his chair, pulled his collar even further up, and blew harder on his hands. The heating had been turned off an hour ago and he was the only one left. He was proud of his progress, not yet able to debate ideas openly, but able to contribute a limited range of opinions, should the opportunity ever present itself.

The four nights he spent there, each week, also served another part of his plan, which was to save enough to emigrate, if things didn't pick up in Germany. It was an unlikely prospect at the moment. He could use someone else's heat, someone else's light, and his concentration took away the nagging hunger pains.

His rigid self denial had seen him put cardboard in his shoes, rather than have them re-soled, coat himself in goose fat for every day of the last four bitter weeks, and, only at the insistence of Mister Hoffmann, had he purchased a new shirt. Reflecting his frugality, it was only new in that he hadn't owned it before, even though the embroidered initials indicated two others had.

He had proved himself indispensable to Mister Hoffmann, and this was another source of satisfaction. His desire to organise, tabulate and schedule any activity in which he was engaged, had enabled him to take control of operations upstairs, occasionally run one of the sections downstairs, whilst at the same time dealing with all correspondence and stock control. His immaculate handwriting had supplemented the skill he had always had- a head for figures. As a result, Mister Hoffmann had increased his hours, but not, Freuntz observed wryly, his hourly rate.

He was unconcerned however, as his hoard of cash was beginning to build. Only one aspect of his job irked him. He had had to re-price every single item three times in the last six months, and the new money exuded cheapness, in comparison to the elegant, pre-war currency which he remembered so fondly. He seemed to have more of it, but was no better off.

As he replaced the book carefully on the shelf, he sighed in anticipatory pleasure at how much learning lay ahead. A 10-8 shift would mean he could go to the bank before work tomorrow. He salivated at the prospect of making another deposit, although not at the prospect of wringing out his socks, once the cardboard had rotted in the slush.

✱ ✱ ✱

He was finding that he had to get to the bank earlier each week, if he was not be late for work. Today was no different. He found himself at the back of a shuffling line, being admitted into the bank which, like so many others, demanded a subservience from its customers, first developed in medieval times.

The slush was now frozen solid, a murky grey, as the polluted air began to release its daily deposits. Snow was beginning to fall, almost reluctantly, as the wind eddied back and forth. Freuntz was reluctant to remove his fingerless mittens, but was glad to be out of the cold.

The Rhineland Cooperative Bank had been designed to reflect the belief that 'nothing was too good for the working class,' and the results were admirable. The porticoed entrance, the high ceilings, and an abundance of mahogany, sought to cow the customers into an awed reverence, more reminiscent of a cathedral. Freuntz gazed upwards, always eager to appreciate the splendour of the design.

The queue was beginning to separate into three lines to approach the tellers, each weighed down, it seemed, by the momentous task which faced them: that of giving the customers some of their own money back. Everything was done slowly, and it gave Freuntz the chance to observe his fellow customers.

A cloth capped workman to his right, clung to the last stub of his cigarette as if to life itself, whilst a buxom woman, in an act of great defiance, actually looked at her watch and tutted. The figure in the military style uniform was what passed for security. Freuntz deduced from the size of his paunch that the cookhouse was probably the nearest he had got to the action, and that his revolver was purely for show.

He was more interested in the two figures at the front of his line. One big, one small. Both were wearing identically styled overcoats which seemed too big for them, their stylish, broad brimmed hats pulled down to their eyebrows. Had he turned round he would have seen a third, stood within feet of the guard. The smaller of the two in front seemed to have what looked like a red towel protruding from one of his pockets.

Just as the realisation was beginning to dawn, the action began. The smaller of the two whipped out the towel with one hand, and draped it over the muzzle of the submachine gun. A brief burst had the desired effect. Shattered glass and splintered fragments of the elaborate stucco embellishments to the ceiling cascaded down like hailstones. The larger figure now took a pistol from his pocket. He blasted away the lock, kicked back the door, and was behind the counter in an instant.

"On the floor now! Now! Now! Get down now!" Freuntz heard from behind. The terrified customers were soon prostrate, accompanied by the low moans and fearful whimpers of the seriously terrified. It suddenly dawned on Freuntz. It had to be. Moeller. Already he was dragging the terrified manager to the first vault, whilst-who else could it be but Kaltz?-began to shovel cash from the tills into a hessian sack. His curses were deafening, the responses panic stricken.

No wonder the overcoats had looked so big, Freuntz thought. He raised his eyes slightly from the floor. The aroma of a freckled teenager, who had soiled himself, was overpowering. He looked in the mirror which ran the length of the wall. The original guard was nowhere to be seen. A different figure was by the door. Bandell!

"Faster! Faster!" Kaltz was screaming now. Notes were spilling all over the floor in the panic. The two tellers looked like they might faint at any moment. Their bodies shuddered. They tried, in vain, to react to the frenzied instructions being yelled at them, it seemed, from all sides.

Moeller released the safety catch, and pressed the muzzle against the skull of the manager. He was already whimpering. A crunch of bone on skull brought it to an end. The clump of a falling body, somewhere behind the counter, gave Freuntz a brief opportunity to observe that Bandell had disappeared.

Kaltz realised that time was running out. He emerged from the vault. His desperate yell to Moeller had barely left his lips. Several hissing canisters exploded. Freuntz knew the drill, but the other customers hadn't a clue. As the vapour quickly filled the hall, they clawed at their eyes, convinced they would be blind for ever.

✯ ✯ ✯

Bandell felt that he had waited long enough. He had to think quickly. Kaltz and Moeller wouldn't escape. Success. But the most important reason for the betrayal, the money, that part of the plan was a failure. As he reached the bottom of the steps, armed police swept by, fingers on triggers, gas masks in place. He had thought they might never arrive. He turned the corner. A moment of panic. The van was still there. Matters had still to be settled with Weber.

Bandell pulled away quietly, and headed for the handover. The bank was half way down one of the streets which led off the square. In no time he was on the far side. He would be at Weber's bakery in under three minutes, just as they had planned. Events there were also starting to go awry.

The wind was now from the east, and the snow was billowing more strongly. The customers stamped their feet and shuffled forward, more in hope than expectation. There were still eight of them on the pavement when the burly figure of Heinz Weber forced his way into the doorway, almost crushing the diminutive frame of Frau Frantzen in the process. He firmed his jaw. He spread his arms to signify that there would be no more bread that day.

This was the final straw for the freezing customers, as his actions had given his father the chance to force the door shut, and to turn the sign around to show 'Closed'. If he thought that was the end of the matter, he was sadly mistaken. He hadn't reckoned with an irate Frau Briedel, who now moved into attack mode.

Weber had felt cheated that the war had finished too soon for him to see action, but his involvement on the fringes of the Fatherland Front helped massage his ego, and assuage his thwarted sense of masculinity. He was to need every resource he could muster as Frau Briedel aimed a wild swipe with her furled umbrella.

His role in the plot was to load the two bread baskets containing the money into the back of the van, once Bandell had arrived, drive back across the square, past the bank and out to the old glassworks, where the others would be waiting. Waiting was something of which Frau Briedel had had enough. Another ferocious swipe caught him a glancing blow, as he realised sanctuary lay on the other side of the door, the wrong side as far as he was concerned.

"Every day, every day queuing up for hours, and then you run out, you fat bastard. You don't look like you're going without, you lump of…" as the effort of launching another swipe left her short of breath to complete the sentence.

Weber realised that safety, at least for a while, now lay in the van, and the hope that Bandell's arrival would save him from a lynching. His flailing arms only just managed to keep Frau Briedel at bay, as she questioned his parentage once again, in even more acrimonious terms.

Through the swirling snow, he could see Bandell approaching. Bandell pulled up, loaded the two baskets into the back, and with a double slap on the roof, indicated that Weber could go. The sight of Bandell in his uniform had brought temporary respite for Weber. He had read how men found religion, when in extreme circumstances-'shellhole religion'- and no longer questioned its existence. With the wheels skidding furiously, he seized his chance and pulled away, as a barrage of snowballs clattered on the roof.

Ten minutes later, he was able to reflect that at least this part of the plan had worked. He inched the van through the snow, but was puzzled by the tyre tracks. He turned into the factory yard, but couldn't see the car, which must have pulled into the plant itself to escape the blizzard. Desperate to show some initiative, he opened the back door. As he lifted the first basket, he reflected on how light money must be.

As he threw the second one onto the snow, crudely cut bundles of newspaper spilled out. The figures emerged from the gloom, rifles raised, gesturing to him to get his hands up.

✯ ✯ ✯

His arrival had been expected for several days, but it came as no surprise, to those who knew him, that he had kept them in the dark as to his whereabouts. Creating an impression was all important to Olivier. Anticipation was all part of the performance.

His new colleagues were anticipating, that much was certain, but each in their own way. For Sophie there was mild curiosity as to just how dashing he was. For Lionel, there was a quiet dread of the harebrained plans which were likely to emerge. For Chalmy, a grudging recognition that the corridors of power would be even more crowded than ever with four of them. How would Trotsky have responded?

His influence had been on the wane ever since Lionel had chosen the childlike designs his nemesis had doodled on her notepad, from within the citadels of power. This was how he saw the manager's office. His hurried reading on the shortcomings of Impressionism had paid no dividends at all. The last planning session had dissolved in acrimony, as the confusion of his attempted critique had come across as small minded jealousy, which was exactly what it was.

For Sophie, work-could she even think of the term career? - could not be going better. Her rudimentary typing skills were sufficient to cope with the correspondence generated, and she often found herself with time on her hands. Her doodlings, as Chalmy referred to them with withering scorn, were actually far more than that. Her love of flowers had seen her spend countless hours as a child, sketching them, smelling them and preserving them in simple notebooks.

Her ideas for simplicity of design were just that, simple. Three basic colours, white, buttermilk yellow, and a mint green, were to be combined with blue cornflowers, red poppies, and sweet peas of varying hues. Lionel had been easy to manipulate. The prospect of any prolonged discussion involving Chalmy made his heart sink.

Simplicity was all, the looms had not been too difficult to re tool, production was slowly increasing, and they were even selling some of the new designs in Germany. The re-tooling itself had been a further triumph, as it had given her the chance to make a series of ever so polite enquiries about progress, whilst a grease encrusted Chalmy toiled beneath the looms.

His eventual arrival did create a stir, and yes it was true. He had a car, and not just any old car. The low slung, burgundy, Renault saloon oozed style, a quality Olivier believed he had in abundance.

For Sophie, first impressions counted, and they were favourable. Broad shouldered, brown eyed, with a dark shock of wavy hair, at close quarters she noticed, that in yet another contrast with Lionel, his tanned forehead was as smooth as a billiard ball. Lionel, in contrast, had a brow which was furrowed on an agricultural scale. Olivier's dazzling smile, as he bowed to Sophie, both alerted and intrigued her.

"Mademoiselle, I have heard so much about you." He paused. "And all of it, all of it was true. That glow, must be from clean living, no?" The colour drained from Chalmy's cheeks. For Sophie, no one had ever enquired about her health in quite that way.

For Lionel, the Parable of The Prodigal Son was one he had been revisiting constantly. The squandered fortune certainly resonated. His brimming good health and unbridled joie de vie only to be expected, thought Lionel. He began to splutter again.

Olivier had contrived to be abroad throughout the conflict, during which time a series of business ventures had been floated, sunk, and re-launched again with bewildering rapidity. The only common thread was that they were all located in those parts of the French Empire where there was no fighting. As far as Lionel was concerned, the only fatted calf would be one for which Olivier paid himself.

Chalmy had grimaced as Olivier launched his charm offensive and the exaggerated "Enchanté", with which he embellished his bow to Sophie, set his teeth grinding. Here was the real class enemy, exploiter of inferior races for whom, no doubt, rape and pillage- well pillage at least- were as natural as breathing. Olivier examined the sketches.

"Oh these are quite marvellous. Quite marvellous. Clean, simple lines. Which Institute did you train at, Mademoiselle? Oh yes. Lionel, you old fox. Where have you been hiding her? Mind, I would want to keep such a talent-still raw I grant you-but a real talent, nevertheless, all to myself. Oh yes. I can tell straight away. We can go places with these. New products need new markets. Raise our horizons."

This suggestion of travel to far flung destinations, added yet another furrow to Lionel's brow. The mention of new machines to increase production were part of a bright, breezy, yet uncosted, plan for expansion he then rattled off to his stunned audience.

For Lionel there would be financial pain if he was not reined in, whilst for Chalmy, yet more time beneath the looms would place him a definite fourth in the pecking order.

Clearly in a hurry, or maybe just bored by the limited canvass onto which he could project his brilliance, Olivier rapidly brought the proceedings to a close.

"Next week we four," at which he stared intensely at Sophie, "We four will meet again." Contradicting him at that moment seemed to be a futile response. His eye contact with Sophie made clear he had all kinds of ideas for what they might do together, whilst a firm handshake suggested there was work to be done to convince his brother. The final "Au revoir, mes amis" made Chalmy want to be sick.

Patronised by the upper classes, just how bad could it get?

# Chapter Eleven

Unfortunately for Sophie, the early feelings of euphoria she had felt at first, did not survive the first month. With production increasing, and her new found responsibilities earning a modicum of respect from her colleagues, Chalmy excepted, her mood should have been brighter than this. Why could she not shake off the nagging doubts?

Her post-natal depression had never gone away, but she had been warned that this was part of the deal. Her new partnership with Madame Chalroix was prospering, but the long hours of rabbit hunting and chicken necking were taking their toll. The latest card had perplexed her as well. The same simple phrase, but in a completely different style of handwriting, and from a different place in Germany. Would there be more?

No, the answer must lie somewhere at work, she concluded. The correspondence the firm received could usually be dealt with in an hour. The rest of her day was spent supervising her looms, and in particular the ones weaving her new designs. The fumes made her eyes water and her head ache. She couldn't let on though, and they were running at full capacity. Natalie's mantra of 'never be off' still resonated.

The plan was to convert two more looms, as Olivier's relentless pleas to ramp up production developed a remorseless momentum. Chalmy's thunderous expression confirmed that such reckless ambition filled him with gloom, and therefore her with glee. Lionel was more and more the passive bystander, and as Olivier finally reappeared, after yet another mysterious expedition, Lionel's heart sank

The burgundy saloon was now replaced by what Lionel recognised was a French Army lorry, which had hauled ammunition during the last months of the war. A cloud of dust was thrown up as he roared into the yard. The brakes were slammed on in flamboyant style. The beginnings of a skid amused him hugely, but infuriated Chalmy. Lionel could see him cursing, as he choked in the dust, whilst checking the bales in the yard below.

The gorge continued to rise, once Olivier leapt from the cab with a flourish. Chalmy suddenly felt quite queasy. The tan overcoat would cost a year's wages, he estimated, whilst the trousers of the double breasted suit billowed like a galleon in full sail.

But the final insult to Chalmy, suddenly deprived of the power of speech or coherent thought, was the rest of his ensemble. Not only was he wearing spats, and carrying an elegant silver topped cane, but, and this was just too much, a cravat, no less. Was there no end to it?

Olivier swept into the mill. A twinkle in the eye here, a question as to a child's welfare there, his self image as a man of the people was further embellished as Chalmy trailed, ineffectually, in his wake. As his process through the machine room slowed, Chalmy couldn't avoid how the besotted female employees were quickly outbidding each other.

"How could you manage that, then, Helene?" swooned Miriam Dubois.

"Any time, any place, you know me. He won't need to ask. When's the next break?! How fortunate, I've got some clean knickers on!"

"Thought you didn't bother with them! It's not your birthday already, is it?"

"They do slow the process down, you're right. But with him, oooh, you don't want a quick in and out, and all over in two minutes. Oh no, take your time with that one." Their day momentarily brightened, they dragged deep on their cigarettes and resumed their routine.

He entered the office. Sophie was typing, laboriously. Lionel focused on the ledger, trying to contain the feelings of dread which resurfaced whenever Olivier reappeared.

He whispered his greetings to Sophie at sufficiently close quarters to look down her blouse, and make a mental note of the colour of her underwear. He hoped to be impressed. He was. Sophie was meant to be impressed by the aroma of his sandalwood, scented soap. She was. Outside in the yard, the tarpaulin was being removed from two machines which were more modern than anything in the factory. Chalmy, having retraced his steps, was beckoning over two colleagues.

"Here we are brother, the key to fame and fortune." Olivier exclaimed with a sweep of his arm. "Faster production, better colour definition and they provide a sheen which will provide the way to you know what –and plenty of it." He continued, with an exaggerated rubbing together of finger and thumb, to indicate the boundless financial bonanza which lay ahead. He was aware that Chalmy was still in the yard. From the window, he observed him closely, examining the new purchases.

"Just look, just look. At a time like this. Of all times. The good ship Lafarge is about to set sail. And where is he? Nowhere. What is he doing? Nit picking, that's what. Demeaning, that's the only word. Demeaning. Mundane matters at a time such as this. Sums up the man. We have to get rid of him. And sooner, rather than later."

Lionel tried to summon strength from a prolonged drag, and immediately asked about price. Olivier's evasive answers confirmed his worst fears. His rambling peroration was short on detail, but long on euphoria. As Lionel attempted to make sense of his proposals, they seemed to boil down in essence to two key elements. The new machinery, and all other expansion, would be financed by the interest paid on a huge purchase of German Government loan stock, paid for through a short term loan he had negotiated. As Lionel cursed his father, silently, for giving them equal control, Olivier drove home the stake by explaining how the mill would be used as security.

"We can't miss. They lost, those bastards, and they are desperate for money. That's why the interest rate is so juicy. But it's a sure thing and they'll still be paying in sixty years. Sixty years! Why wait? Let's grab some now."

Borrowing of any kind was anathema to Lionel, as it had been to his father. As the gravity of the situation began to sink in, a furious row erupted. Lionel's attempts to apply the cold logic of hard cash and conservative accounting smacked to Olivier of the old, the decrepit and the defeated. His attempts to counter Olivier's flights of fancy were strong on logic, but weak on delivery, as each rhetorical counter thrust dissolved into a fit of coughing, which continually interrupted the proceedings like the bell in a boxing match. Sophie knew her future lay with Olivier and his ambitious schemes, but admired the doggedness with which Lionel argued his case.

By now, Chalmy had returned, and he had adopted his most pained expression, 'a double lemon', Natalie had christened it. The arguments now flowed three ways, as Chalmy denounced the new strategy in clinical terms. He and his colleagues knew all about the new machines and their temperamental ways. For once, he was couching his opposition in terms of power to weight ratios, hydraulics and structural mechanics, rather than the impenetrable verbiage of Marxist dialectic.

Despite this, the tide was running with the forces of modernity. Lionel was reeling from the enormity of the gamble being proposed, with the mill as collateral. The papers had already been signed. For Chalmy, the shallow chicanery of high finance, and all its evils, was embodied in the tanned, handsome, sneering face opposite. But eventually the sheer exuberance of Olivier's delivery overwhelmed them.

"You will see. You will see. Speculate to accumulate. We need to expand our horizons beyond…" He managed to stop himself before he belittled his father's life's work, in front of people for whom this was their whole life. He quickly changed tack.

"Come now, come now. Let us put our differences behind us. At a time like this we should all be able to embrace success. Yes, and not just embrace it, celebrate it. I have booked a table for four, at The Hotel Challons in Veziers, 8 for 8-30." He tossed three embossed invitations onto the table.

As he swept down the stairs, he knew there would be no need to alter his reservation for two. Olivier was slumped on the table in despair. In hock to the Germans, a humiliating state of affairs. But for Chalmy, new vistas were opening up once the temperamental machines were under his control.

He was back in the game at last.

✲ ✲ ✲

He had collected her right on time, as Madame Chalroix finished her pleading. Sophie had hastily adapted her only stylish dress to reveal the absolute minimum of flesh. As they accelerated away, the ogling of the habitués of 'Le Parisien' came to an end.

"Six weeks, I reckon. Six weeks. He won't hang about." said Michel Malpain, as he fixed another cigarette between his gums, and the coughing began.

"What makes you the expert on affairs of the heart? No, make that flesh!" smirked Roger Durrand. "I've heard your wife asks you to tap her on the shoulder to let her know when you've finished, so I think we can discount your opinion in these matters!" As Roger savoured the reaction to his salvo, Michel decided to ignore him, and press his point.

"Six weeks, and her Nicole can look forward to the pattering of more tiny feet. French ones, this time. Anyone care to match me?" He tossed a crumpled note onto the table, and enjoyed the satisfaction that none of the others, especially Roger, were prepared to take his bet. Double Ricards were ordered, to toast the happy couple.

The evening passed in a blur for Sophie. She was determined to play it long, and Natalie's advice to "Treat them mean and keep them keen," was about to be tested in the most trying of circumstances She was overwhelmed by his descriptions of exotic climes, and openly confessed that she didn't know vanilla grew in a pod. Did people always send wine back? A click of the fingers in the vague direction of the sommelier was all it had taken. She realised she could get used to this. She had noticed his rapt attention, as she explained how effective ferrets were. His apparent squeamishness on the topic of tripe was a little overdone, but she chuckled anyway.

The drive back to St. Valery passed without words, as if both knew what lay ahead. As they pulled up outside the butchers, Madame Chalroix peered pensively through the curtains. The last of the 'Le Parisien' regulars gawped, as each played their final card.

Sophie waited, as Olivier turned off the engine. He moved round to open the door on her side. She would permit him a chaste kiss on the cheek, and definitely no tongue. To her surprise, he simply bowed his head, thanked her for the evening, and merely brushed her fingers with his lips. Across the street, the rural Romeos acknowledged immediately that they were watching a class act.

As he drove away into the night, Olivier reflected that the evening couldn't have gone better. Play it long with this one. Treat them mean. Keep them keen.

Works every time.

✻ ✻ ✻

"How did it come to this?"

Martin Neumann was there for the third time in a fortnight. A sure sign that he was desperate, Freuntz was convinced. His suit had been stylishly cut, albeit twenty years ago. His upright bearing made him stand out in the queue, which normally consisted of downtrodden housewives.

He pushed the newspaper across the counter, and Freuntz realised that he was merely quoting the banner headline. 'Ruined-For Telegraph Poles'. The article was tracing the schedule of Allied demands, made since 1919, and tracking Germany's slide towards ruin.

"And look at this here. Two thousand… two… thousand printing presses. And running twenty four hours a day, printing so called money. And still they can't keep up."

Neumann placed a canvas bag on the counter. Freuntz could detect the familiar sound of rustling newspaper. Something valuable would be produced soon

"How indeed? And now this. Did you hear about Erlingauer?" Freuntz nodded. "Invading, invading, and all for what? Telegraph poles, 135,000 metres of them, and they invade. Those lads in Erlingauer. They weren't even fighting back, to begin with. Only protecting the mine." Freuntz nodded once more.

"Rumours, rumours, but I bet there is something in them. Arms caches, barricades. It could get even worse. Hard to believe. Even harder to accept."

By now, the contents of the bag had been revealed. Jacob Hoffmann was always on hand, when once wealthy customers appeared. He was not disappointed. The cutlery was the finest Grainer, dated 1870, and even Freuntz could see the porcelain figures and dinner plates were Meissen. The glassware was from Bohemia, whilst the photograph frames contained a series of photographs of Neumann and his wife, taken on various formal occasions. Their expressions indicated that they were besotted with each other. They looked so sophisticated. Even Freuntz could recognise that. Ballroom dancing always looked elegant. Freuntz felt envious. He stepped aside to allow Hoffmann to close the deal.

It didn't take long. The priceless possessions were handed over. Hoffmann delved into the laundry basket, in which he kept the bundles of notes, with their endless noughts. With barely a glance, he made a pile. His expression confirmed that there would be no negotiation. Staring blankly ahead, Neumann stuffed the bundles into the canvas bag and shuffled away.

✷ ✷ ✷

Freuntz awoke early. He needed to be alone. There would be no bread for the ducks. He smeared the merest drizzle of oil onto the brittle crusts, whose component crumbs would require only the slightest encouragement to disintegrate completely. He carefully sliced the remaining half of a softening tomato, wrapped the crusts inside a week old page from the 'Stanheim Courier', grabbed the manual, and headed for the river.

When the wind was from the west, the aroma wafting across from the Rhengrau brewery caused many in Stanheim to salivate. Monks first brewed beer in 1287, on the site now occupied by the castle. The special brew was a treacly brown and sipped with reverence by experienced drinkers, convinced that "it stuck to the ribs". It was force fed to sickly infants by concerned mothers, and consumed with relish by those unfamiliar with its explosive properties. Few finished a third, before being rendered comatose. The glorious amalgam of hops, malt and other mysterious ingredients was the elixir of life for the serious drinkers of Stanheim. There were plenty of those.

Acute powers of observation underpinned his artistic prowess. Freuntz noticed that the crusts he had left last week, beside the rhododendron bush, remained uneaten, and the ochre veined rock hadn't been there either. As he strode purposefully towards his favourite spot, Freuntz wondered why Frau Seeke hadn't been seen lately, but thought he probably knew the answer. He had been aware of the gathering crisis, as he had needed first one, then two, and now three mailbags, just to collect the wages.

He resented strong arming fellow Germans, whose only crime was to be desperate. The new rule of three customers at once had helped to restore order, but business had virtually ground to a halt. They were opening later, and closing earlier, each week.

As the upstairs section had expanded, Hoffmann had been careful to accept only the high quality items. He quickly put a stop to the torrent of ex-military hardware of all shapes, sizes, makes and nationalities. But there was one exception. A wooden crate of what turned out to be ex-army radios had made the old man's face light up. He tapped his nose, and said to Freuntz, with a knowing wink,

"These are the future. Learn to love them." Freuntz was mystified, but the invitation had had the desired effect.

As trade had slowly seized up, prior to his spell on guard duty, Freuntz had plenty of opportunity to empty the crate, sift its components, and in his predictably methodical way try to work out what went where. One seemed to have all its parts, but refused to work. Three others lacked valves, leads, plugs or fascias, but right at the bottom, bizarrely, was a British Army model.

Freuntz had been acutely aware that Britain and her allies had used radio much better than the Germans, and he was eager to unlock its mysteries. The manual was in Swedish, but fortunately had plenty of diagrams, and highlighted the Alexandersen alternator, crucial for improved voice transmission He was determined to get a mental picture of its intricacies, so that if the opportunity offered itself in the future, he could repair, and even build them. Then, he would be able to move on from scheduling and shelf stacking.

Progress was slow, but he persevered. It was half an hour before he put the manual on his knee, and permitted himself the first bite of the crusts. Financial expediency had cut short a growing affection for cumin, and it had been ages since he last ran a moistened finger round the tiny jar of paprika. Times must be hard, he thought, as there wasn't a single duck to be seen.

The break in concentration proved fatal, however. Should he have sent a card? Whose writing style would he have used, and where would he have posted it from? He had given up checking his bank account. The last time he looked he was a millionaire, several times over, but now he was weighing up whether he could afford a stamp, and even if he could, embossed card was now out of the question. He had screwed up his half completed sketch, and thrown it on the fire.

It was getting lighter, when he saw the two figures approach. As they got nearer, he was able to identify that one of them was Neumann. He quickly realised that the other was his wife, still beautiful and stylish. They were arm in arm, locked in deep conversation, dressed as if setting off for a night on the town. They passed right in front of Freuntz, oblivious to him.

They hadn't gone more than twenty metres. They stopped at what seemed to be a pre- arranged spot, right in front of the rhododendron bush. They began to embrace with a passion which unsettled Freuntz. He couldn't turn away, though. Eventually, they stepped back and gave each other a firm nod. Neumann rummaged in his jacket, and produced two sets of handcuffs. They were quickly shackled at the wrist and ankle.

Neumann picked up the rock with his free hand and tucked it under his arm. The pair gazed at each other, as if waiting for the orchestra to strike up. They counted to three. With five, synchronised strides, still face to face, the pair leapt into the gloom. Freuntz heard the splash. Transfixed, it took him several seconds to react. He knew there would be no sign of them. Even if there was, what would be the point of rescuing them?

The chiming of a distant church bell told him he would need to be outside the bank in half an hour. He folded the manual in half, placed it in the inside pocket of his threadbare jacket, and mentally attuned himself to another day of discord and dismay.

The one thing he was pleased about was the outcome of the trial.

✵ ✵ ✵

Repeated delays had served Moeller's purpose perfectly, and conveyed the impression, right from the beginning, that it was he who was in charge of proceedings. Already twice postponed, when outbreaks of violence exacerbated the situation where resentment still seethed, it was felt that a trial, at that time, might add further fuel to the flames. But in addition, Moeller had conducted a skilful guerrilla campaign by constantly claiming the right to be tried in civilian clothes, rather than prison uniform. A series of legal challenges had been decided in his favour, and with medals glinting, the four posed triumphantly on the steps of the courthouse.

What was a straightforward case of robbery with violence was immediately transformed into a piece of political theatre, and with press interest aroused, few were there to have the details of the case rehashed. The facts were clear. The judge selected was renowned for his nationalist sympathies, and his repeated admonitions to the prosecution team undermined them from the start. The Chief Prosecutor, Gottfried Muffner could have been chosen to order. Over promoted due to the disruption caused by the war, a career spent in arguments about the terms of rural tenancies and disputed probate agreements cast him as the bull to Moeller's matador. It was all the jury could do to stop applauding.

When not running rings around the hapless Muffner, Moeller spent much of the trial fixing the Assistant Counsel, Saul Fengel, with a malevolent glare which indicated that today would not be the end of the matter, regardless of the verdict. Whilst Kaltz and Hubert tried to affect an air of detached contempt, Weber looked as if he might burst into tears at any moment.

A series of eye witnesses mumbled their evidence, as if Moeller was deciding their fate, rather than the jury deciding his. Only when the razor sharp Fengel took centre stage was some urgency injected, and his forensic questioning led the jury towards the inevitable decision. But not before Moeller had seized his opportunity.

He had long since decided that he would defend the four of them and had practised a series of gestures he felt would add gravitas to his performance. He had announced to a hushed audience that in fact that he would not cross examine any witnesses, as that would imply they had a case to answer, and needed to defend themselves. They were all agreed that they would plead guilty, and this was the crux of Moeller's case. Guilty in court, yes, but in the court of history a different verdict would be handed down, and he would be vindicated.

The petty nit picking of the prosecution case was derided with unremitting scorn. Their offence was political not criminal and the court therefore lacked all legitimacy. The Weimar Republic had no legitimacy either, and the pygmies of the legal and political establishment would be swept aside by the storm of which he, Moeller, was merely a harbinger.

In the final reckoning, decisive action and strong leadership, not five centuries of jurisprudence, were what would decide Germany's future. Sophisticated argument and reasoned debate would count for nothing, and in time the scales would fall from the eyes of the German people. The flimsy apparatus of democratic consensus would be consumed in a fire which would never be extinguished, once ignited, he added, before fixing Fengel with a glare of unmitigated hatred.

"You have to admit it, he is rather good," whispered the Jury Foreman, under his breath, to nobody in particular, as Moeller, disappointed that this was not a venue where he might receive a standing ovation, turned his back flamboyantly on the judge, the jury and the whole of the despised, democratic edifice they represented

Within forty minutes the jury had returned and the sentences were handed down. Moeller, Kaltz and Hubert were sentenced to seven years, with the possibility of two years parole, dependent on behaviour. Weber was distraught to be given a sentence of six months, which simply emphasised both his minimal contribution, and perceived danger to society. The verdicts were a travesty on a number of counts, but as the defendants were led down, and applause rippled round the courtroom, Moeller was already looking ahead. Five years would be easy, time to plan, time to think, and next time would be a different story.

Democracy was even more spineless than he had imagined.

✯ ✯ ✯

The corpse had been placed with great thought, for maximum effect. The corner of Munchenstrasse and Fiedrichstrasse was where the two main thoroughfares of Stellgahle intersected. Most inhabitants would pass before nine in the morning. Those not there to witness the grisly scene would soon hear about it.

His ears had been sliced off and were placed neatly on cither side of the corpse, from which the eyes had been gouged. His hands had been hacked off. Two fingers were rammed into the sightless sockets. The remains of one hand had been forced into his mouth. The bayonet pinned the message deep into his chest

"Hear no evil, see no evil, speak no evil"

"Oh, Harold. I can't look. What have we become? What have we become?" Marita Kirchen held a handkerchief over her mouth. Her husband, Harold, found it harder to drag himself away. He was not alone. The crowd stood in silence, before the police arrived.

They slowly drifted away. But not before Harold spoke for all of them.

"No in between, any more. People have to decide. Who will they stand with in the decisive hour?" Nobody spoke. They absorbed his point, even though they might not have agreed with him. They were all agreed on one thing, though.

Bandell must have died an agonising death.

# Chapter Twelve

Fine dining was still a novelty for Sophie, and the anticipation of a flourishing relationship with Olivier had helped compensate for the difficulties she faced on a daily basis at work. How long was post-natal depression meant to last? Why were the headaches so searing, unresponsive to any attempted treatment?

Three evenings with Olivier had passed in a haze of knowing moves and counter moves, each sparring in their respective styles, persuading both to be optimistic about future developments, and convince each of them that they were in control of proceedings.

The increasingly ashen complexion which greeted Sophie each morning underlined Lionel's deteriorating health, his wheezing painful to hear. The stridency with which Chalmy exhibited his technical supremacy grated on all who entered his orbit, a process made all the more painful because, as far as the reliability of the new machines was concerned, he had been absolutely correct.

Repeated breakdowns had given Chalmy, and his two colleagues, the opportunity to purse their lips, arch their eyebrows, and suck their pencils in suitably disconsolate fashion. The balance of power had swung back towards the labouring classes and the triumph of the proletariat was at hand. Of that, he was certain.

By dealing with the correspondence on a daily basis, Sophie was aware of the deteriorating situation in Germany as their markets dried up. She feared that one more letter from the bank, in

Basle, would be terminal for the firm. Probably Lionel as well. Sophie had admired his dogged determination to keep the firm afloat, but her own reservoir of determination was being drained rapidly by her ailments.

However, intoxicated by her responsibilities, as well as the attention lavished on her by Olivier, there was little doubt that her head was being turned. She rarely missed an opportunity to embellish his ego, and underpin his conviction that he was a far sighted visionary in the company of pygmies.

The invitation to join him on a picnic ought to have been a chance to lift her spirits, but despite a month of unbroken high summer sunshine her complexion was sallow, and her blonde hair, formerly so lustrous, was surprisingly brittle. She had to force herself to be positive, apply her make up more lavishly, and draw on all her experience to look, and sound, alluring. When Olivier arrived, therefore, she braced herself, prepared for the onslaught of high hopes, daring dreams and ill conceived strategies. He did not disappoint.

No sooner had they passed La Pigalle than the torrent burst forth. Seemingly oblivious to the deteriorating economic situation, he outlined his latest coup.

"And do you know what else? You remember what we have talked about, talked about so many times? Well, it has come to pass. Our own printing press. Swiss made. Top of the range. Top of anyone's for that matter. Yea verily," he continued with a flourish, "the people have asked, and lo, their wishes have been granted! Now you can really give those artistic talents, those creative urges, free rein."

He was undeterred by her momentary grimace, as his plan for her, completely divorced from the minutiae of economics and the practicalities of printing, approached fruition. Both the charm and the engine were at full throttle. He accelerated down the country lanes, one hand on the steering wheel, the other on her lap. He was self deprecating and boastful in equal measure, as always, but somehow the chemistry wasn't there as far as Sophie was concerned. Olivier was oblivious.

The drowsy summer heat shimmered, her beads of perspiration exciting him further, as they began their walk along the river bank. Olivier carried the hamper under one arm, as the other negotiated the small of her back. Sophie couldn't work out why her sense of anticipation was ebbing so rapidly. Surely, here was a chance to escape the limited horizons of her rural isolation, and leave its attendant frustrations behind. A wealthy businessman, a man of the world, a life of exotic travel, and a world of sophistication beckoned. If only.

They had passed by Dreamers Rock on the other side of the river. The path narrowed and the woodland became more dense. The dappled sunlight illuminated a narrow track off towards a small glade, at the bottom of a steep bank. The prolonged heatwave had baked the paths hard. The glade felt spongy under foot, a carpet of moss flourishing in the cool half light.

He laid out the blanket, and delved into the hamper which brimmed with gourmet delights, exquisite pastries and three bottles of top quality Bordeaux. It was a wine about which Olivier had taken pains to educate her, and would, he hoped, lubricate a relationship he now hoped to consummate.

The hazy heat, the wine and the rich food would normally have combined to relax her, make her more receptive to his beguiling charm, but she would quite happily have rolled over and gone to sleep, if she could have ignored his wandering hands. The doubts again. Why did she not simply say no, prolong her campaign and cement the relationship on her own terms and in her own time?

Her knickers were slipped towards her knees. At the same time as he ran his tongue along her exposed thighs, he was removing his trousers, against a background of low, rhythmic moaning. Both knew what the next move would be. Sophie reacted first. She slid backwards, towards the steep bank.

Olivier was perplexed, but was not prepared to see his long nurtured plans thwarted. As she pushed herself against the bank, to help regain her feet, Olivier rose quickly. He forced his weight against her, pinning her against the exposed tree roots.

Her protestations were ignored. Her knickers were on the ground. As Olivier removed his underwear, with what he thought would prove a conclusive flourish, Sophie's scrambled brain concluded that it was now or never. His weight pressed her against the bank. His hands were pulling her towards him. She scrabbled desperately in the undergrowth above her. She grabbed the rock and swung it at him, with all the force she could muster.

The glancing blow stunned him. He staggered backwards, trying to take in what had happened. Sophie needed no second invitation. She darted past him. As she reached the path, the hard ground grated on her feet. Her heart pounded. She gulped frantically for air. But she knew, instinctively, that he would not be far behind.

As the trees thinned, and she emerged into the sunlight by the river, he caught her. He enveloped her in a bear like grasp. Sophie was pleading. He dragged her round and pushed her back further along the track. Blood oozed into his eye. Rage at the indignity he had suffered convulsed him. Her whimpering pleas for mercy energised him. The impact of the blow was rendered even more potent by the rings, which adorned each of his fingers. Sophie reeled backwards. He moved towards her. The afternoon would end on his terms.

He realised that he had complete power over the prostrate figure. Sophie was moaning at his feet. Nobody refused Olivier Lafarge. This country whore would be no different. He raised her skirt. He convinced himself that her moans were those of pleasure. He forced himself inside her.

Once it was over, as the contemptuous sneer faded from his lips, he rapidly appraised the situation. He retraced his steps, gathered his belongings, and trotted towards the car. But only after pausing to spit full in her face.

✵ ✵ ✵

When the teenagers found Sophie, the swelling had already closed her eye, the bruises already assuming a lurid hue. The sun was setting as they bathed her face, before helping her to her feet. Her head was splitting. Although she could see through one eye, the other was impossible to open.

# Chapter Thirteen

Freuntz had always had an eye for talent. The ability to spot potential was something which would endure, unlike the transitory "wealth" he had accumulated which left him unable to afford a stale loaf. Its evaporation was followed by the empty realisation that surely there was little else that could be thrown at the German people. Had he ever really believed all those noughts?

The waste ground by the sawmill was a mixture of cinders and sparse grass, pockmarked by potholes in which rainwater soon collected, the oily film reflecting its polluted origins. Nevertheless it was the venue for 'scratch' football matches for the lads of Stelghalle .The pitch was identifiable only by four oil drums which served as goal posts, and the teams of twenty aside were frequently supplemented by adults of varying degrees of athleticism, desperate to recapture the golden days of their lissom youth.

Freuntz was drawn more frequently as the summer nights began to shorten, and one player immediately stood out. He reflected on his own prowess as a rugged, uncompromising centre half. He had been one who always played better when his side was under pressure, yet always found time to encourage and advise those around him. His normally taciturn approach had concealed a shrewd, tactical appreciation of how the team might play better.

Freuntz noticed the striking blonde hair, but there were others with blonde hair. No, it was his balance and speed, complemented by a toughness which tolerated no attempts at intimidation from the older boys. He was still seething at some indignity as the light finally faded, the keenest half dozen having finally dispersed.

"You need to be half turned before the ball comes, so you can use an arm to hold them off", said Freuntz.

The tide of anger was receding, and as his breathing returned to a more normal rate the boy looked at him suspiciously at first. But then, realising there might be something in what he had heard, replied

"How do you mean then?"

"Defenders expect things their own way. Only needs a short jab, they're off balance and you're away. Makes them less eager to wade in and buys you time. Come on, try and whack me".

The boy, suddenly energised, leapt towards Freuntz, but a playful arm extended at the last second did exactly as had been explained.

"See, if the ball is on this side you're in control. Always use your body. You can make something of yourself, but to get better you need to play organised matches."

"How can we do that? Our ball won't blow up and we don't have a pitch, never mind a kit, or boots. Some of us only have these." He raised each leg in turn to reveal a set of rough hewn clogs which must have rendered any movement painful in the extreme.

Freuntz, sensing another project in which he could absorb himself, replied simply,

"Let's see what we can do."

✯ ✯ ✯

Cathartic, yes that's what it had been, reflected Freuntz as he waited for his first pay packet. He was already looking forward to the crisp notes of the new currency. Money with which he could actually afford something, or more appropriately squirrel away under his re-designed financial plan. By 1931 he would be in America on his own terms. Seven years was a long stretch, but what else was there to look forward to?

Well, quite a few things actually, he told himself. He was expanding his influence within the Hoffman organisation. He had constructed half of his own radio by cannibalising sets he actually chose as being good for spare parts, and he finally had an idea of where The Holy Roman Empire had been. But now it was football which enthused him.

Their initial encounter had been a catalyst. As word spread amongst the players, Freuntz realised that although he was young, his new companion, Wolfgang, had the presence to be the one they listened to and would be prepared to follow. Who would be in the team was now a frequent and heated topic of debate, lending the practise matches an extra edge.

The first training session had been chaotic, with twenty five players to choose from. But within a few weeks he soon whittled the likely candidates down, with none older than fifteen. Not having a decent ball was a problem Freuntz soon overcame with his first pay packet. Despite the scuffs and tears, the T-panel "Weltklasse" was lovingly lavished in dubbin to prolong its life, and served to cement his reputation with his new flock.

This was where he excelled- nurturing the young.

✯ ✯ ✯

Erlingauer wore the scars of its industrial heritage with pride. The ravaged landscape of blast furnaces and slag heaps was criss crossed by a maze of canals from where the acrid fumes, which left eyes streaming and asthmatics wheezing, were wafted across the town. An eloquent testimony to a community which knew the virtues of hard physical labour, the sulphurous atmosphere which enveloped the town was jokingly referred to as the halo which indicated God had favoured them -at the same time as it reduced life expectancy by up to five years.

Pride was the defining feature of its inhabitants, and proudest of the proud were the miners. A community spirit which was almost tangible had seen a range of amenities develop at the same pace as the exploitation of the mineral wealth beneath the town.

The Miners Welfare Hall was grime encrusted, but only served to emphasise the verdant green of the two pitches. Half a dozen teams were regularly fielded, and it was the youngest of these-the Under 15s- who would play host to F.K. Stellgahle, as Freuntz had christened them.

Selection had been an anguished process. A kit of white shirts and navy shorts had been lovingly created by mothers and aunts, whilst eight of the team even had a pair of boots. But, finally, the great day had arrived, and the nervous anticipation communicated itself even to the normally level headed Freuntz.

Only one thing puzzled him, as the boys and half a dozen fathers assembled. Wolfgang was there with his father, who had started attending the training sessions. He rarely spoke; his solemn expression and morose personality made Freuntz resemble a fun loving extrovert in comparison.

The players, and those unlucky enough to miss out on selection, would cram into the back of the bakers van for the four mile trip. Freuntz and the remainder would travel by bus. Eight was the capacity, and once the van was full, the rest of the group trudged into town to commence the twenty minute journey.

Not a word was spoken between Wolfgang and his father, who looked straight ahead, whilst Wolfgang resolutely stared out of the window as the drizzle teemed down. Had Freuntz misjudged him? Would his temperament let him down? Why no nervous banter which the other boys had exchanged amongst themselves?

The bus dropped them at the gate to the mine. There, for the first time, Freuntz set eyes on the sculpture which had been created to commemorate the most recent tragedy in the town's history, an event which had left emotions red raw. The simmering resentment in the town was still barely contained.

Freuntz remembered how vividly Martin Neumann had recounted the story. When Germany had finally been unable to keep up the repayment of reparations, the French had marched in to seize possession of the mines, an act of provocation to which the miners had responded with a programme of passive resistance. Thwarted in their ambitions, as production ground to a halt, an increasingly tense stand off had seen the French attempt to remove some of the newer machinery. The miners responded by launching a pre-dawn raid to re-take possession of the mine, to safeguard their long term future. The attempts to storm the mine, and thereafter quell the uprising, had been predictably chaotic and bloody. Two hours later, six miners lay dead.

The sculpture had been carved from a single, huge block of coal to show the six men in a series of poses which reflected heroism and stoicism in equal measure, each with arms flung upwards, the inscription beneath reading,

"Here we stood, here we fought, here we died."

Freuntz seethed inwardly, and couldn't help noticing how Wolfgang's father visibly straightened his shoulders and consciously clenched his jaw, struggling to keep his emotions under control. However, once in the changing rooms it was time for Freuntz to move into his nurturing role. As the new kit was lovingly fondled, Freuntz went through his soothing pre-match encouragement, as eyes watered under the onslaught of bottles and bottles of ferocious embrocation which were now being liberally applied to limbs of all dimensions, as if the action itself would ensure success. A forlorn hope, as events quickly unfolded.

The pride Freuntz felt, as his flock left the changing rooms amidst a hailstorm of fevered exhortation, was quickly replaced by a feeling of trepidation as their opponents emerged. Under-15 for Freuntz meant a range of ages, whereas their opponents all seemed to have been shaving for at least a couple of years, their rough-hewn physiques representative of those of mining stock.

The pitch sloped from one end, and Freuntz had told Wolfgang that if he won the toss they should kick uphill first, before fatigue inevitably took its toll. He was proved right. Once the whistle had gone Wolfgang was transformed from his apprehensive silence. As he cajoled his team mates unceasingly, he made light of the gulf in age and physique, flitting effortlessly away from a series of shuddering challenges.

At half time, the mixture of elation at the blank score line, and the excitement of their first competitive match, was diluted by the physical effort they had used up in matching their bigger opponents. Freuntz quickly realised that, even with the slope and the driving drizzle at their backs, the outcome was inevitable.

He quickly outlined his plan which was simply to leave Horst, their strapping centre forward, alone up front. The rest would defend the penalty area as if their lives depended on it and, if the opportunity arose, venture out in support. Such tactics served to bemuse their opponents for a while, but soon the siege began.

The heroism of Heinz Strenkel in goal thwarted several attempts, but the turning point came when a deflected shot left him wrong footed. The sudden change of direction momentarily confused him. Although the shot was now heading wide, he flung himself across the sodden turf only to land on the greasy ball, which somehow squirmed from his grasp and, to the horror of his team mates, trickled into the vacant goal.

The cheers of relief, as the dam was finally breached, galvanised the Erlingauer team at the same time as it deflated the Stellgahle boys. From then, play flowed in only one direction, apart from the occasions when Wolfgang, by sheer force of will, managed to support Horst and unleash a series of shots. All, to his disgust, were narrowly off target. Always make the goalie have to save it, Freuntz had drummed into him.

There were only ten minutes to go when Freuntz, peering through the drizzle which was swirling on the strengthening wind, thought he recognised the female newcomer to the ranks of the supporters on the opposite side of the pitch. Right in front of her, from somewhere, Wolfgang found the energy to launch a ferocious, lunging challenge on a boy who was a foot taller than him, only to come off by far the worst, and be left in a writhing heap.

Freuntz located his first aid equipment- the age old combination of bucket, sponge and ice cold water- and made his way gingerly across the greasy turf. Wolfgang was still writhing, but as Freuntz approached, it seemed this was more a mixture of frustration, anger and embarrassment, rather than pain. He was almost there when the woman began to move towards him, causing Wolfgang to wriggle backwards, away from her, at the same time as he emitted a loud series of curses, which Freuntz was amazed to discover featured frequent use of the word, "Mother."

Freuntz was finally there and, as the woman lowered her hood, he realised why he thought he had recognised her. It was Eva, their last encounter having ended with him covered in beer. But, as if that was not alarming enough, he could see that the bundle she was carrying was in fact a baby, who was no older than six months, a baby whose complexion was the colour of cocoa. It was now clear to Freuntz why Wolfgang and his father had been so apprehensive before the game.

Her unfaithfulness had been hard enough to bear, but now, to publicly flaunt it on this of all occasions, even though she had barely any contact other than a birthday card, was a dagger to both their hearts.

Whoring with the French was bad enough, but with a black soldier, the final indignity. The journey home was punctuated by a series of wrenching sobs, and not just from Wolfgang.

# Chapter Fourteen

She stumbled. She grasped. Half blinded, she fumbled her way from window ledge to window ledge. Her condition ought to have melted the hardest of hearts, but an icy contempt, born of anger, submerged but not forgotten, bubbled to the surface. They watched.

"Asking for it," was Madame Poiller's verdict.

"Divine Justice, that's what it is, Divine Justice." Therese Mallion looked heavenwards for confirmation.

"Collaboration horizontale." Chantelle Parcelle spat out the words. "A fitting outcome. It comes to all of them, in the end. Look at Monsieur Chalroix. Caught up with him, didn't it? Siding with the Germans. God has spoken." Madame Poiller nodded sagely. There was little to add, on this occasion.

Eventually, sanctuary was reached. Sophie hammered frantically on the door. The commotion brought Madame Chalroix scurrying to see what was going on. The sight of Sophie shocked her to the core, but the sight of half a dozen animated gossips galvanised her to deliver a volley of ferocious abuse, the contents of which shocked even her.

"Oh Mimi, oh Mimi." was as much as Sophie could splutter, through her swollen lips. Mimi eased her onto the sofa. The gentleness of her tone enhanced the immediate comfort provided by something as simple as cold water. 'Aunty Mimi' gently bathed her face. Shocked by the savagery of the assault, her body yearned to shut down. Sleep came quickly.

✧ ✧ ✧

Dreamers Rock was a testimony to the wonders, fascination and timelessness of Geology, a boulder deposited millions of years ago as the ice sheets first advanced, and then retreated. Its shiny resistance to the forces of nature was in stark contrast to the easily eroded rock on which it was now perched. Its position above the river, a position which long preceded any human settlement, had seen all kind of mythical, semi religious, not to mention completely absurd, properties ascribed to it. Eternal damnation surely awaited anyone who disturbed its timeless guardianship of the village. Few were in any doubt.

For the six teenagers ambling towards it, as summer finally began to lose its furnace like intensity, the shade it offered was the main consideration. Shade, and the opportunities for some exploratory fumbling with the raven haired Laschelle sisters, were what was uppermost in the minds of Andre and Jerome Givet. Less so their younger cousins, Hector and Pierre, who were nevertheless hoping to learn something, however basic, about the opposite sex.

The girls dawdled and gossiped, as they began to climb the slope. Andre had Jerome in a headlock. The girls looked at each other. It looked like it might be a long afternoon. Andre released Jerome, with a playful kick up the backside.

"Glad to be out of there. If I have another day like yesterday I'll... I'll...Well, I don't know what I'll do. But I won't put up with that."

"I know. The curtains being closed all day. That was bad enough. But the crying. All day, and most of the night as well. How do you cry that long?"

"It was father's birthday, and he is supposed to have been a hero, well, you would expect to at least celebrate, remember the good times. She didn't have his photo out, even. And what about his medals? Where were they?"

Jerome didn't answer. He remembered the jibes from Gaston Mirreau. Andre persisted.

"They didn't take them back, did they? You know, like that half-wit, Gaston, said? Why, if he was so brave?"

The telegrams had said that their father had died a hero. But a barely repeated, half believed, rumour intensified their sense of loss. Whispered behind closed hands, the version of events which had gained ground was that their father had been foremost amongst the mutineers, and had refused to obey the suicidal orders at Chemin des Dames. He had been shot as an example to the others.

Denied the solace of a father who had died, but was nevertheless a hero, the mixture of grief and shame intensified an alienation which was common. For many, like Andre and Jerome, the fragility of life had been brutally demonstrated. The only conclusion to draw was to reject the advice of the generation who had caused it, and live life as provocatively, and defiantly, to the full as possible.

"Come on, at least it will be a year until the next one." Jerome's expression began to brighten. "Slow down, let them catch up. Which one are you going to have?"

Their leisurely progress towards the rock continued to be interrupted by bouts of horseplay, and further trials of strength. Arm wrestling, and rolling around in the dust, was as sophisticated as the seduction process was likely to get, thought Monique, the elder of the two girls.

"Laydees and gentlemen. The winner by a fall. Only twenty seven seconds into Round One. I give you Jerome Givet! Now, let's have a warm round of applause for the gallant loser, Andre Givet."

As he levered his brother to one side, Andre grasped that their strenuous exertions had finally lost their appeal. The girls were bare legged, their skirts only just covering their knees. The possibilities were endless. However, the day was in danger of petering out into another missed opportunity, if the stifled yawns of the two girls were not acted upon. Action was needed.

"Look at these muscles," Jerome, the bigger of the brothers exclaimed, as he flexed his biceps. The girls feigned indifference, before Suzanne retorted "I've seen more meat on a sparrow's ankle."

Jerome was not to be thwarted. "See this rock? We can shift it, easy. No problem. Can't we? Can't we, Rickets?" He stared at his brother, who realised he had no option but to agree. "Move the rock? Are you mad?" was all the encouragement they needed.

The brothers rolled up their sleeves. They spat on their hands. They inhaled deeply; they dug in their heels, and put their shoulders to the one part of the rock which jutted out. Finding a firm footing proved difficult as the ground, ravaged and undermined by rabbit burrows, gave way constantly. Sweat poured into their eyes. Any image of measured athletic poise, to impress their female admirers, disappeared amidst a flurry of curses. However, their frenzied efforts finally paid dividends, as the giggling was approaching uncontrollable levels.

To their astonishment, a shallow pit appeared, as the ground in front of the rock collapsed amidst a squealing of rabbits. The rock toppled forward to the sounds of cheers, which were a mixture of the genuine and the ironic.

The rock slowly gathered pace. After a brief moment of disbelief, a frantic yell of, "Come on then!" was met by eager enthusiasm from the two younger boys, and weary resignation from the girls. Their exchange of glances questioned the logic of going back down the steep hill it had taken them so long to climb. The rock was slowly gathering speed. As it did so, the arid earth served to add height to each upward bounce.

Smaller and nimbler, Hector and Pierre were in danger of overtaking, and hence being crushed by, the rock. They were followed by Andre and Jerome, still sweating from their exertions, but unwilling to miss the rock crashing into the river. Half heartedly, the girls ambled down the slope, a bemused expression on their faces. The rock was picking up speed rapidly. Suddenly it bounced onto-and even more quickly off-an exposed slab of limestone. The combination of speed and mass meant that the rock traced a prolonged arc through the air. It was the last thing any of the six were to see.

Had the effects of their exertions not caused such a ferocious pounding in their ears, they could not have missed the splintering of wood, the gouging of metal. The brown cloud, wafted by the late summer breeze, enveloped them. The burning sensation quickly rendered them half blind. The frantic rubbing of their eyes served only to make matters worse. Instinct told them to lie on the ground, in the hope that they could protect themselves. But, instinct was no match for the ingenious minds who had developed the gas. It had been designed to hug the ground, for maximum effect.

They panicked. They shrieked. They clawed at their throats. Their furious intakes of breath served only to deliver ever more fatal doses of the gas. The added agony of burning throats, as their lungs desperately tried to repel the poison, did not last long. Their lips foamed, their breathing became more shallow. The youngest, mercifully, died the quickest. Monique was found furthest up the slope.

Those who were first on the scene would remark on the foetal position each of the six had adopted, as life ebbed agonisingly away. Purple, foam flecked lips, the nail marks from the frenetic clutching at their eyes, were common to all.

As the sun set, the gathering breeze meant that no trace of the acrid, mustard like smell remained.

✳ ✳ ✳

As news of the calamity spread through the village, the crowd outside the church gates grew rapidly.

"Six?"

"Not both the sisters?"

"Gas, you say? Gas?"

"How?"

"The rock. The rock. The legend was true, once it shifted."

"We're cursed."

"You're right, cursed. Cursed by the Boche."

"Yes, even after they are long gone we can't shake free of them."

Further down the street, the curtains were already closed at the Laschelle house.

✳ ✳ ✳

The news eventually reached Sophie and, whilst appalled by the accounts of what had happened, she felt that after a suitable period of mourning, rural life would resume its measured progress. Her headaches were less intense, but her sight still hadn't returned to her right eye. Could she return to work? How? Long days of typing and intricate design work were a strain, with full sight. She was in no doubt that Olivier would have disappeared, once again, but how could she maintain her hard won supremacy over the sneering Chalmy?

The village mourned its loss in time honoured fashion as curtains were drawn, jaws were jutted, and a collective resilience, born of centuries of self-reliance, emerged once again. However, although conversations were hushed and the dead spoken of in reverential terms, the simmering sense of wrong, inflicted on a community who had suffered already, would not disappear. Someone was responsible, and the repressed anger demanded an outlet, something tangible to ease the pain.

Sophie could only navigate the narrow confines of Mimi's living room with difficulty. The news came as a further shock. Mimi, her guardian and soul mate would have to attend her dying Aunt Beatrice in Bordeaux, the only one of her relatives who had ever shown any interest in her. Regaining her independence was now a matter of urgency.

It was common sense for Madame Chalroix to take Nicole with her to Aunt Francoise, in Chemeny. Then, she would commence her long trip across country. Eventually, Sophie had seen the logic in Nicole being looked after properly, until she recovered.

With her customary efficiency, several days' worth of food was provided, along with instructions, simple enough even for Sophie to follow. Tearful farewells were not to the taste of either woman. But for Sophie the loss, even though only temporary, of her mentor and only true friend, along with the most precious thing in her life, left a hollowness and feeling of isolation which she could not shift. The final hug seemed to last for ever.

Self pity was given little chance to take root, however. As soon as Mimi and Nicole had departed, the first of the mourners began taking up position by the church. A good funeral was an opportunity not to be missed, normally, providing as it did the chance to condemn the deceased in the most trenchant terms.

"This is different. This loss is communal. We all feel it."

"Life- and such short lives- snuffed out in the first full bloom of youth."

"The girls, so beautiful. Yes that's the only word. Just like their mother. Look, here she comes."

Conversation came to a halt. Funereal garb and solemn expressions were worn with the practised air of those who relished such occasions. The crowd had grown in size. The slate grey skies provided a perfect summary of the mood, as the rooks provided their own commentary, cawing and hooting from the elms which provided such a regal backdrop to the church. The bereaved led the mourners in. The anguish felt throughout the community, and the timeless dignity of such occasions, at least bound them together, even if only for a short time. Tears were already being shed.

The tributes from the pulpit were heartfelt. The vagaries of fate were cursed, at the same time as the potential which had been extinguished was lamented in the most poignant of terms. However, once the service was over, David Marquand spoke for many as the hearses slowly pulled away.

"God, almighty God. His infinite wisdom, his all-seeing mercy. On occasions such as these, well, you do have to wonder. Where was justice? For those precious six. Gone. No justice for them. Nor will there be, even though we know who was to blame." Madeline Burrand, a church goer for sixty two years, remained silent on this occasion. She feared that many were acquiescing. Silently

Even Sophie, although watching from afar, felt moved by the dignity of the occasion. More importantly, her own predicament was put into a rough and ready perspective which helped resolve the issue. One more week off, and then back to work.

Her well travelled route seemed further than she remembered, as her lack of exercise took its toll. She realised that she would be late, and not just by a couple of minutes. The sweat began to pour down her back as she half trotted in her rough clogs, trying to focus her mind on how to manage her return. Jibes were hastily prepared in anticipation of a withering assault from, well, almost any of her so called colleagues.

However, to her surprise, she entered a deserted factory yard. There was no hissing steam, no muffled curses-nothing. She was aware that the lights on the first floor were on. She raced up the iron staircase, the ringing of her clogs giving advance notice of her arrival. She thrust open the door to find herself face to face with her work mates, but behind a low platform. From there, Lionel and Chalmy were addressing the workforce.

The first faces she saw had the ashen skin tone of the recently bereaved. But whilst glancing across the rest of the room, as she tried to get her breath back, the expressions changed. Their focus was no longer on the speakers. It was impossible to avoid the simmering fury and withering contempt which confronted her

Attempting to make sense of what was happening stunned her temporarily, but Natalie's raised hand offered a momentary refuge at the back of the crowd. It took almost all of her strength to force a path through her colleagues who, it seemed, had squeezed closer together to make her task more difficult. 'Whore' she was ready for, but the 'German' which preceded it alarmed her most. Spat out with a vehemence even she had not encountered before, the shower of spittle and mucus, which covered her back as she eventually reached sanctuary, left no room for misunderstanding.

Her brain was reeling at this turn of events. Indifference-yes, hostility-not unexpected, but this was hatred, a hatred which was naked and unrefined. She turned to Natalie, but she was staring straight ahead. Lionel had now resumed a faltering speech infused with grief, anger, and a recognition of his own complicity.

"I was weak, weak when I should have been strong. Weak in the mind, weak up here." He jabbed a finger into his temple. "It was my father who entrusted the company, your company, to the two of us," he continued, spitting out the last word. "And it is us-the two of us -who have brought about this disaster. After all he taught me, it is I who should have held out. Held out, and listened to the wisdom of Pascal, here." Chalmy puffed out his chest and braced his shoulders.

"This harebrained plan. Invest the company's cash in German bonds, all our cash. Their value is nil. They have suspended payments. Borrowing to buy the printing machine, that is what finished us completely. That, and the collapse of our market in Germany. Regrettably, we are left with no choice."

The atmosphere was funereal as Lionel spelt out the implications. Redundancy was immediate for all but Sophie and Chalmy. They would join him to form a skeleton staff, to try to salvage what was left from the rubble, and try to dispose of the remaining assets. Little, if anything, could be expected was the last thing Lionel managed to say. He was convulsed by a series of sobs, so visceral it looked as if he might faint. Two of his longest serving machinists stepped forward, just in time, and ushered him down the stairs, out into the fresh air.

Chalmy, the person closest to Lionel, should have been aware of what was happening. But his focus was solely on Sophie, an icy glare which managed to combine hostility, superiority, and a sense of self righteousness, in equal measure. It was a stare which could only bode ill for Sophie. Her promotion within the company, and her close relationship with Olivier, were two of the crucial threads which bound together the narrative of disaster. Of that he was certain.

It was a conclusion more and more of the workers were coming to, unprompted, as they began to file out. Her wartime fraternisation, now re-emphasised at every opportunity, after the tragedy at the rock, was the clinching evidence the incensed workers required.

The rise in temperature was palpable. Sophie was speechless. Natalie, attuned to the frenzied atmosphere, grabbed her arm, dragged her out through the rear doors, and ushered her down the fire escape.

"Whatever you do, lock your doors. And above all, watch your back, for God's sake."

✵ ✵ ✵

When the end came, in a flurry of blows, the sepulchral mist of a November morning was their ally. Undeterred, she had taken her regular route at her regular time, despite Natalie's earnest pleas. As her life ebbed away, they used the sheet to suffocate her. When her body was found, the same sheet had been used to cover her. The bright, blue cornflower print could have been interpreted as trying to invest the corpse with a modicum of dignity.

In reality, it was a symbol which combined contempt, and the settling of scores.

# PART TWO

Germany, Northern France, Russia and Poland, 1932-1943

# Chapter Fifteen

"Well this is some birthday," wheezed Freuntz.

Sweat mixed with grime as he heaved another shovel full of coke into the roaring boilers of the dilapidated tramp steamer. Every rivet seemed about to burst from the rusting plates which strained to hold the crashing waves at bay. Mopping his brow merely chafed his skin, whilst coughing up the dust simply emphasised his raging thirst.

"Shut your moaning, you miserable bastard. At least you can go and lie on your bunk to puke your guts up," cackled Hans Denhelm. "Me, I'm down here for the next 12 hours so count your blessings and fuck off. Happy Birthday by the way!" he added with a roguish twinkle which temporarily diffused the despondency which had engulfed Freuntz.

Freuntz, having hurled his shovel at his chortling comrade, began to weave his way along the narrow passageways which bucked and heaved as the storm reached new levels of ferocity. With a grunt he heaved himself onto the sheets, rigid from sweat and coke dust, but sleep refused to come. He dreaded an even more violent burst of sea sickness than normal.

His condition caused endless amusement to Hans, whose constant barbs about being a 'city boy' (a catch all term for someone with less than his own fifteen years at sea), Freuntz had not yet been able to neutralise, let alone counter. This was the world where Hans ruled, and Freuntz had no option but to grit his teeth and bear it.

What he couldn't bear was how it had come to this. How had it gone so wrong when all was set so fair? So wrong, when his dreams had been so close to turning into reality that their evaporation simply added to his anguish?

The ship ploughed onwards, a series of images, fragmentary yet connected, slipping in and out of his memory. The first time Old Man Hoffman had brought him his statement-always on his birthday-seemed to show that the deductions from his wages had somehow been transformed into a growing nest egg, and not a trifling amount either. 1927, when he had sat by the river to double, treble check what the figures said. Hyperinflation had taught him to suspect numbers on paper.

The celebration that same night, to which the old man had treated him, had seen him succumb to the argument that leaving the money where it was would yield ever more riches in the future. The toasts to the far sighted financial wizardry of brother Ezra seemed to be never ending. He had neither the intellect nor willpower to argue, the latter undermined by a mixture of fine brandy, which he had never tasted before, and a dawning realisation that he was a fan of the jazz music which accompanied them into the early hours. Jazz-was he developing a veneer of sophistication in middle age?

But 1929 was the year. He remembered skipping along the street, once his statement had shown him that within six months, eighteen months ahead of schedule, he could actually afford the fare to America. The jazz solos that night had never seemed more serene, the Manhattan skyline almost tangible. If only. A huge wave crashed into the boat and the heaving motion changed the mood of reminiscence. Once the boat achieved a relative stability, the memories were stark.

The Old Man rarely closed, other than on Christmas Day. The last customers were brusquely ushered out at mid-day on the 23$^{rd.}$ There was no denying that the expression he had worn for days was a clue, even to someone as taciturn as Freuntz.

Next morning the biting wind had cut him to the quick as he waited forlornly on the pavement. Eight, then nine o'clock, came and went. Two haggard looking couples shuffled in behind him. After ten minutes the first muttering was heard.

"I bet he knows we're here." An umbrella poked Freuntz between the ribs. "Where is he, then?" Freuntz shrugged. Two minutes of silence ensued. "Can't wait to get our best stuff off us, normally." Freuntz declined to respond. "Not so quick at paying out, though." Further silence. Denied the opportunity to have a good argument, the two couples muttered something about the 'old man' being seriously ill, if he wasn't open for business. Freuntz couldn't make out the rest, and they trudged off down the street.

Finally, as the bells in the distance tolled for 10 o'clock, Freuntz had taken the initiative. In the alley behind the store he built a crude platform from five crates. He wrapped his scarf around his hands. Despite this, the broken glass, cemented into the top of the wall to deter burglars, dug deep as he levered himself over. The blood began to flow.

From the logs stacked in the yard he picked up the heaviest he could hold. After four attempts, his improvised battering ram splintered the door casing. Inside, all was silent. He winced at the pain from his hands. Was Jacob even there? The creaking of the stairs ceased as he tiptoed along the corridor. He pushed open the office door .

There, slumped across the desk, with the top of his skull blown away, lay the old man, the blood which caked his face already brown. Brain tissue, with which Freuntz was so grimly familiar, was splattered on the wall. The papers which covered the desk, for a reason Freuntz couldn't then understand, were also in red. But, unlike the caked blood, they delivered a harsh, unflinching message which couldn't be wiped away.

As another heave of the ship almost made him vomit, it served only to recall the feeling in his stomach when days later he had had chance to talk to the family lawyer, charged with sorting out the situation. Words which had meant little to him as he surveyed the morass of blood soaked papers- prospectus, stock option, preference bonds, margin call- were now seared into his brain. As the situation had been painstakingly explained to him Freuntz had simply slumped further and further into his chair.

"If it is any consolation-and I realise it is not-you are one of thousands. It seems that Ezra was not quite the financial wizard he claimed to be. Trading 'on the margin' is what he- along with many others- has been indulging in. Nothing more than gambling, I am afraid to say. Put ten per cent-the margin- down, and by the time you are due to pay the full amount, prices have risen, so you pay the margin and pocket the profits. Radio shares, they are the ones where speculation has been most rampant." Freuntz winced as he pictured Jacob and his advice to, "Learn to love them."

"Philadelphia Electric, RKO Chicago, Texas Communications, they have been the most widely traded. Now completely worthless. I am afraid the most exposed have taken the most calamitous losses." The lawyer read out two of the latters he had sent to Jacob. As he began a third, Freuntz indicated that he couldn't bear to hear any more.

Freuntz realised that only one prospect awaited those like him- unskilled, poor and embittered- ruin. In such circumstances, shovelling coke on a tramp steamer was progress of a kind.

On that depressing note, sleep finally came.

✵ ✵ ✵

Three days was usually the limit. One day of relief to be back on dry land. One day to undertake a futile search for work. Then another, only for the realisation to dawn that his future prospects still consisted of twelve hours of sweat and toil in the engine room, interspersed with frequent bouts of vomiting, to the huge amusement of his guffawing shipmate.

The Mannfred Granze Naval Mission was only a couple of blocks back from the Hamburg quayside. Its outline was grimly familiar. November 1932 was now the fourth time in two years he had shuffled up the sandstone steps. Set up, originally, to provide bed and board to seamen who were destitute, homeless or bereaved, its capacity was stretched to bursting point as the economic crisis engulfed Germany.

Having handed over the crumpled notes in return for his food tokens, he wearily climbed the stairs to the twelve bed dormitory. Through a fog of cigarette smoke and condensation, he could make out at least a dozen other men sprawled across any surface which was available. The smell was overpowering, but something he always quickly got used to, and far superior to that of his own vomit. He launched his canvas bag onto the one vacant bed, clambered up the flimsy ladder, and rolled onto his side. He was asleep in minutes. Conditions which would have appalled many had a warm familiarity, which took Freuntz back to his time in France.

After what seemed minutes, but was actually hours, Freuntz was awoken by a ferocious argument from the bunk below.

"This is fucking useless. A blind man can see these are fakes. We can't just storm in any more, they will be expecting us. We need to get in first. Who did these? Tell him I'll rip his arm off and use it as a quill pen if he sends any more of these. Christ, how difficult can they be to fake? They're Communist cards for fucks sake. Give me that pen. I'll do it myself."

The storm was starting to abate, but none of his comrades seemed willing to challenge the outpouring of fury. Curious to see what had caused the uproar, Freuntz lowered himself gently to the floor, and tried to find out what was going on. The bunk below was covered in a jumble of leaflets, cheap cigarettes and filthy underwear, on top of which was a brown shirt, a brown forage cap and some knuckledusters. But what caught his eye, on the cheap cabinet, made his chest swell with pride- an iron Cross.

"Freuntz, 1st Grenadiers," he said, thrusting out his hand

"Greber 9th Hessians," came the response. "What's it to you?" he grunted, without looking up.

Even in the half gloom of the dormitory, and just back after six months at sea, Freuntz was grimly familiar with what was going on. He had devoured the newspapers. Yet more elections were set for later that month. The political paralysis, in the face of six million unemployed, played right into the hands of the two mortal foes.

The Communist Party on one side, and the Nazi Party, in the shape of their para military force, the SA, on the other, had been forcing the issue. Despite their seminal differences their methods were identical. By reducing Germany to a state of anarchy and chaos, they both hoped to show that democracy was incapable of coping with the escalating crisis.

Once this had been achieved, the field would be clear for the final showdown between the two, their battles raw and brutal. Streets, rather than drawing rooms and salons, muscle not brain power were where, and how, the issue would be decided. Just like Moeller had predicted.

"Let me see what you are trying to do," said Freuntz, with the result that Greber, unused to any response to his volcanic outbursts, meekly handed over the flimsy cards.

"Well, you're right about one thing, these are diabolical. I can do better left handed. Any card? Any printing blocks? Leave it with me."

Freuntz rummaged in his bag and found two blunt, but trusty, calligraphy pens. Glad to be escaping the odour of stale sweat and foetid underwear which seemed to seep from the walls, he headed downstairs to the reading room.

Reality did not match up to its rather grandiose description, consisting as it did of four crude wooden tables in an alcove. He relished a task more sophisticated than shovelling. Once the materials were assembled, he began with enthusiasm. After a couple of clumsy attempts, he began to flow.

Within three hours the task was complete. A sense of pride coursed through his veins as he handed over the cards. Greber almost drooled in admiration.

"Perfect. Now we can really stick it to them."

✣ ✣ ✣

The Luther Matthaus Memorial Hall had seen better days. But, bathed in gas light and drizzle, its solidity seemed to impose an impressive air of foreboding upon its neighbours. Even as he had watched from across the street, the atmosphere had been heavy with a mixture of tension, anticipation and adrenalin. Red banners festooned the streets. Every wall was plastered with posters, already sodden in the drizzle. The primal rhythms of the marching bands could be heard in the distance. The hammer and sickle was everywhere.

It was now an hour since the animated hordes had finally filed in. All that Freuntz could glean about what was happening inside, was based on the series of muffled roars, underpinned by the stamping of feet, which punctuated proceedings at regular intervals.

Suddenly, an explosion at the rear of the building was quickly followed by the unmistakeable orange hue of flames. Freuntz set off towards the action. But as he dashed into the cobbled side street, he was knocked to the floor by four burly figures, fleeing in the opposite direction.

Half crouching, he tried to regain both his breath and his senses in the half light. He caught sight of a brown forage cap, dislodged as the men fled. Flames were now starting to shoot skywards, illuminating the scene more clearly.

To his amazement, there were up to thirty policemen massed beyond the emergency exit from the hall, yet making no attempt to intervene. Muscular figures continued to emerge, curses and commands shrieked in equal measure. The smell of smoke became more acrid. His eyes were beginning to sting.

From the smouldering doorway, two sinewy figures emerged. Half dragging a third, whose clothing seemed to be on fire, their shrieks indicated the urgency of the situation. Within ten staggering paces, they in turn were overtaken by a group of four others. They were wrestled to the ground. The smouldering figure cringed in anticipation, his hands clasped around his head. Others quickly emerged from the smoke to join in the assault. But then, as if ordered by some invisible command, the police leapt forward and began to administer even more ferocious beatings to anyone they could lay their hands-or boots-on.

Amidst the mayhem, the situation clarified itself to Freuntz. It was an ambush. But not only an ambush, an ambush in which the police had actively colluded, and were now participating with relish. The explosion was obviously the work of the S.A. The trap had been set with military precision. The Communists were taking a real beating.

The smouldering figure had somehow managed to detach himself from the melee, and was rolling towards what little shadow there was. Training again kicked in for Freuntz. Fortified by his years of shovelling, he threw the groaning figure over one shoulder, and stumbled into the main street, as the arrival of the fire brigade offered a perfect distraction.

✯ ✯ ✯

Through blackened lips and a mass of bandages the words were a barely audible rasp, each word an ordeal. But Greber was determined to recruit his saviour, as Freuntz ushered the Ward Sister away.

"You get a wage, not much." After a while he continued. "Some food as well." He was convulsed by a series of coughs which Freuntz thought might never end. "Got to stand up for Germany. He is definitely the man…our time is coming." He fell silent.

The commitment to the disjointed, rambling message was undeniable, the pain involved in delivering it excruciating. But in truth, Freuntz needed little persuading. Another voyage, incarcerated with the smirking Dunhelm, was more even than a martial spirit such as his could bear.

✯ ✯ ✯

If Nicole was to impress Guillaume, it was now or never. The air in the classroom was heavy. Sunlight blazed through the windows, windows which remained resolutely closed under the rigid regime of Monsieur Lagland. Another seventy minutes was almost too much to bear. Richard Gravaux was slumped forward on the table. Angelique Balmain's eyes were almost closed. David Pernier stroked his groin and lusted after Angelique. Monsieur Lagland was oblivious.

His lungs had never functioned properly since he had inhaled the first gas the Germans had used on the unsuspecting French.

He found it difficult to speak for more than ten seconds at a time, rendering his delivery both monotonous and relentless. He constantly seemed to be rushing to complete his sermons, in case he finally ran out of breath before he could convert all his students, students who were part of the future of France. It was a future which could only hold out promise if the ideas which had led to catastrophe, for him and thousands of others, were finally and decisively rejected.

For Nicole, however, the constant diet of apology and self-abasement had first rankled, and then infuriated her. Her fiery spirit could not accommodate such an insipid view of the future, or the caustic rejection of what France had done in the past. If France could not summon the stomach to confront the apologists and defeatists, then only one future was possible .

This was where Guillaume had come in. She instinctively wanted, felt compelled almost, to rebel. But she was struggling to articulate how, or against whom. For guidance, he was therefore the best bet.

Ever since their first day in class together, she had been taken by his languid air of superiority, his mocking tone and refusal to get too close to his fellow students, whether male or female. He had been the first to smoke, the first to challenge Monsieur Lagland, and the first to try to charm the platinum blonde, Genevive Gerbanne, whose family wealth afforded an icy air of superiority which deterred all but the most self-confident.

However, Guillaume did not fit the characteristic profile of gilded youth from a bohemian background, dabbling with extreme politics to confirm their supremacy over their intellectual inferiors. Quite the opposite.

The youngest of five sons, a future on the family farm held no attraction whatsoever. He had been sickened when, as a rite of passage his father had insisted on for all his brothers at the age of five, he had been forced to watch the slaughter of the beef cattle. Their passivity had amazed and horrified him in equal measure.

Such a visceral and brutal process fuelled his opposition to his father. The ritual abuse of him as a 'pansy' only entrenched his defiance. He hadn't eaten meat for four years. As he read more and more about Communism, he revelled in the fact that there would be no role for the peasantry.

This was a line of argument he knew would provoke his father to fury, once he found the courage to articulate it. He was prepared for the hail of flying fists. Beatings were part of the price to pay for the true believer, he convinced himself, as the bruises began to blacken. And as for joining in all that digging of those two pits in the barn, at all hours of the night, even on Sundays, they were dreaming.

Matters of the flesh were only part of the attraction for Nicole, as her hormones raged, however. She was first attracted by the workmans caps he, and his small group of disciples, had taken to wearing. They convinced themselves that it was a sign of solidarity with the working classes. But it was the practised air with which he espoused his views about the inevitable demise of France which impressed her most.

The ideas flowed seamlessly. The names, references and ideology transfixed her. Bourgeois, Trotsky, class conflict, triumph of the proletariat, were all delivered with an ease which deterred debate. His fluent articulation meant that he could also play off his string of admirers, one against the other. She hung on his every word, and tried to marshal the arguments in her head, so that they might be plausible as her own. Such sophistication!

Her sense of rebellion had been finding an outlet at home. Challenges to the rigid limits Aunt Francoise had tried to enforce, provided daily, even hourly, trials of strength. The box she had received on her birthday added to her sense of rootlessness and alienation. It fuelled her embitterment at her orphaned state, at the same time as it reinforced her role as an outsider. Challenge was what she thrived on. The moment had finally arrived.

She cast a glance at Guillaume. He nodded his approval. She gulped, and launched into her tirade.

"Monsieur, there are many things wrong with France, but the biggest problem is you, and all the people like you! Look around you, France is finished. France is broken. France is no more." This outburst had achieved the first objective of all speakers. Command the attention of the audience.

Momentarily taken aback by her own audacity, she seized the opportunity to deny him his chance to respond by moving fully onto the attack.

"We are bored by your lessons, we are bored by your opinions, and we are bored by your spinelessness! Your view of the future has nothing for us. You fought against Germany, and for what? They are on the march again. Fifteen years ago, we had supposedly beaten them, but here they are again."

Momentarily, she tried to coordinate her chronology and vocabulary, before she ploughed on. "You lacked the stomach to finish them once and for all, but you also lack the guts, the know-how, the…" and as her brain swirled, she blurted out, "Balls!"

Richard was now sat bolt upright. Angelique was fully awake. David had stopped stroking. Her use of such profanity caused jaws to drop and the sniggering to start. Monsieur Lagland had to regain the initiative. His repertoire of strategies to control the class was inevitably limited, as he rarely encountered any challenge to his authority.

"The only way to resist them is to unify the international working cla…" The sentence remained unfinished. With a surprisingly fluent motion, for one so frail, the chalk hurtled towards Nicole. It whistled past her left ear. It served only to enrage, and then embolden her.

"You are weak. You are old. You are finished you old, you old … bastard!" The last word was spat out, fuelled by contempt and surging adrenalin. "We are the future. There will be no more…" she raged. Monsieur Lagland, his complexion florid, his professionalism dissolving in the face of this flagrant challenge, hurled the board cleaner at her with all the force he could muster.

His aim was perfect, but the outcome was not. It struck Nicole on the point of her shoulder, bounced against the back wall, and came to rest on Guillaume's desk, across the aisle. Relishing his role as the orchestrator of this frontal assault, he thrust the board cleaner into her hand. The red mist had descended. Rational thought was impossible. With a grimace, she hurled it back.

To her amazement, the missile struck him right in the middle of his forehead. Completely unprepared for any retaliation, his veins bulged, his breath rasped and the colour drained from his cheeks. He crumpled behind the desk. The stunned silence which followed the resounding thump, as he hit the floor, offered the perfect moment.

With a dramatic throw back of her blonde hair, she stalked out of the classroom, eyes blazing. But not before she had cast a lingering glance over her shoulder at Guillaume. He reinforced her sense of a mission accomplished by a nod of the head. And an almost imperceptible smirk.

✻ ✻ ✻

"These uniforms, fine if it's below zero, but Jesus, it's like a steam bath today." Freuntz ignored the comment, and tugged at the coarse brown collar of his uniform. He, too, was itching.

"It's like I've got lice." Michael Heinze continued, wriggling to try to avoid scratching. "Potato sacks, that's what they must be made of."

The humidity served only to emphasise how pungent the fumes from the Erlingauer chemical plant were. Their eyes streamed. Rubbing them made it worse. Freuntz rested in the limited shade provided by the requisitioned bakers van, mopped his brow, and tried to fathom out what the purpose of the next activities might be.

He could still taste the coarse sausage, and even coarser bread, on which he and his comrades survived. "Ninety per cent tendon!" was Andreas Schumann's opinion. Clear thinking was difficult. Even more depressing was the sight of the dried bloodstains and clumsy shackles, as he sought refuge from the searing heat in the back of the van.

The daily round of intimidating anyone who questioned Nazi rule had appealed in the first heady months of power, the previous year. Now that had begun to pall. Beating up anyone who might be a Communist was just about acceptable, but it was the endless hours stood outside Jewish businesses which grated. Nowhere near as much, though, as the attitudes of his erstwhile comrades.

War stories had their appeal, but on a limited basis, as far as Freuntz was concerned. The beer swilling camaraderie felt forced, especially as its most vocal proponents were the two former criminals, Heinze and Schumann, who had ascended through the ranks and now commanded the S.A. detachment.

Their command was based on no more than a propensity for a casual brutality they relished a little too openly, as far as Freuntz was concerned. Neither had seen action and, as was always the case, they were now the most belligerent. They relished their swaggering mastery of the streets, and were determined to exploit their immunity from prosecution.

"Time to settle some scores, Kamerad! Saddle up!" was their rallying cry. It reflected both their self-appointed status as avengers of wrong, and their affection for the sub-titled Westerns which had offered cheap escapism to so many during Germany's darkest period. Their clearly defined sense of right served to underpin their warped version of morality

Not only were they belligerent however, they were, as far as Freuntz was concerned, completely deluded. Trampling on civilians was certainly no preparation for the discipline required in a real army.

The rally two nights earlier, dominated by tub thumping oratory, interspersed with raucous applause, had left him shaking his head. Equality of esteem, rank, and resources was their increasingly strident demand. If it came to a trial of strength with the regular army there could only be one winner. Their self-absorption in the cause left them oblivious to the jibes, made with increasing frequency behind their backs, about their fondness for doing everything together.

"Come on, then, face ache. Cheer up. You'll enjoy this," leered Heinze. "We're whore hunting."

✡ ✡ ✡

Freuntz was invaluable to the pair for his local knowledge. He gazed forlornly at the list of six names, and wondered what their 'crimes' could possibly be. He didn't need to wonder what their immediate fate would be. As he studied their ages, he was certain that any youthful beauty they might still possess would not endure for much longer.

Their first stop was a grimy pharmacy on a busy side street. Early afternoon, with plenty of spectators was perfect for sending a message to the cowed onlookers. With a theatricality they could only have got from the cinema, they screeched to a halt and leapt out. A young mother with a pram was sent sprawling, amidst a flurry of profanities. Freuntz tried to see what was happening inside. He didn't have long to wait. Heinze reappeared with a stockily built brunette draped over his shoulder. Her frenetic screeching and flapping legs made the attempts to scratch out his eyes even more difficult.

Great theatre, Heinze thought to himself. As the small crowd tried to work out what was going on, but knew better than to try to intervene, he flung her into the back of the van. Before she could gather her senses, Schumann had her chained up. The door was slammed shut and, ever with an eye on their audience, they roared away from the pavement. Their role as impartial avengers and dispensers of justice was off to a flying start.

On each occasion the script was followed. A blustering entrance, a forceful removal and a dramatic exit. Hilda Klensmann had offered the most resistance, as the teethmarks on Schumann's cheek showed, whilst bakery owner Anneka Jensen had come along so meekly that the pair felt cheated.

Their task was almost complete. The sounds of impotent resistance in the back dwindled, apart from a muffled sob. Only one of the six on the list remained. After that, they could look forward to an evening of boasting about their prowess, and swooning over the dashing exploits of Tom Mix.

The location was perplexing Freuntz. Twice they crawled the maze of streets and alleyways in the Glenfeld area of town. Run down didn't even begin to do it justice, and Freuntz found it difficult to accept that someone with so little was having even more taken away.

Eventually the address was identified. The script was adhered to. Freuntz had feigned indifference to the last couple, but this was different. Through the open doorway came anguished screeches, those of an adolescent. A yelp followed a thump.

Immediately, a blonde haired figure was scrambling to her feet, having been knocked into the street. As she got to her feet, she made no effort to flee, but instead headed back inside to confront her assailant. An unwise choice as it turned out. A swinging fist from the gloomy interior knocked her backwards. Still she tried to resist. It took two of them to subdue her. The leering pair were energised by such spirited resistance. A quick glance between them confirmed to Freuntz how they loved the job.

As they pulled away, he was aware of a figure, desperately trying to catch up with the van, as it gathered speed. In the wing mirror, Freuntz was staggered to see a dark skinned teenager, with his hands on his hips, realising his attempts were forlorn. Freuntz sat bolt upright in his seat. His scalp prickled. He scanned the list to try to make sense of things. He recognised the Christian name- Eva- but not the surname.

The blonde hair, the fiery attitude, the mixed race son, he had to ask. Previously, the focus on their mission had led to long periods of silence which Freuntz had been unwilling to pierce. Now, he felt he had no choice.

"What's going to happen to them?" he asked, as Eva cursed with all her might in the back.

"Whores. Collaborators. Fraternising with the enemy. Defilers of German motherhood. Nigger lovers, all of them" said Heinze, with a tone which managed to combine a snigger and a sneer. As they passed the colliery, its pitches straw coloured in the heat, the reply made Freuntz feel sick.

"They're going to be sterilised, what do, you think?" drawled Schumann, the relish in his tone undeniable.

✭ ✭ ✭

The storm clouds gathered menacingly in the distance. Freuntz realised that his decision to head back to Clensburg was a wise one. Tramping through the rolling countryside for the last two days, parched as it was, had offered a chance to escape the humidity which had blighted Erlingauer for almost a month. The half-timbered houses which greeted arrivals in the village harked back to a peaceful, pastoral past, in contrast to the grimy, urban reality of Erlingauer. It had also offered the opportunity to reflect on what had happened

The Clensburg Hotel offered shade and cold beer. Just one. As he made his way towards the shaded seats, his eye was taken by a newspaper hoarding which screamed 'Plot Foiled', in the densest of black print. Intrigued, he scanned the papers on sale at the stall, all of which carried the same message, 'Threat to the Nation Thwarted', 'The Fuhrer Safe', 'Plotters Crushed'. Beneath all the headlines loomed the same unflattering photograph of SA leader Ernst Rohm, whilst a phrase he couldn't quite make sense of, featured in at least two of them, 'Night of the Long Knives'.

He quickly paid for his copy of the Frankfurter Dagenblatt, and his furrowed brow disappeared as he scanned the less prominent articles. 'Threat to national security', 'unstable elements', 'decisive action'-the messages were rammed home with the unmistakable conformity of a censored press, as was the most lurid of the messages which had to be conveyed to the German populace-'Depraved Homosexual Plotters'.

The column of those murdered was headed by a photograph of Moeller and Kaltz, handcuffed but defiant, ready to embrace whatever fate might have in store for them. When both Heinze and Schumann were also listed, he could barely contain a self-satisfied grin.

The sense of release made his body go limp.

# Chapter Sixteen

For Nicole, 'The Red Flag' was a tune capable of stirring a range of emotions Depending on her mood, it could generate a fierce confidence in the future, whilst on other occasions, a melancholy sense of foreboding could threaten to overwhelm her. The population of Veziers, dependent as they were on the jobs generated by the railway yards, were overwhelmingly in the confident camp.

Elections in 1936 had seen its voters deliver the second highest number of votes for the Popular Front in the whole of France. May Day was a chance to flaunt their power. The stirring martial music provided the backing to a sea of banners which described the ancient, craft origins of so many modern occupations. Boiler makers, wheelwrights, carpenters and printers, the list was endless. The linked arms of the leading ranks of the marchers portrayed a convincing image of unity.

The choreography was impressive, but her doubts were growing. The tenor of the daily conversations at Monsieur Orvet's grocery encouraged her contrarian opinions. 'The workers this', 'The workers that'. The more she heard praise for anything, the more antagonistic and confrontational she became. She didn't mean to, but she couldn't help it. The previous week, a furious row with a bristling Madame Forceaux had cost her half her wages-and all about the price of sugar!

The stinging rebuke, which Monsieur Orvet had delivered in front of a shop full of customers, had had the opposite effect to the many she had received since she could walk. This time she backed down, she wilted, she shrivelled inside-and she hated it. Her latest encounter with Uncle Charles had shaken her.

In a swirl of emotions she tried to trace the root cause, as she sat beneath the awning, toying half-heartedly with a glass of the coarsest vin blanc. It was Guillaume who had set in motion this draining of confidence. He was late again. He rarely turned up on time now, and on three occasions he hadn't turned up at all.

However, the efforts to snare him made the series of humiliations worth it. The bouquets of flowers, home made perfume from those same flowers, and even poetry, had flattered her ego. It was almost too fluent and stylish not have been copied from some obscure poet he had come across, whilst seeking to goad his father. But it had worked. However, being manipulated had run its course. She tried to marshal her arguments.

The noise around her increased, as the exhilaration of a blue sky, a holiday, and the potency of the local cider, combined to produce a mixture of animated conversation and raucous laughter, interspersed with ever more frequent calls of,

"Encore, garcon, quatre bouteilles s'il vous plait."

Suddenly he appeared. His languid lope appeared to part the animated crowds which thronged the pavement, like a biblical scene she half remembered drawing at school. His chin, thrust upwards, emphasised his sophisticated air, but the image was compromised by the insipid stubble which represented his first attempt at a moustache. The inevitable cap was accompanied by a sleeveless leather tunic, but his puny biceps rendered his attempts to portray working class masculinity slightly risible.

His lukewarm embrace signified straight away that there were explanations to be made, and business to be done. Her heart began to flutter. He gulped back a second Ricard in a couple of minutes, and launched first into a series of explanations as to his neglect of her. He was part of a covert Communist cell. He was instrumental in the planning to take over the local branch of the

Union, with a view to strangling rail traffic in the North East. Or so he said. Total secrecy was crucial, hence keeping her in the dark.

"Classic tactics," he enthused. "Straight from the text book. A small elite, focused and well motivated can achieve so much more than …this." He swept his arm dismissively towards the ranks of honest toilers, who, now the march had finished, were heading towards the bars around the square for some well deserved thirst slaking.

"Lumpen, obedient dupes, ox-like in their obedience, cavalry in a machine age. I loved it, there have been just six of us, but now…" The relish in his role, as an intellectual amongst the horny handed working classes, was undeniable.

His words tailed away, and it was clear that he was summoning up his courage to deliver some unpalatable truth. He was softening her up, with what she knew to be at best a half believable yarn.

"In the morning I'm off to Spain. That's where the real action is. Austria is just the first step," his fascination with membership of a revolutionary cell now dissipating like morning mist. "It's confront Fascism now, there. Or, confront it later… here," he continued, with another sweep of his arm around the teeming square. "Confront it we must. It is the duty of our generation," he continued with the youthful certainty of someone who believed totally in the power of historic forces and class conflict, not individuals.

The rhetoric flowed, as her eyes slowly filled with tears. She couldn't bring herself to beg him not to go, as she knew the die was cast. She instinctively knew her blubbering amidst the animated crowds would only draw attention to her, compounding her sense of humiliation. She knew the ache of being deserted once again would come later.

She grasped at his wrist, as his oratorical tour de force drew to a close. But he slipped away, realising further words would only complicate matters. He paused momentarily to kiss her on the forehead.

He didn't look back, and as he quickened his pace, he couldn't help but smirk as he told himself with a sense of relief,

"Well, that was easier than I expected."

☆ ☆ ☆

The consistent deductions from her wages, meagre enough to begin with, had forced her to seek a couple of shifts at the Café Gasquet. She did not dare to be late and as a result, as she dashed past the entrance to Parc de Marshall Foch, still packed with couples, red faced children and family picnics, she slowed only momentarily.

The platinum blonde was entwined in the arms of a scrawny figure, who, despite the passion of their embrace, was still wearing a workmans cap. Revolutionary Cell? Ha! It all made sense, and this public display of lust was akin to announcing it in the town square. After the painful encounter that morning, her heart was already beginning to harden, and confrontation would achieve little.

Revenge was a dish best served cold. She had always found a way to get even, and if the chance ever came this would be no different. Uncle Charles and his wandering hands were no longer her only concern.

☆ ☆ ☆

Exercise had always invigorated Freuntz. He sunk into his seat. The rattling of the train became more rhythmic and induced a warm feeling of contentment, feelings he hadn't had since the halcyon days at the Hoffman Emporium.

The countryside around Clensburg could not possibly have been more verdant. Indeed, he could easily have fallen for the legend that simply bathing in the spring water which supplied the spa, on which the village based its prosperity, could actually rejuvenate even the most haggard. Nowadays his muscles ached after twelve miles, but it was a fatigue born of exercise which was beneficial, not punitive.

Even better, the week had been topped off by promotion at work, a reward, he was convinced, for the assiduous attention to detail he had exhibited since starting at OKB Electricals. The firm, whose production of radios was achieving new peaks each week, was expanding at a breakneck pace.

Few in Germany could escape its power to cow and indoctrinate. The loudspeakers which blared forth the latest propaganda in every communal space had long been the staple product of the firm. But it was radio which could help enslave a people. Built to order, they only had a range of fifteen miles, thereby excluding any alternative or subversive message.

Virtually everyone in Germany had one. Now, since Anschluss, there was the prospect of a new captive market in Austria. A firm grip on orders and rigorous stock control were essential. He might have designed the requirements of the job himself. Meticulous organisation, assiduous attention to detail, and effectively his own boss-perfect! He began to doze, as rays from the fading sun delivered a milky heat to all in the carriage.

All this, and Pastor Neumann tomorrow.

✯ ✯ ✯

Known simply as 'Die Kirke', it implied there were no other churches in Stelghalle, and to all intents and purposes there weren't. Under the onslaught of propaganda and coercion, attendances had plummeted at The Blessed Saint Mary, whilst the synagogue remained a ravaged shell, unaltered since it was set ablaze, three years earlier. Standing proud and unbowed in the corner of Karl Hoffman Platz, 'Die Kirke' seemed to be Pastor Neumann embodied in brick, stone and mortar.

The Pastor had been decorated for his valour in France, a valour which had bordered on the reckless, and had cost him his arm during the black days of August 1918. Undeterred, he had shunned the comfortable life he could have had in the affluent suburbs. In contrast, he had sought out the most deprived areas. The most challenging appointment available was a prospect to relish, and he had been in the heart of Stelghalle for over ten years.

He was Muscular Christianity made flesh, and his fierce devotion to his congregation was rewarded by ever increasing attendances.

His outreach and pastoral work were his greatest strengths, and few churches could equal the collections he organised, whenever tragedy struck.

Freuntz had never had any interest in religion, but he had occasionally thought that there must be something in it. He had seen how frequently the terrified young lads had discovered it, before a bombardment, or the dismembered ones afterwards, once their agonised cries for their mother came to an end. His long nights in the library at The Workmans Academy had led him to wonder what drove the martyrs of The Reformation.

What had originally led him into contact with the Pastor was his support for FK Stelghalle. The Pastor had been an accomplished player himself, in his youth, and he didn't take long to concur with Freuntz that Wolfgang had the talent to go far. He ran the line, he ran on with the bucket to treat the injured, and occasionally cursed under his breath as another indiscretion against his boys went unpunished.

There had been three teams eventually, but 1933 changed all that. Almost as successful had been the rudimentary art instruction, and calligraphy classes, which Freuntz had provided before he had been forced to go to sea. The embrace of all creeds and classes was at the heart of The Pastor's philosophy, all were God's children and this was where his philosophy had, up until now, flourished.

As the street battles had disfigured the streets around Die Kirke, legend had it that on at least three occasions his arrival on the scene had caused the brawling thugs to back off shamefacedly. The table leg he carried on such occasions he jokingly referred to as his 'mighty sword of righteousness'. Simply brandishing it seemed to have a tranquilising effect on the bloodied combatants.

But now, the teams and the classes had dwindled. Now, The Hitler Youth monopolised any spare time the local teenagers had. To his dismay, Wolfgang had been one of the first to enrol as an instructor, and Freuntz had seen little of him for years. The brutalising of any opposition had appalled The Pastor. He had not been afraid to speak out about the divisions and hatred which disfigured his beloved community. His favourite parable had been that of The Widows Mite-a person with nothing, giving their all-summed up what Germany should be about. But in recent weeks his theme had changed.

The congregation were still shuffling in, expectant in the dappled sunlight which filtered through the high windows. Fire and brimstone was what they liked. He had the perfect raw material. It was May Day tomorrow, and the previous evening had offered an ideal opportunity for yet more ritualised, state sponsored, humiliation of the local Jewish population. On this occasion, it was for their alleged Communist sympathies.

A supine press reported that in a series of assaults by 'upstanding citizens of The Reich', whose supposedly spontaneous defence of 'the national character' had been provoked by the 'increasingly brazen displays by perverted disciples of a verminous Bolshevism', three Jews were dead and another twelve in need of medical treatment. Such treatment was even beyond the powers of The Pastor. That hadn't stopped him trying. The tears had flowed as he cradled seventy year old Levi Reiner, and he knew what must be done.

As the congregation sat back and waited for the fireworks, he confounded them by talking in such a calm, quiet, and measured tone that those at the back had to crane their necks to hear. Slowly, it became clear what he was doing. He was describing, in great detail, the qualities and achievements of the casualties and the deceased. His detailed knowledge of their upbringing and background was a tribute to his view of them as good Germans, one and all.

"Sarah Rosenfeldt, Ward Sister. Ezra Warzmann, craftsman, jeweller and war veteran. Jacob Siegel, accomplished violinist and father of four, Moshe Hartz, engineering draughtsman." The list continued. The volume slowly increased, his tone colder, more caustic.

"These were Germans… these were good Germans, killed and maimed here on our own streets, their blood on our cobbles, their only crime to be deemed unfit and by who? By who? What kind of perverted creed permits, no encourages, no enforces the unwarranted assaults on our friends, our countrymen, our fellow Germans? The guilty ones, and by that I do not mean the deluded dupes who carry out their bidding, for they are no better than chimpanzees who perform for bananas. No, the guilty ones are perverted. They are ever ready to condemn homosexuals as perverted, but they are unfit to walk the same streets as such people. For they, at least, are genuine in their motives."

Eyebrows were being raised, and eyes averted from The Pastor, as the implications of what he was saying began to sink in. The oration approached its climax. With a series of sweeping gestures with his one arm, eyes ablaze, he bellowed,

"Only God can choose to take life, only almighty God, not the posturing thugs who rule our once proud nation. They are no better than the gangsters of Chicago, cowering before an Austrian corporal. Our country, your country, the country of Ezra and Sarah is heading for disaster if you forget The Parable of The Good Samaritan. Do not pass by on the other side. No, do not avert your eyes. One day they will come for you, and then who will you turn to? Only God. Now is the time to prove yourselves as true Germans, for this criminal gang are no better than the Communists they encourage you to hate. They long since forfeited the right to consider themselves genuine Germans."

The force of his oratory slowly dissipated. He looked longingly around his flock. Freuntz was sure The Pastor believed this to be his last sermon, and beseeched them,

"Get up! Stand up! For Germany, for yourselves, for our Jewish brothers and sisters!"

✵ ✵ ✵

The store room was subdued and the atmosphere morose. Stares were blank as the news was digested. The events of Sunday evening were still etched in lurid hue in their memories.

To a man they had stood back, they had averted their eyes, they had passed by on the other side, as The Pastor was dragged past the congregation, gathering in anticipation of a second onslaught that evening. Had his silence been in mute protest, or was his jaw already broken? The size of the police contingent suggested that they expected trouble, but the mere implication of brutal force usually intimidated all but the most foolhardy. This occasion was no different.

"Anyone know where Dieter is?" asked Freuntz, curious as to the absence of his foreman.

An uncomfortable silence ensued before the answer came haltingly,

"Turned in ... by his son, Gunther. Only his fourth time at The Hitler Youth. Poor sod."

Conversation ceased until the siren blew for lunch time.

In the light of what had happened, Freuntz was ever more resolved to continue with his plan. Work late, alter the figures, sneak out the latest high specification components. Owning your own radio was dangerous, building one doubly so.

Freuntz was in no mood to waver.

# Chapter Seventeen

"Christ that was a cold one. That was the coldest I've ever been."

"Listen, soft balls. You can't even begin to imagine what real cold is, so shut your rattle. Did the lubricating oil actually freeze? No. Did anybody freeze to death, stood up? No. Did anyone get a frozen anus because they couldn't get their trousers up quickly enough? No. So unless you were here last winter, you know fuck all about cold. This is like Spring." Rolf Schwerner sank further into his greatcoat. He took the hint, and closed his eyes.

Silence descended. Russian vodka didn't have the same warming properties as Schnapps, Freuntz reflected, rubbing his temple. But at least it helped dull his senses. Another day, grimly collating the eradication of yet more Russian villages, stretched ahead. His new colleagues, attached to The Cologne Police Battalion, appeared to relish the statistical discipline implicit in recording every last detail of the genocidal havoc being wreaked upon the Russian countryside. The cumulative effects of the last twenty one months were finally grinding him down. Bohme had been shot the previous week for drinking brake fluid, his fate noted with a mere shrug of the shoulders.

"You know what? That first summer it seemed so easy. Just like they told us. A walk over. Kick the door in and the house will collapse. Do you remember that? Do you?" Martin Pohl was getting no response. He pressed on. "It was all so quick. Do you remember?

We couldn't keep up. And so many of them. How many fucking Russians can there be? And another thing. How can you tell a Russian from a fucking Latvian from a fucking ... Who cares? They were right about one thing though. You have to admit. They are only one step removed from animals. I mean look at the shacks they live in. No question. They're only fit to be serfs."

Freuntz thought back to Poland, a trial run, where the phrase 'The Wild East' was first coined. There, the chaotic, harebrained plans were first pursued with a maniacal glee. He remembered the contempt with which the Russians were viewed. Tales of the capture of Orel in 1941, whose citizens were so taken by surprise that the trams were still running, as the Panzers roared into the town centre, seemed to encapsulate their 'dumbkopf', peasant stupidity. Untermensch indeed. It was a tale they never tired of repeating. Spirits needed to be bolstered, the faith kept burning bright, he recognised. Now, the stories had lost their triumphal tone. Twenty one months on. No end in sight.

Unlike his colleagues, Freuntz knew about military matters- and he knew about history. The euphoria had grown as victory had followed victory. But the vastness of Russia had eroded the complacency.

"Much further and we'll be in Asia. Another fucking horizon. Always another horizon. Is there no end to the fucking place?" Pohl had been the first to express what some of them had started to think. The supply lines were lengthening. Freuntz knew it was starting to gnaw at them. "Many more 'victories' like this and we are finished," Freuntz had once confided to his colleagues. They had ignored him. They were still drunk on the mission to record every last detail, as the theories behind Master Race supremacy were put into brutal practice.

They cheered themselves up any way they could. "You know, don't you, that future generations will venerate our work. They will see us as accomplished scholars of the human condition, there to record the creation of a new model society. There, when the experiment was conducted. There, at the creation. Witnesses, participants, recorders of the truth."

Joachim Hessler was tolerated only up to a point. After all, he had been a school teacher. All of them had hated school. Long words and pomposity irritated them. But one thing they could all agree on. The derided 'Ivans' didn't know when they were beaten. Freuntz recognised that their refusal to give in was wearing down German men, material and morale.

No wonder he had turned to drink.

✵ ✵ ✵

"Do you ever smile?" wheezed Hans Zemmer, the scowling sergeant, turned bureaucrat.

"Why bother? More time for frowning!" chuckled Remnick in response, as he pulled the collar of his greatcoat even further over his ears.

The sun was low in the East. The lorry alternated between skidding on patches of thawed mud and juddering across still frozen ruts. The fields of winter wheat were already exhibiting a lattice work of tank tracks, pock marked by shell bursts.

Last night's session was one Freuntz had been regretting all morning, until it provided the opportunity to spew the remaining residue into the lap of the yawning Remnick. At least it put a temporary halt to his salivation at the prospects which lay ahead. It seemed that Schwerner might burst, as he tried to conceal his sniggering.

It was left to Zemmer to outline the plans. The blank expressions could have told him. The same as every other day. Follow in the wake of the marauding SS units, and then detail the death tolls. Age, gender, occupation were fairly straightforward. The far more complex task was trying to fit the deceased, often unrecognisable, into one or more of the myriad, racial categories the deranged theorists had dreamt up. How to categorise a charred infant, or an emaciated seventy five year old, had quickly proved impossible. Once the lunacy of repeatedly trying to achieve the unachievable had sunk in, drinking oneself unconscious made perfect sense.

## Will

✯ ✯ ✯

Zhubrevno was, or had been, a typical, yet substantial, peasant village. The rolling landscape was showing only the barest signs of emerging from its hibernation. Any sense of a rural idyll had been obliterated, as the 21$^{st}$ Battalion had visited all the horror of modern warfare upon it. Self-propelled guns, and lorries laden with supplies, were haphazardly parked by the side of the track, which was rapidly turning into a morass. The first field kitchens were being assembled. The troops queued for breakfast or some rudimentary first aid.

The billowing, black smoke stung their eyes, and served to confirm that The Blowtorch Battalion had indeed carried out their mission. A third battle for the strategically vital city of Kharkov was looming. No mercy was to be shown in the preliminaries, they had heard.

The crudely painted blowtorches adorned every vehicle, but most brazenly the hulls of the Panzers, their gun barrels finally cooling. The name had been given to the unit to describe their tactics of using their overwhelming firepower to obliterate anything and anybody who stood in their path. Their tactics regularly turned the villages of straw roofed, wooden buildings into one blazing inferno after another. Zhubrevno was simply the most recent.

They inched down the street. A prolonged rat tat tat came from behind the smouldering ruins of the Orthodox Church. "No Geneva Convention here, boys. Wasted on them, anyway. Civilised, that's what you need to be." Pohl was glad of at least one nod of agreement. "Hmm, is that roast meat I can smell?" Freuntz knew there had been little sanctuary for the civilians who had cowered inside. He felt like punching Pohl. Carnage had never bothered Freuntz in France, but licensed mayhem against civilians chilled him to his marrow. The village school, at the end of what passed for a main street, collapsed with a gentle whimper, an eloquent testimony to its ramshackle construction.

A group of traumatised survivors were sat, cross legged in the road. The raised rifle butts underlined the urgency with which the crudely translated questions were bellowed at them.

"Partisans? When? Who is Commisar? Who?"

Three elderly men slumped backwards, their answers neither quick nor informative enough. The children in the group screamed in terror, and clutched the nearest adult. Their blank stares indicated that they knew what fate had in store.

As their driver presented his papers, a column of civilians shambled towards them, cringing in expectation of a beating. They carried shovels 'at the slope', in a pitiful parody of military discipline. It was a parody which their new masters found hilarious.

As the lorry pulled away, two flaxen haired children, clutching hands for reassurance, also carrying shovels at the slope, turned to stare at the lorry. Freuntz couldn't take his eyes off them. They stared plaintively right at him, or so it seemed. They had him fixed, as in the viewfinder of a camera. Their expressions combined accusation with a serene fatalism. It quickly dawned on Freuntz. The reason the bigger one seemed to stare straight through him was that he was blind. Both children searched tentatively for the hand of the other, as if their interlinked fingers would ensure salvation. If only. They would be the first to be shovelled into the burial pit that day. But not the last.

✷ ✷ ✷

Eventually they left the last of the smouldering ruins behind, and were soon past the orchards, the splintered stumps bearing the same scars as the village. Freuntz looked at Remnick quizzically, but Remnick could anticipate what Freuntz was thinking.

"Form filling later, Mister Methodical. He's initiating some of his cubs- and he's invited us to watch."

✷ ✷ ✷

The Dreznhya River was dappled by the sun, still low in the sky. Suddenly, the temperature dropped. An ethereal mist enveloped the river. Their progress along the bank slowed to walking pace. Freuntz thought he saw a rowing boat disappear into the mist. They finally reached the saw mill.

The swirling mist provided a ghostly backdrop, as Freuntz and his colleagues jumped down. They immediately began some frenzied arm waving and foot stamping. Was the dreaded Russian cold about to return for one last assault on their morale, and their marrow?

Knowing their place, Freuntz and his colleagues stepped back, beside the pile of half cut logs, to allow Hitler's elite to occupy centre stage. Orders were barked from inside the mill. The padlocked door was thrust open. To the astonishment of Freuntz, although not his smirking colleagues, eight naked women were propelled forward into the freezing mist.

They ranged from the plump to the sylph like, some broad shouldered, some narrow hipped. None of them were older than forty, Freuntz guessed, but the privations of war were evidenced by their protruding ribs. All had their hands bound. It was clear that they had been forced into the open air by the boots of the guffawing black clad troops, who now followed them into the yard. As the women slowly adjusted to their predicament, the troops suddenly clicked heels to attention.

From the recesses of the mill their commanding officer appeared. The women shuffled into two lines. They hadn't needed any encouragement. After a theatrical pause, he inspected the ranks. His whip forced up the chin of each woman in turn, women who knew better than to make eye contact with a German officer.

From behind, he barked into the ears of each in turn.

"You swim Ivana? You like to swim? You will soon learn, let me assure you of that. You want to live don't you?"

He didn't know many Russian names, but his tone mixed lascivious relish with acidic contempt. He allocated each a name at random, eight names in total. Each was subjected to their own prelude to the main event-the group address.

"Ladies, daughters of Mother Russia, bearers of the revolutionary flame, you may not know this, but you are at the frontier. Not a frontier on a map, not a frontier with a barrier across the road, or a checkpoint. No, the frontier between civilisation and... and...barbarism," He swept his arm towards the mist shrouded river bank. He had to pause for his oratory to be translated. The delivery was halting, the message undeniable.

"We, the German people, are as the frontiersmen of the American West. We bring civilisation to the unenlightened, to the primitive, the savage, the inferior. We are as doctors sent to combat a plague, a medieval disease, a pandemic, the answer to which is a cleansing, a fumigation, a total eradication of what went before if a normal, healthy civilisation is to emerge from such polluted raw material. We are the ambassadors of enlightenment, the disciples, the missionaries. Our message is of renewal, regeneration... renaissance," at which he paused to consider the image of himself as a Venetian patron of the fine arts.

"And, just as in 1917 we allowed Lenin his sealed train, to spread the Bolshevik virus, we want to allow you, my fair damsels, to spread a message. Here it is. You are free to go. We want you to spread our message. A blowtorch is being applied to the whole of your lice ridden ideology. Go tell them we are here, we will be with them soon. But not to despair. After all, we Germans are not barbarians."

Even he found it hard to conceal a smirk. As the translation finished, the ropes which bound the women were severed. They were ushered towards the freezing river. The women rubbed their wrists, red raw from their incarceration. Their dilemma was becoming clear. Each, instinctively, turned to Anna Khuzhnova for guidance. The deal was sanctioned as their only chance to survive, by the briefest of nods.

As they slithered and slipped down the bank, the sun began to break through the mist. Their predicament aroused a chorus of hysterical laughter amongst the German troops. Five ancient canvas deck chairs were produced, on which the commander, and four of the youngest soldiers, sat.

The women tip toed their way into the icy water. Each felt gently for a secure footing, constantly fighting the urge to scream in the presence of their captors. Maria Yemneva was the oldest, a heavily built woman, who hated water. A shot whistled past her ear. No further encouragement was needed, or hesitation contemplated. At Anna's command, the women threw themselves into the shallows, and began to thrash furiously in an effort to gain some momentum. The current was increasing in strength as they got into deeper water.

Panic set in immediately for Maria, and her fate was sealed at once. As she half turned back towards the bank, a burst of machine gun fire left her limp in the water. The current carried her into the shallows, her buttocks protruding through the surface.

Immediately, the SS men began to throw wads of money onto the ground, at the same time as they engaged in animated discussion. Freuntz quickly grasped the fact that they were betting on the outcome. The seven survivors ploughed on. But the frequency with which Olga and Natalia Bremynko sank beneath the waves indicated they wouldn't last much longer. They quickly disappeared.

"You fucking lazy Russian bitch. Two weeks wages," met with little sympathy. The money was added to the pot by the fellow gamblers, now becoming more animated as the field thinned.

"Watch the blonde. Built like an ox, that one."

"But can an ox swim, you moron?" simply added to the general hysteria. Unnoticed, Catarina Grezhneva, the task made impossible by her emphysema, gave up the ghost and floated down stream.

The survivors, clearly becoming weaker with each stroke, were now approaching the far bank, as the sun began to disperse the mist.

"Just in time, we might have missed it."

Freuntz could now see the rowing boat. The exhausted women flopped onto the bank in relief. Six black clad troops emerged from the woods. At the same time as the women were dragged up the banking, the troops began to strip off their uniforms. On the opposite bank, their cheering comrades produced binoculars. The running commentary commenced.

"Come on Gutzmann. How long does it take?"

"Look at Horst, going at it like a bull!"

"Look… two of them on the redhead."

Eventually the rape finished. The troops on the far bank gave a synchronised "Heil Hitler" to their cheering comrades in the deckchairs. There was to be little time for further hilarity, although that did not dissuade Remnick and Zemmer. Their wheezing simply made Freuntz despise them even more.

Freuntz had but the briefest of flashbacks to La Pigalle, but was quickly jolted back to the present, as the four women were dragged towards the distant bank. Commands? Insults? Abuse?- Who could tell?- were being yelled into the faces of the women. But what was undeniable was that the women were being thrust back into the river. They began, even more wearily, to swim back.

The commander, clearly the winner of the bet, waved the bundle of notes above his head. The derision of his comrades reached a crescendo. Four ancient hunting rifles were produced.

"Now then, boys. All this." He waved the bundle in an even more exaggerated fashion. "All this for the top marksman. Let the games commence!"

The women, understandably traumatised by their experiences, were flapping ineffectively. The first shots hit the water. Irina Provenkya could take no more, and simply sank beneath the waves. Martha Durtseva was only hit a glancing blow, but understandably was in no mood to resist any longer.

Fatigue, shame, and blind panic now immobilised Helena Ghorzhova. As she vainly tried to tread water, Helena turned to watch Martha drift down stream, resigned to her fate. Her head was only turned momentarily. In that instant she offered a clear target, and the shot blew away half her face. Her red hair quickly darkened further, as her life blood gushed away.

On the bank, the whoops of glee seemed to last forever. The money was eagerly grasped by the decisive marksman, Werner Briedel. Remnick and Zemmer slapped each other on the back, as if they themselves had been active participants. They edged forward, so as to bask fully in the raucous celebrations.

The mood of elation was beginning to subside, as the feeling of anti-climax that there would be no more sport that day began to set in. Suddenly, a bedraggled, blonde haired figure broke the surface of the water. She began to stumble through the shallows, to the amazement of the assembled onlookers. They had assumed that all the women were dead. The opportunity for an encore re-energised them, and they focused on her as she staggered across the rocks.

The animal determination with which she was pursuing her course added an edge to the proceedings. As she reached the flatter part of the bank, she straightened up and made straight for the commander. Her eyes blazing, shoulders back, no longer the victim, she was oblivious to her nakedness.

Briedel leapt forward and pinned her arms behind her. Freuntz realised that the lone survivor was Anna Khuzhnova, to whom the women had looked for guidance, as their ordeal had begun. She struggled and strained with such force that it was all Briedel could do to keep her in check. She was focused on the commander, who remained seated, his legs languidly crossed.

Briedel finally dragged Anna to a halt, feet from her intended target, towards who she now directed a stream of virulent invective in a breathless, heavily accented language Freuntz thought may well have been Ukrainian. He couldn't help but admire the raw courage of the woman, for whom no experience could possibly be worse than the one she had endured during the last hour.

"West, west, west now! Remember those days when it was all east, east, east? All for the Austrian corporal. Remember those days? Remember those days? How many of those fresh faced boys are with you now? Look around. The veterans... replaced by boys. But don't worry, Herr General, we are famous for our hospitality. After all, we welcomed you with black bread and salt. Oh yes, we will take care of them. They will remain here with us- frozen in winter, but warm in summer. So far away from Germany."

"Stalingrad, Herr General. We won't forget. That is what Berlin will look like. We are going there. And when we get there, we're going to fuck your wives. Then your daughters, then your..." She fell silent. With all her remaining energy, she threw back her head and braced her shoulders.

"Herr Komandant, Ich bin ein Komiss..."

The sentence was never finished. The Commander whipped out his Luger and shot her straight between the eyes. Brains splattered Briedel, who knew that he couldn't afford to weaken or, even more crucially, vomit. Briedel felt immense pride that he hadn't let down his mentor. He let the woman fall lifelessly to the ground, and each fleetingly held the gaze of the other. The commander held out his arm rigidly for maximum effect, his SS blood type clearly tattooed on his forearm.

An eerie silence now pervaded the scene. What would happen, if the Russians ever got to Berlin, haunted them all when alone with their thoughts. After what seemed an age, he leapt from the chair to signify there was more deadly work to be done that day. As he swept past his colleagues, now slowly readjusting to the grim realities ahead, he re-holstered his Luger. Their eyes met.

"Freuntz."

"Wolfgang."

# Chapter Eighteen

Nicole knew that he was rarely late. He didn't disappoint her. Four drunks interrupted their animated debate. They fell silent as he passed, already removing his gloves. Despite their inebriation, they knew how things worked.

Her face brightened, as he sat down beside her. He lent forward, as if to whisper in her ear. The four drunks looked on in admiration. She knew there would be no physical contact, but was accustomed to the routine. She slipped into her role, as he placed the oblong box on the table.

"I do so hope you will like them. They are extremely rare, you know." Nicole removed the lid, and dutifully allowed her eyes to widen in appreciation. "They are from Slovakia. 'Maravna 1870', Centenary Collection, the finest craftsmanship. Look, there is their mark, their coat of arms."

Nicole stroked the stems of the champagne glasses, before turning each one up in turn. He knew she was feigning her expertise, but her avid appreciation made it all worthwhile. She placed the glasses back in the box.

"Shall we go upstairs?"

✲ ✲ ✲

For Gerhard Werner, The Café Gasquet was a perfect stage to continue his pretence. A large audience in a public place, the company of an attractive woman, but above all the authority conferred by his uniform, which served to project an air of unchallenged authority he rarely felt deep down inside.

He could hold the future of an individual, a family, even on some occasions an entire village, in his hands. He had realised that the Roman Emperors had held similar power, and this should have emboldened him. His rise through the ranks had been rapid. Still in his early forties, his grip on his French fiefdom was now complete.

As was the grip on his emotions. He dreaded the revelation of any personal foible, and had not hesitated to use his position to avenge any slight, although the two who had hurt him most were beyond his reach, killed in an air raid on Wuppertal the previous year. He hadn't even attended the funeral.

Returning to the scene of his humiliation would have been more than he could face. The humiliation of growing up with blonde hair, when that of his father, Jurgen, was black, was just the start. Together with his step mother, Else, they had presented the perfect image of lower class suburban respectability, as they strove to build up their shoe repair business.

Jurgen was a stern, scowling autocrat, and Else had no answer to the sarcastic barbs which cascaded down upon her. Gerhard was the result of a drunken fling on New Year's Eve, 1899, hardly the most auspicious start to the new century. Even less auspicious, his mother had given birth beneath the railway arches, dumped him on the shop step, then disappeared. Outward representations of normality drew Jurgen to Else. Fear that she would never marry drew Else to Jurgen.

Their mutual desperation made little impact outwardly, as bourgeois respectability, the front pew at church, and order in all things ranked far higher than any outward show of emotion. Inwardly, Jurgen was mortified. The choice was to face social humiliation or soldier on. Soldier on it was, but at a cost to those around him. For Else, the choice was stark- stick and endure- or face a spinster's life, thereby confirming all her mother had ever said about her. She chose to stick, and in order to cement their relationship she sought to become more like him.

Unfortunately, Gerhard was the focus of this doomed attempt at marital harmony, as well as a constant reminder of the barren nature of their relationship. As they competed to outdo each other, the constant verbal assaults were the only time any emotion was exhibited, their relationship otherwise conducted amidst an arid civility.

He had first wet the bed at the age of two, and was still suffering in his teens. On his fourteenth birthday he was daring to hope he was over it, when disaster struck. He made the mistake of chatting too long in the town square with the daughter of a family friend. When he compounded the error of coming home late, by lying, the outcome was inevitable.

Still slightly built for his age, he was no match for the flailing boots and fists. His sobs met only with further, ferocious assaults, in which his step mother joined with enthusiasm. He was thrown down the cellar steps. No sooner was the door slammed shut, than his bladder began to empty. The only two meals he ate that week had a familiar smell and a ghastly taste. Dog meat.

By the fourth day, there was no more urine left to flow.

✲ ✲ ✲

Nicole looked forward to Tuesday evenings, because with Gerhard things were straightforward. She had been looking forward even more than normal, as she had to put him off last week. He only wanted company, he only wanted conversation. She now knew that being seen in her company was sufficient.

She ensured she made regular eye contact during their snatched conversations, but couldn't forget how his whole body had stiffened when she made her only attempt to sit on his lap. The first time he had accompanied her back to her apartment had been interrupted by constant dashes to the toilet, a sequence of events completely outside her experience. Over the weeks, bewilderment had led to a gentle inquisition, as the explanations were teased out. She had begun to empathise, a process he had started to embrace, as tentatively as he dared.

Occasionally she had kept him waiting an extra five minutes at the end of her shift, time during which attention was focused on him by his comrades, most of who couldn't work out his secret, but nevertheless wished him all the best. The constant onslaught of their foul mouthed tirades deadened his senses. They reminded him too much of his youth. He had become adept at conveying the minimum of agreement, whilst scanning the bar for one of her glances, regardless of how brief.

For Nicole, foul mouthed tirades about France, the French, and their manifest weaknesses, were meat and drink. Being French had done nothing for her, so what was the point of loyalty? The collapse in 1940 had confirmed her youthful premonitions and prejudices, whilst enabling a convenient veil to be drawn over her left wing convictions. Here was a country which had seized command of its destiny. Backing the winning side was no more than simple common sense.

Unlike her fellow citizens, she had not dreaded the arrival of the Wehrmacht, and, accustomed to living on her wits, she had quickly embraced the new realities. Cafe Gasquet was where the new masters drank. She missed no opportunity to ingratiate herself. Here, blonde hair was an asset beyond price.

Gerhard was perfect- non threatening, powerful, not unattractive- but above all generous. Her apartment had been transformed, and now she couldn't find room to store the fine wine and cognac. Weekly bouquets were par for the course. Silk sheets and expensive furnishings arrived from Germany on a regular basis. Given that the screw was being tightened on Germany, it was obvious which ethnic group was providing the constant stream of luxuries.

She convinced herself that it was their tough luck to be on the wrong side of events, something Nicole was determined would not happen to her. Information was power, and she was prepared to use it to assure her future. A grudge to be settled, and the father figure she had longed for. Perfect.

All that remained was to bring the two together.

✭ ✭ ✭

Their time together rarely extended beyond an hour. Nicole was acutely aware of his dread that, if he stayed longer, he might reveal a secret so shocking that yet more trips to the toilet would ruin any chance of intimacy. Verbal responses had come more easily, as the weeks had passed, but she realised that anything physical was completely out of the question. She had just begun to tease out why this might be, but that was a long term project. Here was an opportunity to see how much influence she actually had.

Gerhard was aware of the domestic arrangements which had prevailed, ever since Nicole had been young. The sudden death of Uncle Jerome had left Aunt Francoise devastated, and it was only her religious faith which had seen the clouds lift after eighteen months.

Determined to fulfil the pledge they had each made to each other-that whoever died first, the survivor would find someone else-she had met Charles LeVin at an art class, at the local college. His wry sense of humour was coupled with an easy, self-deprecating approach to most things, and at her stage in life Aunt Francoise had decided that this was as good as it might get. They were married on St Valentine's Day, in 1935. Other than that he knew little.

"You remember I told you about Uncle Charles. Well, I haven't told you everything about the wedding. That was where it started," Nicole began abruptly. "It had been one of the happiest days I could remember. That is until it happened. I cringe every time I relive it."

She allowed her eyes to moisten before continuing. "In my own mind, the bridesmaids dress made me princess for a day, I have never felt more beautiful. I can still smell the scent of the freesias aunty provided. But now, now it is only the shame that I can remember. Forever stained. That's how I remember that day. Not that I try to remember it."

She continued in a hesitant, faltering manner to which he was unaccustomed.

"The reception, it was only simple. Simple but perfect, somehow. Or it was until he... The reception was in full swing. LeVin.

Eughh! His name makes me want to be sick. I didn't know he was there. I should have. You could usually smell him- stale sweat, garlic and locomotive smoke. He had sneaked up behind me. He placed his hand on my, on my left buttock. I didn't know what to do. And you know what? He kept it there. Kept it there for ages. Because I didn't know how to react, he must have felt that I was enjoying it. I moaned, yes I moaned. Moaned in panic. Yes, he thought I was enjoying it."

Nicole looked at Gerhard for a reaction, but he seemed lost in thought. The confines of the cramped apartment had meant that physical contact was virtually unavoidable when the three of them had been together, Nicole continued. "Nowhere to get away from him. Brushing past me in the kitchen was too good a chance to miss. He never cooked. Not once. Never out of the kitchen, though. Couldn't be in there often enough."

"Why did I not do anything to deter him? That's a question I am always asking myself. I have spent many nights awake, trying to work out why I did nothing. The best I can come up with is that I longed for security, I longed to be part of a proper family, I suppose. But it was me. It was me. No, I was in on it. I was part of the bargain, a pawn in his plans. He begged me not to tell, and I went along. It would be our secret. I thought it would make him stop, some time. But his hands, his hands. What does that make me worth?"

A pause for dramatic effect followed, but Gerhard remained unmoved, working out the implications of why she was telling him this now. How could it be used to his advantage? Perplexed by his apparent indifference, Nicole changed tack.

"He has been back a week, and you should hear the things he says. He has always been a Communist you know." Gerhard registered marginally more interest. She rested her head on his shoulder for a moment. She knew that anything other than momentary contact would send him over the edge, interrupting the unfolding melodrama, as he dashed along the corridor to relieve himself.

"He says the Russians are trampling on the Germans, and the war is only going one way. If the British and Americans had more about them, and invaded now, it would be over in six weeks.

He has a bottle of 1921 champagne from somewhere, under the floorboards. He can't wait for the Red Flag to be run up in Veziers. Then it will be time to settle some scores, he says. Communism has proved stronger than Nazism, and soon all the world will see for themselves. He heard about Stalingrad on the BBC." She paused for the last sentence to register.

"Not here, at least I don't think so. It was while he was in the yards in Paris." Gerhard recognised that this was a seam which could be mined here and now, but truth and allegation needed to be sieved carefully, if it was to provide him with protection. Her knowledge of Communism seemed to be contrived, he felt. Uncle Charles could always be arrested later, if need be. He opted for later, and allowed her to continue.

"Then, on Tuesday, Aunty had to go to work, and so I was there on my own. I didn't know he was there. He was upstairs and just as I was going…I couldn't find my purse…I could hear his footsteps… I couldn't leave my purse there… he was coming," she gulped, "And just as I found it down the sofa…"

She was beginning to sob, a lot more convincingly Gerhard felt. He contemplated stroking her hair, but decided against it. Experience was a harsh teacher. His bladder was on the brink. This was turning into a full confessional, as opposed to the usual meandering chats he enjoyed so much, as a release from the daily grind.

"Just as I got it… I was so glad… I looked up and there he was…the most moth eaten dressing gown… his black socks, his hairy chest and the …and then… guess what he did. The look… the look …the look on his face," she gasped. "As if he had won a fantastic prize. He was smirking, he was licking his lips and then… and then…" Nicole gulped, as if taking in enough air to stay under water for an hour.

"He said 'Nicole…' and really dragged it out. 'Nicole, sweet Nicole. Have you missed me? My, how you have grown.' He started coming towards me. 'You can't imagine how much I've missed you, but here's a clue.' And with that, he dropped his dressing gown. And you know what? You know what? You couldn't miss it."

Gerhard made eye contact directly for the first time.

"He's Jewish."

✳ ✳ ✳

It took a while for her to regain her composure, and Gerhard was convinced that the story was true. More information to be stored away. Eventually, she regained her composure and started again.

"I couldn't bear it. The slimy bastard. I had to go back and get even. Next day, I was there before seven, and once he was at work, and Aunty was out baby minding, I got in. And you know what? I would have demolished that place with my bare hands. I was determined to find his fucking champagne." She paused, to imply that she was shocked that she had been reduced to swearing, "But, but, I found something even better."

"It took a while, but behind the oven is a so called ventilation vent, covered up with a wooden board, which he has had plastered. That's where his champagne is. Or was! Because I sprayed it all over the living room! I enjoyed it so much!"

"Solid cast iron, that oven. It nearly broke my back moving it just far enough to get my head in the gap. I wriggled my shoulders in, and that made a bit bigger space. And behind the champagne was a box, all covered in dust. Well, it wouldn't be there for nothing would it?"

She looked at Gerhard for approval of her deductive skills, a confirmation indicated by a gentle nodding of the head, and a pursing of his lips in anticipation of the clinching evidence.

"He is not even called LeVin-his name is Levy. It's on his card from the last war. It has a Star of David on it."

She began to gabble. Amidst the morass of splenetic abuse and supporting evidence, the bit which registered most clearly was the newspaper article which acclaimed "Levy the Hero," a faded account of a football match from 1925. Beneath the headline was a photograph of the victorious side, clutching the cup, with Levy holding the match ball triumphally aloft.

"Not only him. The rest of them were Jewish as well. You could tell from the names." She paused, dabbed her eyes, and then, back in control, looked expectantly straight at Gerhard.

To her astonishment, their farewell was curt and formal. No words were expressed, and he was gone.

✫ ✫ ✫

The sultry warmth of the August evening still hung in the air, as the church bell tolled eleven. He allowed himself the luxury of a roundabout route back to the house of the former textile magnate, his base for the last three years. It was the grandest of villas, on a secluded road which was full of them.

A lot to consider, Gerhard told himself. Not just tonight, invaluable though it was. Amidst the deluge of information he was presented with each week, this could be gold dust. But, using it would take careful planning if his back was to be covered.

News from Russia was bad, and not much better from Italy. If the British and Americans ever landed, Veziers was certain to be a major target. Resistance activity was increasing, and if it continued, questions would be asked and the finger pointed. He could always use Uncle Charles for a summary hanging in the town square, but instinct told him not to play this card yet.

No, if the pressure came from Berlin there would be subordinates to blame, superiors to implicate and reputations to impugn. No, he would leave Charles where he was for now, and use him as a pawn to lure Nicole further into his plans.

The guards opened the wrought iron gate to the villa, and clicked to attention. He gave his usual immaculate salute in response to "Heil Hitler." Regardless of the situation Germany was facing, his loyalty was total. The gravel under his feet gave a satisfying crunch, as he pondered his last dilemma of the day.

The approach of his birthday, as well as Nicole's gentle encouragement, had prompted him to see if he could find out who his real mother was. Wuppertal was becoming a more intense focus for R.A.F attacks, and he held out little hope of success. To his amazement, having almost forgotten about his enquiry, the carbon copy had arrived within a week.

There was his father, but his attention focused on his mother, his real mother- Eva Carlsson- Date of Birth, April 7, 1881. Place of Birth-Wolfsburg.

The names of her parents, and the date of their deaths, had been included at a later date. He had allowed himself, briefly, to consider using his influence to try to track her down, but had immediately thought better of it. What would he have to say, after all?

A matter of much greater urgency loomed. Was there an informer at Headquarters?

# Chapter Nineteen

By noon, the heat in the carriage had become unbearable. Across the tracks the swarms of flies were multiplying. Four Polish labourers were ushered towards the first wagon. Freuntz and Wolfgang watched as they approached. Suddenly all four, in a sequence of macabre choreography, threw back their heads in unison. Two collapsed, retching by the side of the tracks.

German soldiers immediately forced them to their feet, and they began to remove the heavy bolts with one hand, whilst covering their mouths with the other. Progress was laborious. Others in the carriage were watching now.

Finally, one of the central doors was forced back. A woman gasped, as the nearest of the labourers was buried by six skeletal figures which toppled lifelessly from the wagon. The commands of the German soldiers were becoming more frenetic. A rifle butt was raised.

Eventually, the labourer, mortified by the experience, extricated himself from the decaying heap of humanity. A brief glance indicated his bewilderment. But it was only brief. Another labourer was thrust forward. Immediately, they began to force the corpses back into the wagon. The task became more difficult by the minute, as other corpses toppled into the space left by the first six.

Three frail hands, thrust out from the wagon in search of supplication, could be observed. Those in the carriage watched, as if in a trance. The original corpses were eventually heaved back into the wagon, and the door slammed shut.

By now, the wagons were being doused liberally with petrol. Once the task had been completed, the central wagon was ignited, and soon all seven were ablaze. Such was the speed with which the fire took hold, that the groans of the surviving Jews inside were unlikely be heard above the roaring flames. The smell of roast flesh, mixed with the clouds of smoke, wafted towards the carriage. Freuntz, Wolfgang and their fellow passengers still watched in silence, still enthralled by the spectacle.

Originally diverted to the Lodz goods yards ten days earlier, the wagons had been shunted into a siding and then forgotten about in the chaos of war. The conflagration began to burn itself out, leaving only the smouldering, metal skeletons of the wagons.

The onlookers considered what they had seen, still spell bound.

"Not as good as Zyklon B. Wouldn't have missed it for the world, though," observed Wolfgang.

The tension broken, conversation slowly returned to cursing the delay they had been subjected to, and speculating as to how much longer it would be.

Staring, transfixed, across the tracks, Freuntz found it impossible to join in.

✫ ✫ ✫

Freuntz had been unable to resist the offer, but had regretted it ever since. Personal aide to an SS Fuhrer offered a chance to escape the mind numbing work with the Police Battalion. But more importantly, as far as he was concerned, it was a chance to moderate the behaviour of his former protégé, who, since the battle for the bridge, had become even more erratic in behaviour, more outlandish in his pronouncements. How naïve he had been.

Their journey from Orel to their ultimate destination, Dresden, had already taken eight days, as partisan action in Russia had caused repeated delays and diversions. Once the train picked up speed, the rhythm ignited another of his rambling orations.

"It's about will, Freuntz, the will, nothing more, nothing less. Who has the will to endure, to inflict, the will to rule, the will to take what is rightfully yours, the will to suffer and, even more important, the will to inflict suffering. What may seem cruel, even inhumane, to an outsider or a detached observer, is a part of the struggle- and the ultimate arbiter of who will emerge triumphant. Nature is like that-red in tooth and claw-and so is any struggle between races. Just like a lion devours an impala, weaker races will be eliminated so that a stronger, purer, humankind emerges. We are on a sacred mission."

Freuntz couldn't concentrate any longer. He nodded intermittently, as he recalled the taunts Anna Khuzhnova had spat at him. He was forced to refocus his attention, as Wolfgang prodded his leg.

"You know what convinced me, finally? When we were in the Hitler Youth, lots of kids used to drop out of those thirty mile marches, but with will you could get there. None of my recruits ever failed to get round. Not one. Elite of the elite that was us, just like now," he added. He smoothed down his uniform, crumpled and dusty from their interminable journey.

"But the moment…the moment… was when I was on sentry duty, and this fourteen year old lad arrived back late at camp. It was almost dark, and he was way behind the others. He couldn't remember the password and, even though I asked him lots of times, he couldn't remember. Three of the other sentries were with me. We were all shouting at him. No good. And you know what he did? Burst into tears. I shot him on the spot. He lacked the will, you see, lacked the will…"

Wolfgang looked wistfully out of the window, as if yearning to return to a simpler, purer time. He returned to his theme.

"And it was the look they gave me, the look. Respect? Awe? I don't really know, but what I do know is the rush of adrenalin, the surge of pride. I felt tall, so tall. My skin tingled. I had acted. I wasn't weak, I had the will…you see, don't you Freuntz? I got it from you, all those years ago in the 'halle. Never give up. Endure. Keep fighting. Any game can be won. You see, you were ahead of your time. The will, that's what you taught us. Look, here I am."

Wolfgang leaned forward, his body rigid. "Your prize pupil. Your Germany. Our Germany. Where we're going, I'm going to need you to organise things. Do you remember, just before we used to run out, you always said the same thing? 'Make them have it.' Well, that's what we're going to do Freuntz-we're going to make them have it. Together once more."

Wolfgang began to rub his neck again, as he grimaced, an action that was repeated more frequently each day. The implication of what Wolfgang had said sank in. Freuntz stared blankly ahead.

✲ ✲ ✲

They parted outside Dresden's Central Station, three days later. Wolfgang was to remain for a week long briefing. Security procedures in key communications centres, was as much as Freuntz had been able to glean. Freuntz had the day to himself, before beginning what was sure to be another lengthy trek across country to Emmingen. Then, on to re-join Wolfgang in his new posting.

The city was a hive of activity as the drizzle drifted across the Elbe. A constant stream of vehicles was heading east. But the city exhibited none of the scars of the war, borne by those within bombing range in the west. The militarisation of the city was undeniable, but there were soldiers mingling on the streets or drinking in the cafes. It lent an air of normality Freuntz wanted to wallow in, so different from the ravaged landscapes of Russia.

The radio components, carefully concealed in the secret compartments, rendered the bag too heavy to carry any distance. Once he had forced it into the left luggage locker, he set off. He had no definite plan or destination. He simply wanted to wander the streets in order to embrace the splendours of the city. He knew little about architecture, other than that baroque and classical applied somehow.

He lingered outside the castle of the Saxon kings, gawped at the sweeping lines of the Frauenkirche, the ornate grandeur the Opera House. All of them filled him with a swelling sense of national pride. This was Germany, the real Germany, a city which fully deserved its label as 'The Florence of the North'. He was saddened to think how the refined scholars, whose knowledge underpinned the advances made in the last two hundred years, would look upon the barbarism which so many Germans-their descendants- had not only indulged in, but participated in with such sadistic relish.

He headed for the river. But, as he wandered aimlessly along the sweeping promenade, he couldn't avoid the way pedestrians lowered their gaze, lowered their voices, and steered a wide berth around him. The uniform, with its distinctive insignia, sent a message. On at least two occasions, mothers dragged their small children away from his path. Fear? Respect? Or contempt? Freuntz was unsure which, but well aware that if they knew what he knew, their contempt would be the least of his worries.

His feet were beginning to ache, and he was finally tempted to rest. He reached inside his overcoat, and took the first frantic gulp of vodka. It was a taste he had become accustomed to in the last twelve months. He knew full well that he would consume half the bottle before its first effects began to register.

Long before then, the images began to swirl. One of the most frequent was the execution. The Battle of Kursk had sent the undeniable message that the initiative now lay with the Russians. Freuntz recalled the reactions of his colleagues now that the tables were turned. From then on, they hadn't just recorded the death toll. On at least three occasions they had contributed to it. The screams of the partisans, thrust into the acid bath at the tanning factory, meant that two hours of uninterrupted sleep was now a bonus.

The new sophistication and improvisation in the Russian tactics had stunned the Germans, and in the retreat from Prokhorovka, the Blowtorch Battalion had almost been encircled by an unexpected Russian breakthrough. Having fought their way out of the trap, Wolfgang was ordered to detach the battalion, and race to the last remaining bridge across the River Kreshev. Its loss would maroon thousands of Germans on the wrong side of the river, facing annihilation.

Freuntz had listened to the blizzard of fragmented commentary which poured into headquarters, as the drama unfolded. On at least four occasions the sudden disappearance of radio contact signified that the T-34s had managed to neutralise the superior fire power of the Tiger tanks, as they closed alongside and blasted the less heavily armoured sides. Frenzied shrieks signified that tanks had caught fire. The prolonged incineration of their comrades shook even the most hardened radio operators.

But it was not fire, but shrapnel, which had almost done for Wolfgang. He always commanded, bare headed, in full view of his unit-and the enemy. Between the blazing hulks of two disabled tanks, the T-34 emerged from the inferno, as Wolfgang was concentrating his fire on a crippled opponent. The first Russian shell splintered the gun barrel as it recoiled, and the blast threw him backwards in the turret.

From his own experience Freuntz had learnt to fear the deadly neutrality of shrapnel. Its red hot fragments were capable of cutting a man in half, severing a blood vessel or maiming permanently, whilst remaining blindly impassive to the skill, bravery or morality of those on the receiving end of the lethal hailstorm.

Before the T-34 had a chance to finish its prey, it disappeared in a ball of flame, as the well-honed marksmanship of Wolfgang's protégé, Briedel, claimed a fourth kill of the battle. As if protecting a wounded cub, Briedel offered covering fire. The battle had ebbed and flowed, before finally being decided by superior German firepower.

The attack having been repulsed, the withdrawal across the bridge could resume in a semblance of good order. But Wolfgang was not finished. There was vengeance to be visited upon those deemed responsible for the debacle.

The operation to remove the shrapnel was short, but not totally successful, leaving several slivers in inaccessible areas of his skull and spine. Further operations would be out of the question. The implications were clear. His career as a fighting commander was over. He had no more than two years to live. Once the verdict been delivered, and the consequences absorbed, Wolfgang had thrust past the protesting doctors, and headed back to his unit.

The thunderstorm eventually broke. The endless column of tanks, guns and tramping infantry moved inexorably through the pine forest, westwards across yet another bridge. At gunpoint, Wolfgang had forced two hundred weary soldiers to form a semicircle in the clearing, surrounding the focus of his fury.

Oberleutnant Denmann and his four subordinates were marched into the centre, as the ground rapidly became a morass. The teeming rain beat a tattoo on the puddles. When combined with the roar of engines from the bridge, Wolfgang's condemnation was rendered inaudible. Those still approaching the bridge shrugged their shoulders, perplexed by this spectacle. They weren't perplexed for long, however. Wolfgang executed the five, one by one, their blood darkening further the ever growing puddles.

As he strode away, the spectators were unsure how to react, until barked commands urged them back to the trucks. The message had been sent in the starkest and most brutal of terms.

It was simply a matter of will.

✯ ✯ ✯

Freuntz was brusquely awoken by a series of shots. He peered from the shelter, the gathering gloom and drifting drizzle making it hard to see at first. Almost as soon as he poked his head out, more shots zipped over the heads of four fleeing figures. Their grunting indicated that they were feeling the effects of their exertions, as they lumbered past him. At least one was a stoutly built young woman.

They disappeared into the swirling mist. Right in front of Freuntz, two burly figures took aim once more, this time from a standing position. From somewhere further down the promenade, screams indicated that at least two of the shots had found their target. Satisfied that at least some of their prey were disabled, they trotted off to examine the result of their efforts.

A thudding headache convinced Freuntz to head off in the opposite direction. Slowly he gathered his senses, and tried to make sense of what had happened. It did not take him long. At the foot of a group of six elm trees was a mass of pamphlets which had clearly been dumped in haste. Others had been hurriedly torn down, but the purpose of those still there was clear. "No more Stalingrads! Germans resist!" The typeface indicated the crudeness of their production, whilst emphasising the incendiary nature of the message.

The authors' final provocation was to add their supposed contact address-that of the local Gestapo chief Hans Kruger- along with the name of their organisation-'The Friends of Morny Siegel.' It all fell in to place. The pursued were part of an embryonic protest movement, centred on a number of universities. Their members were determined to protest at what was going on in Eastern Europe, driven by the fear that Germany faced disaster if something wasn't done.

Their choice of name was deliberately provocative. Siegel played clarinet in the Woody Gemson band. The Nazis hated the nigger music-jazz-they played with such verve. Listening to it was a criminal offence. Understandably, this had provided a perfect vehicle by which young people could demonstrate their resistance to the regime. His flamboyant lifestyle embellished his reputation further. The clinching feature was that he was Jewish.

His head was beginning to clear, as dusk descended. He couldn't avoid the voices which had been growing ever stronger in recent weeks. At least the protestors were doing something. He was increasingly desperate to do something as well, but depressed that he couldn't think what.

Drink had become one way of coping with the situation, but its effectiveness was diminishing. It was dawning on him that he didn't really enjoy it at all. In contrast, what did seem to work was rough treatment at the hands of a woman, the rougher the better. With this in mind, he fumbled in his pocket for the crumpled notes, threw the bottle with all his vigour into the Elbe, and headed for Koenig Strasse. He had been assured he wouldn't be disappointed.

✷ ✷ ✷

As he stumbled into the glare of the early morning sun, his wrists were still red raw. His breath rasped. It took a while for him to regain his customary forceful stride pattern, but it slowly returned. He would book Helga every time if last night had been typical. The bruising extended right across his ribs, and so his nocturnal activities could remain his secret. Secret vice? He wasn't bothered any more. Given what he had been through, any notion of normality or acceptable behaviour had been jettisoned long ago. What was there left to regret?

Deep in his sub-conscious, a small part of him still recoiled at his sordid interests. The salve of immersion in culture needed to be applied, and quickly. Once again he set off, rendering himself conspicuous as he gazed at the soaring monuments to German–not Nazi-culture and erudition. As the streets began to fill, his eyes were fixed upwards, confident that he was immune from collisions. The uniform guaranteed that.

He was beginning to enjoy the rising temperature, and after forcing down two bratwurst, which were nearly all gristle, he shortened his stride and meandered towards the Garden Suburb of Noringen. Neat lawns, Bauhaus design, and curved three storey apartment blocks emphasised once again to Freuntz that Germany had been at the cutting edge of modern design, when they were planned in the 1920s. Their futuristic style seemed to place Germany at the heart of a common European fraternity, determined to put 1914-18 behind them, and embrace the future. Freuntz shook his head at what had become of his beloved country.

As he was about to cross the junction, the sound of a brass band, playing somewhere to the left, injected a new vigour into his stride. The tunes were militaristic in tone. As he began to hum to himself, without realising, he began to march in rhythm.

The park had been renamed in honour of the 'November Heroes', killed in the Beer Hall Putsch of 1923. But the crass rebranding couldn't detract from the intricate artistry of the wrought iron gates. The sound gradually grew in volume. He realised that he was almost at the band stand, as 'Lilly Marlene' approached its climax.

Eventually, he turned into an avenue of neatly clipped, brittle, green hedges. The sight made his heart sink. The band, to a man, consisted of ex-servicemen, all of whom were maimed, blinded, or disabled in some way. Their uniforms lent an air of poignancy to the whole affair which became almost unbearable, even for Freuntz.

The tune finally finished. All that could be heard was the sobbing of the spectators.

✲ ✲ ✲

The train was due to leave at four. As he rushed past the Nordmann Department Stores, which monopolised the prime locations on the approach to the station, he realised he had cut it fine. More importantly, those pushing past him were ignoring his uniform, something to which he was unaccustomed in recent weeks. Virtually all the voices were louder than normal. Fevered argument seemed to accompany animated head shaking, wherever he looked.

The square opened up before him, and he could see what had animated them. The last of the crowd were drifting away, as the bodies swung in the wind. Notices were being nailed to the crudely erected gallows, and a larger one hung round each of the corpses. He didn't want to look, but he couldn't avoid it on his way into the station. He couldn't avert his eyes. Blood stains could be seen on clothes of the stoutly built blonde haired girl, rotating gently on the right of the four.

✲ ✲ ✲

As the train pulled out, right on time, he felt himself moved by their courage, but above all, their youth. They had taken risks, and it had cost them everything. Would he have had the courage, if he had been in their place? He would like to have thought so, but wasn't sure. After all, his life had been built on doing as asked, as told, as his inner voices dictated. A better Germany though, who wouldn't want that? If that wasn't something worth taking risks for, what was?

The train jerked to a halt in order to allow two trains, packed with troops, to pass. A smartly dressed woman began to applaud, the sound echoing, the carriage silent. Eyes were averted and heads shaken. An elderly couple dabbed their eyes. Briefly, he allowed himself a soldier's sympathy, but the memories he couldn't suppress quickly extinguished any warmer sentiments, before they could take hold. With a shriek on the whistle, the train lurched into motion.

If this place ever comes within bombing range, what a prize target it would make, he thought, as his eyes lowered.

# Chapter Twenty

How much longer would he be? The evening had begun to drag, even before his latest dash along the corridor. Nicole was becoming over familiar with the travails of his childhood, and feigning interest was only made more bearable by the money it paid, the gifts she received. Did he never even consider taking things further? Was it time to look for another father figure, if the revelations about Uncle Charles didn't bear fruit? Maybe she would get her box out, but in her current mood it might depress her further.

Another ten minutes, and time would be up. Don't be too hasty, she thought, as he reappeared, smoothing down his hair, and trying to re-establish a semblance of poise and control. He settled beside her. It was obvious he had also been doing some thinking.

"Nicole," he began hesitantly, "You know how much I enjoy our time together. The chance to talk. You don't know, you just don't know how much I ... appreciate it, look forward to it. There is so much going on, and sometimes my head spins. The pressure is building up, here in Veziers, the railways, you see. It is such an important hub, so much going on. Such a focus for the so called Resistance." The venom with which he spat out the word gave the first hint as to where this might be leading.

"The pressure from Berlin, it never stops, they are never off the phone. The Resistance... they are trying to make a nuisance of themselves..."

Nicole was struck by the quaint description of alleged activities which had seen five men hung in the last two months, none of whom, it was widely acknowledged, had anything to do with any kind of resistance, secret or otherwise.

"My job is at stake if things don't quieten down- and fast. They will send someone to take over from me, and that will be that. Russia?" His tone of voice indicated the mortal dread the prospect instilled.

"I need to stamp it out, stamp it out before it is too late. I am sure they have an informer, and this is where you can help. There are big things happening, and we need to be absolutely secure. What I would like you to do is...when you have finished...." The hesitant tone signified the discomfort he was experiencing.

He began again. "When you have finished," at which he nodded with a leaden theatricality towards the bed, "When you have finished, you know...you know, it is easier to talk about things, and you might be able to find out some things, you know...when their guard is down," he gulped. "I will make it worth your while, I promise. There are three I would like you to start with." He thrust a typed list towards her in a manner which indicated refusal was not something with which he was familiar.

"The first one is downstairs now, sat by the piano. Shaven head, drinks Ricard, a bit dumpy, I am afraid."

She was already calculating that this was an opportunity too good to miss, the chance to strike a blow at France- and be paid in the bargain. Who knew where it might lead?

She tentatively patted his shoulder, and left the request unanswered. He continued his outpourings, which were as frank as they were unexpected. Eventually she decided to respond, as it looked as if he might have to dash out once more.

"Don't worry Gerhard," she cooed, knowing full well that the use of his first name had such a reassuring effect on him that she could ask for almost anything. It worked again. The anxiety seemed to drain away and he was back in charge, his defences erect, his bladder back under control. Ahead, that evening, there was serious business to be done.

As he placed his cap firmly on his head, he turned towards her. "I haven't forgotten Uncle Charles."

✵ ✵ ✵

The armoured Mercedes swept into the marshalling yards, oblivious to the blackout. Four lorries carrying regular troops followed in its wake, bouncing along the gravel between the tracks. The convoy screeched to a halt outside the repair shop, and the troops fanned out across the yards, each under the command of one of Gerhard's trusted henchmen. Gerhard stood back to allow the vanguard to reinforce the aura of intimidation, as they leapt to the ground amidst a cacophony of barked commands.

For the weary engineers, events took a painfully predictable course. They lined up, their arms spread above them against the wall, with the minimum of fuss. Alain Leclerc had discovered that counting how many bricks made a row helped pass the time until some of their number were selected for the inevitable beating. Michel Parvaux closed his eyes and tried to work out how many days he had worked in the yards since 1922. Pierre Toussin prayed it wouldn't be him that they chose. Three beatings in a fortnight would be more than he could take. They had become familiar with the grimy whitewash which flaked from the walls, and realised that what seemed like hours were actually only minutes when you were terrified.

Gerhard studied the list which was thrust into his hand, and soon realised that one person was missing. For Pierre Navanne, his third night of diarrhoea had been the most severe. The result was that the agony he was experiencing from stomach cramps loomed far larger than yet another random swoop from the hated Boche. He was determined to let nature take its course. Then he would face his oppressors.

Unfortunately, prolonging the feeling of release was not his choice to make, that night. He had only time for three drags of his cigarette before he was hauled from the stall with his overalls round his ankles. The tell-tale splattering of his thighs and underwear bore graphic testimony to the violence with which his ablutions had been interrupted.

He was dragged past his workmates, their arms already aching, all secretly hoping that Pierre's insubordination would now make him the focus of the latest raid. They were disappointed. Four of them were clubbed between the shoulder blades, before slumping to the floor. But it was the hapless Pierre who was to be the main focus for Gerhard.

Boots met ribs amidst the synchronised combination of interrogation and intimidation. The four groaned, and tried to give answers to questions they couldn't understand. Gerhard was about to begin his own performance in customary style, by screeching straight into the face of the accused, before clubbing him across the jaw with the handle of his Luger. He knew full well that this theatricality was purely for public consumption. The serious work would begin at headquarters.

However, this occasion would be different, the severity of his predicament producing an altogether predictable response from Pierre. As he was dragged towards Gerhard, he soiled himself once more. The two soldiers recoiled, as their boots were splattered with diluted excrement, and they left him to slump, face down, at Gerhard's feet. Gerhard contemplated getting on his knees to begin the assault. But the flabby buttocks and greying, stained underwear led to a rapid reappraisal.

He knew he could not recoil, and as he bent to bark at the whimpering Pierre, the smell was almost strong enough to make him retch. It was made more potent, he quickly realised, by the infusion of a competing aroma which he could not place, but which had a faintly exotic scent to it. He realised that he was about to be sick. He straightened up with as much dignity as he could summon. He inhaled deeply.

Fortunately, the dispensing of summary brutality by his junior officers had ended, and the four recipients were left slumped amidst the congealed oil and grease. One of them was making a valiant attempt to haul himself upright. A parting blow brought an end to his endeavours. He spat out three teeth, and collapsed.

Gerhard clicked his fingers. Two more soldiers grabbed Pierre's wrists and dragged him from the dimly lit workshop, into the pitch black night, still groaning, still semi naked. With a final round of commands, Gerhard swept out behind them, relieved beyond measure that it was not he who would be inhaling Pierre's pungent aroma for the moment. He headed for the Mercedes.

A night in the cells would allow his victim to regain a semblance of stability. Then he could begin. He was never averse to using the electrodes, but baulked at the simulated drowning. The amount of water swilling about had led to a predictable, and potentially embarrassing, outcome for Gerhard the first time he had been involved. Fortunately, he had been able to pass off the spreading wet patch around his groin as a by-product of the violence with which the suspect had resisted her immersion.

Something told him that no such extremes would be needed for Pierre. Equally, little would be yielded. What was that other smell, though? It hinted at some kind of spice he thought, an aroma he associated with Christmas.

A Christmas which had existed for others, but never in his house.

✻ ✻ ✻

The bar area was becoming more boisterous. The raucous conversations were interspersed with sporadic attempts to generate some martial spirit through faltering renditions of the 'Horst Wessel'. The number of would be choristers was almost balanced by those engaged in morose reflection. They stared into the dregs of their glasses, they slumped face down on the table. They had been in France for twelve months now. They dreaded their next deployment. There was a smattering of elderly local people who, necessarily, kept their conversation subdued, and fixed their gaze no further than across the table.

Nicole was trying to identify her first target, and finally spotted him, precariously propping himself against the wall with one hand, embroiled in a heated argument with a fellow officer. A swift appraisal indicated that dumpy described him perfectly. He was well under two metres in height, and his florid expression did little to compensate for his ginger hair. His belt strained to encase his gut, and the sight of his double chins made her heart sink. To cap it all, a moustache, a sign of the deluded and the desperate, she believed. Nevertheless, this was business.

Having located him, she stood still momentarily, so as to be fully prepared to launch her campaign. She smoothed down her dress so as to emphasise her ample cleavage. She moistened her lips so as to add to her allure, although she realised that this one wouldn't need much, if any, luring.

Having composed herself, and fixed her gaze, she was half way through her first stride when she was knocked sideways by a wiry figure. They both collapsed amidst a tangle of ankles, accompanied by a growing chorus of guffaws from the nearest tables.

Eyes blazing, she hauled herself half upright as she prepared to let fly at the clown who had ruined her opening moves. Her head was spinning, as she realised that the pain on the way down had been from a bony kneecap. Instinct told her to avoid lashing out. If her equilibrium was lost completely, and she collapsed again, her humiliation would be complete.

She was suddenly aware that the person now assisting her to her feet, whispering soothing words into her ear, was in fact her 'assailant'. He smelt of something she associated with farmyards. But, as he completed his apologies and straightened up from his elaborate bow, she realised that on this occasion she would have to revise her opinions about moustaches. Not only that, but his lop sided grin made him look like a guilty, but cheeky, school boy. There was something about this one, she thought, as he began.

"Mademoiselle, mademoiselle, please accept my most humble and profuse apologies."

Profuse, she thought, a touch of class that. The alluring stranger, his composure regained, thrust forward his hand. With a twinkle in his eye introduced himself,

"Alain."

# Chapter Twenty One

As the train emerged slowly from the tunnel, the effects of the raid were clear to all. The billowing palls of smoke indicated that it would be days, not hours, before the fires burnt themselves out. As he glanced out of the window, he couldn't avoid the awed silence which had descended on his fellow passengers. They contemplated the scene in disbelief.

Ahead, the track curved through almost ninety degrees, and it was obvious that their journey would come to an end very soon. The viaduct, which towered above Emmingen, had embodied the pride of its citizens, a pride with which Freuntz had been imbued from infancy. It had represented progress and modernity when constructed in the nineteenth century. His grandfather had helped build it, and Freuntz had never been allowed to forget it.

It was the means by the town was connected to the wider world, a world eager to buy the raw materials and precision engineered products which poured forth from its foundries and factories. No longer. Direct hits had blasted away two of the arches, the rubble piled at the foot of the massive columns, the tracks dangling uselessly in the void, as if ripped apart by some malevolent giant.

The train ground to a halt, and the passengers began to scramble down the banking. The prospect of carrying his case all the way to the home of Aunt Agne was making his arms ache in anticipation, especially as his wrists hadn't healed from his evening with

Helga. Slithering and scrambling came easier to some more than others, but none could avoid the acrid cloud which assaulted their eyes and their nostrils.

A pungent mix of smoke, ash, masonry dust and who knew what else, was beginning to envelop the passengers. Flames erupted in the middle distance, indicating that a gas main had exploded. The oily consistency of the swirling clouds confirmed to Freuntz that the rubber factory had taken a direct hit. The river, normally little more than a polluted open sewer, foamed and steamed as the early morning sun seemed to create a rainbow above the curdled froth. As he reached the bottom of the banking, he was torn between helping the more elderly passengers, or adhering to the strict timetable he had allowed himself to complete his quest.

Local Party officials were assembling to assist the infirm. With a grunt, he hurled his case over the wall, hauled himself up on to the top, and dropped down onto the pavement. Or what remained of it. He immediately felt the heat through the soles of his boots, and it took a dozen frantic strides before he could cool them in the torrent which gushed from a fractured mains pipe. He could only imagine the inferno which had incinerated the apartment blocks opposite, the rubble still smouldering. Everywhere he looked, he was confronted by the desperate attempts of the regime, intent on maintaining its grip in the face of the devastating retribution its policies had brought upon Germany.

He set off towards the centre of town, mountains of smoking debris on either side of him. Shell shocked civilians began to pick through the ruins. Chains formed to pass usable masonry along the lines to the waiting lorries. Frenzied exhortations blared forth from loudspeaker vans. Local officials, armed with loud hailers, demanded more effort. Extra rations were being distributed as an incentive. Everywhere Freuntz looked, the bread was being ripped in half, before being traded for the real currency, cigarettes.

Incredibly, parts of the town were unscathed, apart from scorched paintwork and windows which had been shattered. He had seen ambulances parked down a side street, and soon worked out why they were reluctant to enter the square. The prospect of asphalt melting their tyres was not a danger here, but the commandeering of their vehicles by desperate civilians was. And there was an even more depressing reason.

Approaching were two elderly men, desperately trying to keep their wheelbarrows from tipping over. One was filled with severed arms, the other with severed legs. The two staggered past. One observed laconically,

"They'll be lucky to make a full set out of any of this lot."

Even more poignantly, two women knelt in the dust, on what had once been an ornately patterned hearth rug. They spread out a collection of tiny limbs from a blood smeared waste bucket. Their faces indicated that they were beyond tears.

As he began to move away from the square, the procession of spectral figures, their remaining possessions wrapped in grubby blankets, young children on their shoulders, reduced to a trickle. The familiar sights of his childhood began to reappear. Frickes Butchers defiantly declared that they were 'Open as Usual', despite the fact that their counter was buried in glass and dust. Outside Junger Brothers, grim faced housewives were beginning to queue.

Finally, he turned the corner into Munster Allee, and realised he was home. The three storey block appeared to be unscathed, and, incredibly, the Gorsden Steelworks did as well. He shook his head in a mixture of bewilderment and relief. Outside the entrance, two elderly women were knitting socks, as if in a trance, rocking rhythmically backwards and forwards.

"For the boys. For the boys in Russia," the first one muttered, in a tone devoid of expression or emotion.

"How are the boys? Anyone heard from the boys?" asked the second one, resigned to her question going unanswered, her gaze unwavering. The surreal scene was completed by their ghostly appearance, covered as they were, from head to toe, in white dust. Freuntz navigated around them as delicately as he could, dumped his bag in the entrance, and climbed slowly up to the first floor. He knocked on the door, and could eventually hear laboured shuffling, accompanied by incoherent muttering.

The door creaked open.

"Aunty, Aunty," Freuntz began, before realising why Aunt Agne was not able to respond with any alacrity. Her face was swollen to twice its normal size, and she was clearly in agony.

He led her into the darkened room, and sat her down. The pain was clearly intense as she massaged her cheeks, as forcefully as she dared. Freuntz abandoned his efforts to find anything to drink, and sat down beside her, cradling her in his arms. Suddenly she launched into a furious tirade which was difficult to understand, although the cascade of profanities offered a clue.

"Three days, three days in absolute agony. Never, never, have I known anything fucking like it. Never! Four fillings he said I needed, four." She paused to rub her cheeks again. "Four. And you know what were the only things he had? The only fucking things. The only stuff he had? Go on, go on, fucking guess!" Freuntz shrugged. "I'll show you shall I? Fucking show you. Show you!"

She produced a leather purse and grasped some of the bronze coins in a clenched fist. She waved her hand back and forth, before hurling the coins at the ceiling. She aimed a furious kick at the coins as they cascaded back onto the carpet. She buried her head in his chest.

"Bronze fillings. What a state. What a state. Is this what it has come to? Oh the pain, the pain. Thank you to our mighty Fuhrer. Fuck him."

Astonished by such raw emotion, Freuntz cradled her in his arms until her body went limp.

✱ ✱ ✱

An hour passed. Eventually she sat upright, and Freuntz began to tease out how she had been managing on her own for the last seven years. The answers came so fitfully and painfully that he realised he might never get the information he sought, in the time available. He swallowed hard, and blurted out the question which had haunted him all his life.

"Aunty, why did my mother hate me so?"

The anguished expression on her face barely changed, but the change of topic registered with her. She swallowed and braced her shoulders, determined to do the enquiry justice. Unfortunately, the pain resumed immediately, and she began to sob even more. Her explanation was prolonged and tortuous, as she reassured the sobbing Freuntz that his mother hadn't hated him. She had simply never recovered from the trauma of giving birth to him, but also his twin sister.

Freuntz sat bolt upright, unable to believe what he had heard.

"A twin? A twin? Who? Where?"

He was about to shake her in order to get more sense out of her, before thinking better of it. He made a conscious effort to lower his rocketing pulse rate, and allowed her to tell the story in her own time.

"You, you were the first to be born, five weeks early, the pair of you. Her waters broke whilst she was serving in the shop. It was complicated, really complicated. And drawn out. Doctor Jakobs, he had blood up to his elbows. He was pulling and sweating and..." She paused for a moment. "Almost three hours before they got you out. Just imagine what it must have been like for your mother. Just imagine. And there was still your sister to come. He tried his best. He really did. He got her out, finally."

"But it was the chord, the chord. Wrapped round her tiny neck. She was blue. Your mother cradled her in her arms, cradled her. Twelve hours it must have been. Had to prise the little one out of her grasp, eventually. Oh, the screams. She didn't mean to ignore you that day, I'm sure she didn't. It was just too much."

"She didn't mean it really, you know, didn't blame you. No, not blame you. It was just the shock, the hurt, the disappointment. She had always wanted a girl...and somehow she never got over ... Your father, Alphonse, well you know, don't you, he was no good at dealing with that kind of thing, so it was no good talking to him. I did my best, but it was just like a permanent black cloud that nobody could shift. We even suggested going to church, but that got her going even more. She couldn't see how there was a God after what had happened. And who's to say she was wrong? She didn't mean to blame you, but she never come to terms..."

At that moment Freuntz heard furious screaming all along the corridor, accompanied by frantic knocking.

"Out! Out! Quick! Everyone out! Quick! Bomb! Bomb! Unexploded bomb!"

Freuntz ushered her towards the staircase, as the trickle of panic stricken civilians from the upper floors threatened to become a flood. They emerged into the sunlight. Members of the Hitler Youth were already directing the throng towards the steelworks. Freuntz held her hand briefly before she was swept away by the crowd.

As he turned to look at his cherished childhood refuge for the last time, he observed ruefully that the crowd were having to skirt round the two dust covered women, still rocking, still knitting, as serenely oblivious to the immediate danger as to the situation in Russia.

All in all, it was probably for the best, he thought.

✯ ✯ ✯

Fifteen hours later, fifteen miles to the west, he finally resumed his journey. He slumped wearily into his seat, and reaffirmed his conclusions. The speed of the clouds, scudding across the glowering autumnal sky, was in stark contrast to his plodding thought processes.

The countless evenings spent in melancholy, drink sodden introspection were over. No longer did he feel loyalty to a regime which had wrecked his country; a country for the promotion of whose ambitions he had been prepared to lay down his life. Now he was prepared to lay it down, in order to thwart them. A token gesture to be sure, but inspired by 'The Friends of Morny Siegel', the decision had crystallised into 'If not now, when? If not me, who?' He nodded slowly, as if to convince himself. He was rocking backwards and forwards. On the seat opposite, a twelve year old girl nudged her mother.

His long hours in the Workmans Academy had embedded the notion that Germany did indeed belong amongst the first rank of European nations. The soaring architectural splendour of Dresden had confirmed it for him at first hand. But a thousand Dresdens would never compensate for the barbaric onslaught which had been unleashed in the East. He was now tapping his head against the window, arms folded, eyes bloodshot. The girl tried not to stare.

On Armistice Day in 1918, he had been two days older than Denmann, executed by the bridge. An honourable, much decorated officer, doing his best amidst carnage and chaos, his life had been snuffed out to assuage the rage of the Aryan elite who swaggered, strutted and slaughtered. The girl covered her eyes with her pig tails.

Their perverted philosophy and messianic self-certainty rendered them immune to even the most basic tenets of civilisation. Of that, he was now convinced. By now, his expression was contorted. The girl buried her face in the arm of her mother.

The balance had been tipped irreversibly. Yes, at first he had been seduced by the casual brutality and simplistic remedies of The S.A. Yes, he had been part of the bureaucratic caravan which had trailed The S.S. And what about Wolfgang, who he had nurtured as his own, imbued with self-belief, and fostered in him the idea that Germany was the supreme nation? He embodied that perversion of Germany's sense of nationhood. Freuntz winced. But was Wolfgang to be blamed for what his older, and supposedly wiser, mentor had drummed into him? When given the opportunity, why not put theory into practice?

Freuntz heard the mother try to reassure the girl. "It's the war Edith. It's all to do with the war."

The blustering wind hurled the rain against the window of the carriage, with such force that it resembled a hail of machine gun bullets. The clattering took him back to the main street of Zhubrevno. That removed the final vestige of doubt. The head banging ceased. He was staring straight ahead, his body rigid.

He wasn't sure how, but he knew where. France.

# PART THREE

Northern France,
August to December, 1943

# Chapter Twenty Two

The wait no longer grated for Gerhard. It was now solidifying into a seething antagonism. He glowered at nobody in particular, and dug his nails into the palms of his hands, clasped behind his back. Clearing his desk and re-locating his staff, in anticipation, had been bad enough. Forming up as a guard of honour was the ultimate insult.

For the previous three years he had been able to survey the hive of activity on the floor of the Town Hall below, with an air of olympian detachment. The clatter of typewriters, the frantic ringing of telephones, and the frequent outbursts of splenetic abuse whenever a crisis erupted, had been the background accompaniment to his reign. By simply descending the staircase he could still a dozen animated conversations

But now it would be stripped away. And he would have to take his place amongst those who kept the machinery of terror oiled, its reputation for brutality burnished. He absorbed the final insult, as he gazed at his new-smaller-desk, tucked behind an ornate column near the entrance, out of eye contact with his minions.

The two lines of uniformed staff clicked to attention as Wolfgang and his cohorts swept past, oblivious to Gerhard, any attempt at eye contact, or even the most cursory attempt to return the salute. Desperately trying to keep up, Freuntz and Briedel were sweating and panting, as Wolfgang bounded up the magnificent staircase to the balcony. He handed his leather greatcoat to Briedel, and smoothed down his close cropped hair. He paused for a moment, before spelling out that drastic changes were imminent, inevitable due to the hapless performance of those previously in charge. Gerhard's nails drew blood.

Freuntz knew what was coming, and so focused on the expressions of those below. Yet more faux messianic rhetoric held no appeal for him. Not one dared allow their attention to wander. Their expressions were fixed, their brows furrowed, their nodding seemingly synchronised by some unseen puppet master. National destiny and the futility of resistance were recurrent themes. The methods which would be utilised were outlined in only the sketchiest detail.

Behind the column, Gerhard felt himself more diminished by the minute. He clenched his jaw as his record was derided, his capabilities disparaged. Weak was the message which was hammered home relentlessly. He maintained the same blank expression throughout, duty above all dictated it be so. The public humiliation would not go unchallenged. How and when were for another day. After all, he was being retained. All was not yet lost. Events could still be shaped to his advantage.

Freuntz was about to steal a glance at the delicately painted dome which dominated the hall, but was forced to refocus his attention. Wolfgang reached inside his uniform and produced a glass jar, which he then produced to hold aloft, as if carrying the Olympic Torch. After a prolonged pause he rattled the jar of metal fragments fiercely, the sound echoing around the hall.

"That is what sacrifice is. That is what it means. That is what they pulled out of me in Russia. They could have pulled out ten times more and I would still endure. That is what we are about, what The Reich is about. Endure, survive, flourish. A thousand years, that is what The Fuhrer has asserted. We are at the beginning. France is at an end. The matter is decided. It is simply a matter of will."

He turned on his heel and swept towards his new office. Freuntz followed behind, but as Briedel was about to follow them in, Wolfgang turned and gesticulated that he and the remaining staff would be working down the corridor. Freuntz turned, and noticed how this public sleight produced from Briedel a look of what could only be described as betrayal. Only momentary, but there for all to see. Freuntz was convinced he saw a moistening in Briedel's remaining eye.

Once inside, Wolfgang sank into the luxuriously embroidered sofa. Freuntz offered a huge glass of cognac, which he downed in one. The rubbing of his neck began, as he slumped in silence, his emotional well run dry for the day.

For Freuntz, a night alone with his radio was just what he needed.

✻ ✻ ✻

Returning to work had been a painful process for Pierre. As he crossed the tracks, his coughing was aggravated by the mixture of fog and locomotive smoke which now hugged the ground each morning. His ribs ached, his hips ached, but at least the diarrhoea was gone. He dreaded a prod from a rifle butt, as he and his colleagues were marched between the wagons.

He clambered the wrought iron fire escape, wiped his hands on his grimy overalls, and checked that he had his cigarettes. Turning briefly, he realised that he could see no more than ten yards. The lights of the canteen gave off an ethereal light, but once inside there was a fog of a different kind. Under Wolfgang's new regime, this was the only opportunity the men in the yards would have to smoke. He peered through the man-made murk for his father, Raymond, and as usual he was the target of ribald abuse from a cluster of German troops.

Raymond was wearing yet another of his berets, along with his usual outfit of brown corduroy trousers and a blue jacket, shiny and threadbare. On his left breast he wore the three medals which had been awarded for valour in 'The Battles of the Tunnels', fought under German lines in The Great War. Friedrich Gamser and Horst Wensel orchestrated the daily ritual of ridicule, kicks to the backside, and the malignly playful removal of his beret. Taunting 'The Hero' was the highlight of their day.

Raymond forced a smile, and delved into the slop bucket to remove his beret yet again. This time it was unfit to wear, even for the proudest Frenchman. He saluted his tormentors, put the beret in his inside pocket, and shuffled down the long, refectory style tables to continue his chores. Pierre averted his eyes, fighting hard to ignore the systematic humiliation. Eventually, Raymond slid in beside him. Pierre could not avoid his wheezing.

Conversation could only be perfunctory, and include the most basic of topics. German troops vastly outnumbered the railway workers, and were supported by Gestapo men in plain clothes. Once both had consumed their rations, a glance at the clock indicated that fifteen minutes were up.

Pierre fumbled in his jacket and offered his father a cigarette. Raymond placed it behind his ear, before shuffling off to finish his shift. Determined to make the most of his final couple of minutes, Pierre leaned back. In a forlorn attempt to combine sophistication and defiance, he began to blow rings of smoke towards the ceiling. Pieter Meyerling, assigned by Gerhard to report anything remotely suspicious, had already lost interest.

Freuntz couldn't stand the smell of cigarette smoke, normally. However, there was something exotic about the aroma which lingered, even after Pierre was marched out with his colleagues. The presence of a fellow veteran was what first attracted his attention. This was the fifth day Freuntz had watched the same routine. Why did Raymond never light them there and then?

Freuntz had been curious to discover what happened when Raymond left the yard. There was a familiar pattern to his activities. Freuntz set off in pursuit once again, following some distance behind. Raymond was well known to local people. Sweeping bows to all with whom he exchanged even the shortest conversation, elicited a knowing jocularity. It confirmed to Freuntz that he must have some kind of history, or condition, with which they were familiar.

His journey home was punctuated by regular bouts of basic stretching and toe touching, which suggested some kind of sporting background. Jogging on the spot, accompanied by frequent bouts of sharp shadow boxing confirmed what the background was. Could too many punches explain his behaviour as the benign fool in the canteen?

The frequency with which Raymond's journey was interrupted made it difficult to follow him without detection. Was it deliberate? The steep, cobbled side street which climbed away from the yard posed no problem to him. Freuntz was starting to perspire, despite the autumnal chill, and was struggling to keep up. As he approached the top of the hill, a final performance in front of 'Le Café de Monaco' culminated in the casual dropping of a cigarette packet in the doorway.

Freuntz speeded up. He bent to examine the packet, aware of the aroma it gave off, even though it was empty. The packet showed two palm trees, either side of a pyramid, the writing Arabic. Freuntz straightened up and realised that he had lost sight of Pierre. Quickening his stride, he could see the street drop down to the bridge across the railway tracks.

At that moment the whole bridge was enveloped in smoke, as a goods train began the long haul out of Veziers. The smoke began to clear. Pierre was well into his routine, but now it was clear that this performance was not for passing pedestrians. Now he was oblivious to them. Lots of rhythmic punching upwards was alternated with a series of straight jabs, first one arm and then the other.

At that moment the smoke from a second train enveloped him. Freuntz could only admire the stubborn pride with which he was wearing the red beret. No fool like an old fool, thought Freuntz, as he was about to sidle past, feigning indifference.

From the flats opposite, a broad shouldered woman appeared, and began to put on her bicycle clips.

✵ ✵ ✵

Briedel fumbled forlornly in his inside pocket. Once he had finally located it, he began to stroke the silver cigarette case. The inscription, "Thanks for EVERYTHING. Siggi." took him back to those glorious early days in Russia. For him to be hand picked by a General had been the proudest day of his life, the nights before his redeployment the happiest, the days following their parting the saddest.

He was roused from his reminiscences, as Gerhard slumped into the seat beside him. Briedel immediately realised he needed a distraction from the dreadful alternative, that of having to engage Gerhard in any conversation, beyond the curtest of civilities. He only had one of the cigarettes left, so at least he was spared having to offer one to Gerhard. He lingered over the process of removing it from the case. He tapped it gently on the table, pausing to savour what lay ahead, before eventually lighting it.He inhaled deeply, pausing as long as he dared before exhaling. The effects were immediate. He felt himself begin to gag. He felt himself go faint. He fought to avoid spluttering. The feeling of light headedness took him back to his first trip to Vienna. He had never appreciated how thrilling it could be to almost, but not quite, pass out. The feeling intensified every sensation, electrified his emotions. It was a feeling he had experienced several times with Siggi.

There was little chance of any repetition, as Gerhard, also bereft of company, pondered the dilemma of making conversation with one of his recently imposed superiors. He sat down. He narrowly resisted the urge to complain that this was his first night off in ten, since Wolfgang had assumed control. He realised who he was sat next to.

Briedel inhaled whilst Gerhard stared. Both were focused on Nicole, engaged in deep conversation with Alain. The conversation was accompanied by girlish giggling on her part, and wolfish glances on his. They were spared any further suffering as, from behind them, a slurring voice indicated that Wolfgang was approaching.

Thierry Parsan began to panic. "How many did he say? Was it three glasses and one bottle?" His wife, Marie, shrugged her shoulders. "Bordeaux, woman? Bordeaux or Burgundy?" Marie was speechless. Thierry swallowed and took down the last bottle. He could see in the mirror that the colour had drained from his cheeks. St Emillion. 1927. He had hoped to save it. Just one more imposition. "No chance for it to breathe Marie, no chance!"

Her look indicated they had no alternative. He twisted the corkscrew. He swallowed hard in relief, and said a silent prayer. Her hands were already trembling. With a gulp, she carried the tray across, her breathing shallow, her palms moist. Wolfgang gesticulated that the bottle be left, along with the glasses. He knew there would only be a need for one.

"Of course you don't, do you," he sneered at Gerhard, "Needs a clear head to out think these peasants, cunning these peasants. What with their terroir, their hairy women, their fucking equalité... egalité, and all the fucking rest of it. They can obviously out think Germany's finest analytical minds. Also makes me wonder, and I am not an unreasonable man, what exactly has been going on here these last eighteen months?"

His sweeping gesture left little doubt about who he was referring to, at the same time as it tipped the contents of his glass into Gerhard's lap. Panic set in, as the wine soaked into his uniform. Fearing total humiliation, he felt the jabbing pain from his bladder. He mumbled his excuses and fled to the toilets.

"Well that didn't take long did it? Weak, weak, weak. No wonder the peasants have been having it their own way before I arrived. Weak. But he's gone now, and there's just the two of us."

Briedel dreaded these moments. The alcohol induced a tone of sneering menace he was unable to counteract, being junior to Wolfgang in every respect. His scalp prickled. He had a premonition about how it would go

"Well then, Phar Lap, any passing trade for me? Any trade for me? You need to step up your efforts or it's back to Russia for you. And we wouldn't like that at all, would we now? Going... to... have... to... try... a bit... harder... aren't we?" The staccato delivery, and the rhythmic thumping of the glass on the table, reduced Briedel to silence.

Briedel hated the nickname, as most people thought Phar Lap was a stallion, when he knew the horse had been a gelding. The veering between drink induced sarcasm, calculating brutality, and a maudlin sentimentality, was wearing him down. Briedel's breathing slowly returned to normal. He knew it was impossible to predict his moods, and even more difficult to cope with them. He had learnt to put up with them. The relationship they had forged in Russia encouraged him to endure. One day, the good times would return.

Fortunately for Briedel, the onslaught was cut short, as Wolfgang caught sight of Nicole. He rose to his feet, staggered between the tables, and slumped into the chair beside her. Alain was taken aback by this abrupt intrusion into his plans for the evening. But he was aware of where the power lay. Acquiescence was best for now.

Wolfgang's glassy stare suggested he might be more amenable if the first offer came from Alain. As he began to offer the packet, panic set in. How many were left? How could he be sure to offer the right ones? Offering the wrong ones would be fatal. He struggled to remember how he had been told to set up the packets. Were the safe ones in the middle? No, they were at the end. Weren't they?

His palms were sweating. As he fumbled with the packet, he gambled. He offered the middle one of five, offered to light it as he lent forward, and felt his buttocks clench. Nicole was no longer paying him attention. Fortunately, neither was Wolfgang, now enthusiastically inhaling the scented smoke, with all the zeal of a new convert.

The next seconds seemed like minutes to Alain, but slowly he relaxed. Wolfgang divided his attention between the delicious aroma and Nicole's ample décolletage.

"These, these…where do you get them from? Obviously not France. Much smoother, much, much smoother than the usual French shit. Sorry my dear." He apologised with a ham actor's insincerity. "No, seriously, they are really good. You can let me have some."

There was menace in the glance, edge in the tone, a tone Alain realised he would be wise to act upon. He swallowed hard and was about to offer Wolfgang the crumpled packet. Now, turned fully to engage Nicole, Wolfgang waved him away.

"I don't want any you have had for any length of time. Originals. Ten o'clock in the morning. You would be wise not to disappoint me. Let's start with two hundred."

From the deepest recesses of his mind, Alain summoned up a mumbled acceptance, with as much grace as he could muster. He slid from his seat, bidding a respectful farewell. Wolfgang ignored him.

Alain tried to reconcile the narrowness of his escape with the potential loss of such a lucrative income stream. He would be dead soon enough, but wasn't ready to die yet, he thought. Accept it, he told himself. There were other ways he could make money. He felt inside his jacket. The wad of notes offered reassurance. For now. Plus he could always conceal a few more packets for his own private enterprise.

His next move would have to be on Saturday. He would need to dig out his suit, if he was to stay in the game. He was aware of the contrast between the glossy, intimidating, smoothness of this intruder, in comparison to his rough and ready garb. He nodded to Nicole, and headed towards the door.

He brushed past a glowering Gerhard, the damp patch almost dry, his calculations complete, but fascinated by the prolonged conversation he had observed. The first three leads he had given to Nicole had yielded nothing, and if he was to get back into her orbit he would have to raise his game, given the emergence of two serious rivals.

Doctoring the files on the 'Failed Three', to make them more incriminating, was crucial. Gerhard's resolve hardened as he sidled past Wolfgang, already engaged in the light hearted repartee he could never produce. His humiliation could have been worse, he realised. "Bide your time, bide your time," he repeated through gritted teeth, a reckoning with his nemesis inevitable.

Suddenly, the familiar drone of the klaxon told them that they had two minutes to get to the shelter. As he fastened his jacket, Wolfgang recognised that the allure of Nicole might prove irresistible. Nicole savoured the last of the Bordeaux. She glanced briefly at Gerhard, already forcing his way through the crowd by the door, grateful for the generosity which enabled her to appreciate the finer things in life. The new opportunity to extend her sphere of influence was too good to turn down, though.

Briedel was the last to leave, the urge to acquire more of the special cigarettes intensifying already.

✲ ✲ ✲

His head had cleared now, and as he surveyed the wreckage one thing was unclear to Wolfgang. Only six bombs had been dropped, but three had had a devastating effect, not least in blasting the chasm from which the rear half of the shattered locomotive protruded. Those wagons not destroyed immediately had been shaken from the tracks by the blast.

The crane crews were already setting up the heavy machinery, amidst a drizzle of cement dust from the bags, ripped apart by the explosions. At the rear of the train, the remainder of the prefabricated panels were being reduced to ash, despite desperate attempts to hose down the blazing wagons. Strewn everywhere were hundreds of giant rivets and tent pegs.

Only six, though. A deliberate strike? Or just a lightening of the load, before turning for England? He was inclined to the latter. Regardless, a message had to be sent. He would spell out the cost of informing. Three would suffice. Five would have more impact, though. Above all, if he was to deliver, he had to step up the pace on 'Operation Whuffy'. Another fifty needed to be conscripted. He would start in the morning.

✲ ✲ ✲

Back in Veziers, Freuntz was scratching his head. The radio had been easy to assemble, but now the transcripts threatened to cover his bed completely. Quicker triangulation of where the replies were being broadcast from was already in evidence. The messages to The Resistance had been decoded easily enough. Working out what they meant, though, was a different matter entirely. He had the pieces, but didn't know what the puzzle was.

✯ ✯ ✯

It was not yet light. But at first glance it looked as if the plan had finally paid dividends. The wheels of the motor cycle were spinning slowly. Two bodies lay crumpled against the wall, whilst the third groaned in agony by the roadside.

As usual, it had taken the five miles of cycling for the pain in his hip to disappear. But now Guillaume's pulse was racing, a mixture of the effort he had put in to his daily pre-dawn tour, and a heightened sense of anticipation. He had been sceptical that Olivier's plan would ever produce results but now, who knew what it might yield?

The motor cycle and sidecar had crashed into the wall instead of negotiating the right hand bend. As Guillaume dismounted, he became aware of the film of frost which had provided an extra, lethal ingredient to Olivier's mixture. Olivier had correctly anticipated that with the RAF ensuring that travelling in daylight was too hazardous an undertaking, more and more communication would take place, not only under the cover of darkness, but by using the maze of high hedged, country lanes.

This was their weak point, according to Olivier. The Resistance had a duty to render it more fraught. "And here's the proof. You were right, you old bastard." Guillaume chuckled, a mixture of acknowledgement and anticipation. The combination of manure, hydraulic fluid and oil was impossible to detect at night. Even better, it could be deposited at will, whilst appearing to be part and parcel of rural life. 'The Elixir'. Guillaume remembered how Olivier whistled as he stirred the vats, composing an imaginary advertising campaign for his deadly potion. The approaches to bends, before braking began, were the most lethal.

He realised that he would have to act quickly. The first pink hues of dawn were appearing to the east. It would not be long before the lanes were crawling with German troops. The first decision was a quick one. His hip had loosened up now. Two fierce kicks to the ribs of the prostrate German elicited only the faintest of grunts. He didn't have long to go. Not worth the risk. Guillaume forced an oily handkerchief down his throat. After smothering him with his jacket for a further minute, the groaning stopped.

Guillaume quickly checked the pulses of the other two-gone as well. As he emerged from the ditch, from the corner of his eye, he spotted a rectangular object which had been thrown across the road in the collision. He realised that it was a briefcase, but now faced a dilemma. There was no sound, other than his laboured breathing. Stealing it was the easy option. However, if it was important, and it was missing, the retribution would be indiscriminate and brutal.

To his relief he didn't need to force it open. He removed the documents. He realised that he could either try to read and remember as much detail as possible, or skim read the whole contents, and try to piece together anything he had missed. He chose the latter. Illuminated by the headlight of the crashed bike, he struggled to interpret the blueprints. A series of low buildings? Embedded in a hillside of some kind? Tunnels, passageways and storage facilities would be below ground. Outside, there would be some sort of inclined platform. A birds eye view seemed to show three such platforms.

In the distance he heard the low hum of vehicles. They could only be military. He realised time was short. He rifled through the remaining documents. Dates were listed. Veziers was mentioned in all of them. There seemed to be four destinations, the dates spread over the rest of the year. The growl of the engines was louder now, and he was fumbling ineffectively. One last frantic skim. He placed the documents back in the briefcase, snapped it shut and tossed it into the middle of the road.

He glanced back. The yellow beam was stronger now. They would soon be on to the long, straight stretch. He would be spotted. He quickly re-mounted and pedalled into a patch of mist, pausing briefly to smile in satisfaction at a job well done.

The spirals of smoke, beyond the woods in the distance, indicated that the raid last night had been a heavy one. Once safely clear of the scene, he adopted a more leisurely pace. He tried to make sense of what he had learnt. Anything? It made no sense to him. But then why send it by special courier-three of them?

He needed to find out what 'Vergeltungswaffen' meant.

✲ ✲ ✲

"Not again. We drove up from Marseilles quicker than this," Olivier rasped as he clamped his fourth cigarette of the day between his lips. Unfortunately for Guillaume, these were the dirt cheap ones and he faced a dilemma. Choke in the fumes? Or wind down the window and endure the gusting wind, now approaching gale force? Freezing was better than choking, and the window was duly lowered.

"Lungs of leather, you! That mucus you cough up, though. Could mend a puncture with it. Is it meant to be yellow?" Olivier ignored him. His next three drags were deliberately prolonged. Guillaume inched the aging lorry to the side of the road and joined the queue for the third time that day. He winced each time he felt the threadbare tyres crunching the shattered glass which carpeted the main street.

"Quick! Cough some up! I'm sure that's air escaping. Quick!Cough !" Guillaume smirked. More deep drags ensued.

The queue of what remained of the available workforce of Veziers snaked ahead. The air of grim fatalism was palpable, as stragglers joined the back of the queue, heads bowed, shoulders sagging, staring at their reflections in the puddles.

Guillaume fumbled for his papers and settled in for a long wait.

"Half an hour. Half an hour at least. And then we've got to get through the roadblock." The muttering ceased as soldiers checked the back of the lorry for the third time. The chickens in the back behaved as chickens always behaved. The sacks of vegetables were ransacked once more, and were now strewn all over the floor, impossible to sell had people not been so desperate.

"Looks like it was a big one last night," Olivier muttered, without removing the cigarette, nodding towards the pall of smoke rising from the rubble of the Credit de Paris, and beyond, towards the rail yards. "Tell me something, do you ever wonder if it is worth it? This…all this… I mean, look at these poor sods in front. They won't be seeing Veziers again any time soon. Just think, if that boat to Beirut had left on time, you wouldn't have been in that bar, and you would be out of all this." He nodded towards the rubble once again.

"I mean, look at her." He pointed to a middle aged woman, desperately trying to sweep her pavement clean of the shattered glass from the window of her milliners shop. Boxes of stock were precariously stacked on top of each other, when a sudden gust of wind blew the whole pile over, and they cartwheeled down the street. The woman collapsed to her knees, her head in her hands. "Do you think she thinks it's worth it? I haven't long left, but you, you're still young, you could be well out of it." For a few moments Guillaume replayed their first meeting, and the long trip up through France.

"It is worth it. They always clamp down after a raid. They are getting desperate. Of course it's worth it."

✵ ✵ ✵

Forty minutes later they were allowed through the checkpoint, before being directed towards the courtyard behind the Town Hall. From the balcony, Freuntz watched as the line shuffled forwards towards the row of low tables. The resignation on their faces was clearly visible. The unpredictable eddies of the howling gale threatened to blow away the piles of forms, spread out in front of Gerhard's assistants. They were right to be apprehensive, Freuntz thought.

Heels clicked. An immediate snap to attention indicated that Wolfgang was about to appear below. He duly did. Completely ignoring the methodical system Gerhard had set up in preparation, he began to march up and down the line of fearful civilians.

Five of the first ten were thrust to one side, after the briefest of examinations. Sixty three year old Giscard Lamence didn't make it back to his feet, and began to froth at the mouth. The queue remained immobile. Freuntz couldn't help but notice that Wolfgang's immaculate black uniform was streaked with grey dust. He knew that another unfortunate would be getting the full blast, before long.

Trying to remain oblivious to Giscard's distress were two chubby workmen, also covered in grey dust. Wolfgang ignored them. But then he gesticulated to the next in line to accompany him to the corner of the courtyard. A dismissive gesture and a clicking of fingers signalled to Gerhard that he could take over now. He arched his eyebrows at Meyerling. He walked as slowly as he dared towards Guillaume. Medical papers produced, Guillaume was safe.

After five minutes, their negotiations concluded, Olivier rejoined the queue. Wolfgang dismissed Gerhard back to the tables with a limp wristed wave, indicating to all just where Gerhard fitted in. Suddenly, another downpour drenched those who remained in the courtyard, a situation Wolfgang was not prepared to endure, whilst ensuring that Gerhard would. Having hardly had time to sit down, he was ordered back to his feet. Wolfgang swept past and disappeared inside.

As the rain began to drip from the peak of his cap, he vowed that once he was dry he would make it his business to find out why the conversation had taken so long. Why so amenable? The suspect unharmed? The inspection of documents so cursory? Gerhard's mood began to lighten.

Freuntz watched as the first lorries backed into the courtyard. Those selected for forced labour began to clamber in. As they were doing so, Briedel hauled three more out of the line, and led them towards the main square, their fate decided.

The deluge continued. The puddles began to form around him. Giscard continued to tremble and twitch.

✫ ✫ ✫

As they shuffled out of the courtyard, Olivier and Guillaume found themselves abreast of the two dust covered workmen. Both were whistling, one responding to the other.

"Relief?" asked Guillaume

"You bet, what with last night, and now that. Can't help thinking our luck won't hold much longer."

They resumed whistling with increased gusto, and suddenly it dawned on Olivier.

"I used to sing that when I was little. How do you know it?"

"Last night-all night-those bastard Germans were singing it, and it gets into your head. Why, what is it?"

"It's a nursery rhyme. It's about Whuffy."

The two workmen shrugged their shoulders, and set off to look for an undamaged bar.

"Whuffy?" said Guillaume, quizzically.

"Yes, he's a scarecrow. Lads, let me buy you a drink."

✲ ✲ ✲

An hour later Guillaume spotted Olivier in the darkest corner of Le Café d'Annecy, its front windows blown out by the raid, the proprietor attempting to carry on, unperturbed. Olivier noticed that Guillaume had arrived. As he clapped the two men on the shoulders, he gave each of them a cigarette.

Back on the lorry, Guillaume struggled to contain his frustration.

"You stupid bastard. Right under their noses. It's crawling with troops and plain clothes men. Still you're at it. Just can't leave it alone can you? It won't just be forced labour if they catch you. Why run the risk-put everything at risk-everyone?"

"The deal. Always the deal. That's what gets me out of bed. The deal. Always the deal. Relax, mon brave, a couple of petrol coupons each. A small price to pay for what I've found out."

# Chapter Twenty Three

Nicole attempted to remain positive, despite the rise and fall of the flabby white breasts and the overpowering odour. She examined herself in the full length mirror in her bathroom. It had been one of Gerhard's latest gifts, its ornate carving hinting at fine craftsmanship. She smoothed down her dress as she reflected that it was one of the last useful things he had given her, in stark contrast to this latest potential suspect. No sooner had he finished, than his snoring was making the glasses on her dressing table vibrate. Five minutes maximum it had taken. She would inform Gerhard that the news was that there was no news.

She supposed there must be better ways to make a living but couldn't fathom out what they were. It would take more than simply a tap on the arm to rouse this one, she realised. Once she was happy that she was looking at her best again, she screamed so loudly, directly into his ear, that it seemed to take ages before his flabby, white breasts stopped wobbling.

She stroked his ego by accompanying him down the staircase, arm in arm. She waved him goodbye. Something strong was required to erase the memory. A stiff brandy usually did the trick. It took two on this occasion.

Fortunately, as she rinsed the last mouthful around the back of her throat, Alain spotted her, and immediately her spirits lifted. He had clearly made an effort. A sophisticated man of the world approached. In stark contrast to the grubby overalls he often wore, the broad lapelled navy suit was complemented perfectly by a crisp, white shirt, and a diamond patterned tie, burgundy and blue. The handkerchief which protruded from his top pocket completed the ensemble with a flourish.

She smiled warmly as their eyes met. But it was as he made his way towards her that her suspicions were confirmed. He had obviously been measured for the suit when much younger, and crucially, much healthier. During their previous light hearted encounters she could not avoid the pinched lines around his mouth and a hint of sallowness in his eyes. His hair had probably once been lustrous, but the liberal application of brilliantine couldn't conceal the fact that it was now thinning, flecked with grey. His coughing, whilst not frequent, was obviously a clue that he was not in the best of health. But many were no better. The rations had been reduced again.

He approached. She couldn't help but notice that the suit seemed at least two sizes too big for him, the clear space between his stomach and his trousers made braces essential. He seemed to have shrunk physically, and his drawn features made him seem much older. He was probably quite handsome when he was younger, she mused. She couldn't help but notice the rings, chunky and ostentatious, he wore on each finger. Not exactly to her taste. But enough to excite her interest, unusual as they were for a farm labourer.

She quickly cast such reservations to the back of her mind, and decided to make the best of it. His witty repartee and colourful, if mysterious, past offered the prospect of an entertaining end to the evening.

He didn't disappoint her. The red wine flowed. Half an hour seemed to pass in an instant. He knew a lot about foreign countries, but was evasive on details of actual visits. He knew a lot about high living, but was sparse on details of when he had actually experienced it. After all- on a farm labourers wages? As she continued to giggle, she concluded that this was a line of patter which had invariably proved successful in the past, so why change now?

As they finally drained the bottle, a sudden change in mood descended on Alain. From being the gregarious extrovert, he plunged into a morose introspection during which he was silent for what seemed like ages. Nicole was unsure how to alter the mood but it was Alain who did it for her.

"Mademoiselle. I am so sorry. So rude. Do forgive me, I must apologise."

"No, no, something is clearly wrong, monsieur, are you unwell? It is not something I said? Some unhappy memory, perhaps?" She stroked his hand, by now surprisingly clammy.

"Of course not, of course not. How could it be? These evenings are the happiest times of the week for me. I am coming to terms with the fact that there won't be many more."

He didn't cast a sideways glance to appraise what effect his words had had, unlike so many of her clients who tried all manner of opening gambits. She concluded that he was genuine, and would soon be asking her to play her part. She was right.

"I do not have long to live, and you could make me even happier than you already do. I will make it worth your while."

He pulled back his jacket and revealed the top half of a bulky bundle of bank notes. Nicole tried to conceal her surprise at this lucrative offer. Having composed herself, she took him warmly by the hand.

It was impossible to avoid how loud his wheezing became as they mounted the stairs. He might not be able to manage it, she thought ruefully.

✯ ✯ ✯

He hadn't been able to. He was her last client of the night, but despite all her words of encouragement and well honed techniques he couldn't satisfy her, nor she him. The combination of his wheezing, sobbing, and self-lacerating criticism had conspired against them. She had never heard anyone use the word 'emasculated' before, but could guess what it meant.

Normally, she kicked them out without a second thought. But something inside her stirred, an urge to succour, to shelter and protect. After all, that was what a daughter would do when their father was vulnerable-wasn't it? It was certainly what she would have done, if only she had had the chance, had events conspired differently.

As he dozed contentedly, she slipped out of bed, still fascinated by the quality of his suit. Every item of clothing had been placed with meticulous precision. Even the handkerchief protruded with a flamboyance the setting didn't merit.

The label inside confirmed it, Hausmann of Paris. He clearly had, or had had, class. The notes protruded from the inside pocket and she removed the bundle, never having had so much money in her hands at one time. Something about them struck her. They seemed to be in pristine condition, but were somehow rough to the touch, fibrous rather than smooth. In the semi darkness she couldn't make out whether the colour had faded, but how, if the notes were new?

He rolled over. She paused. Once she was sure he was asleep, she searched in his other pocket and felt two oblong shapes, removing them both with one smooth movement. She sighed. The first one was probably what was killing him, and also gave the suit its unusual aroma.

But it was the second which aroused her interest further-a huge bundle of petrol coupons. Her heart had softened towards him. Even his moustache hadn't put her off. But now such sentiments were redundant, replaced by hard headed calculation.

How could she use these discoveries to her advantage?

✫ ✫ ✫

They had been pedalling for twenty minutes, and the realisation was dawning that the woman in the distance probably did this weekly, even daily. He hadn't done it for twenty years. Last night, Marianne had used the red hot wax for the first time. It wouldn't be the last, but the pain still lingered. Physical exertion was making Freuntz wince, his eyes water.

A chance to allow the woman to get ahead on the long straight helped him to recover his breath, as well as avoid detection. It also allowed him to reflect on what his next move would be, as well as on what he had seen earlier.

The switch, how had he missed it before? Admittedly, it was only the second time that Pierre and Raymond had been joined by a third workman. The cigarette packets were placed in the centre of the table. After the briefest of conversations, the three had separated. But not before Raymond, who hadn't produced a packet, put one in his pocket before resuming his duties.

After a series of elaborate farewells to his German tormentors, he headed for the bridge, replacing his green beret with the red one, as he dropped the packet. Was it a delaying tactic or a decoy? Once again, Freuntz had bent to pick up the packet, but this time it contained two cigarettes.

By now, Raymond was on the bridge and commencing his routine with all his usual vigour. Freuntz watched from the doorway of a photography studio as he examined the packet. Once the routine was over, he watched as Raymond hurriedly lit the cigarette, but didn't actually inhale. Of course, burn the evidence!

The woman emerged. He commandeered the first passing bike, and set off in pursuit.

✯ ✯ ✯

A trial run the previous week now proved its worth. He closed on the woman. He rounded the final bend and accelerated, providing the momentum to send her tumbling into the ditch. The plan worked to perfection. She lay face down in the pungent mud. Freuntz dismounted rapidly, and placed the knife by her throat.

"Madame, I could kill you here and now, but it is not you I am interested in. I am here to help you, providing you help me. Do exactly as I say, and you will come to no harm. I need your coat and your hat. Quickly! Hurry up!"

Her senses still reeled from the force of the collision. She struggled to remove her coat. Eventually, he wrenched it free, placed the hat on his head, and removed her rough clogs.

"Remember, don't dare move. I will find you and kill you if you do. Stay here and you are safe. Now, what is the message? What is it?" he hissed in her face, flecking her with spittle. The colour drained from her cheeks. A gentle trace of the knife across her jugular vein was all it took.

"Devant.11.Htmn," she gasped, before passing out.

Freuntz fastened the coat, put on the hat as carefully as time permitted, and threw the clogs over the hedge. He pedalled slowly up the drive to the farm.

He dismounted behind the cattle shed, and removed his disguise with a wry shake of the head. He allowed his heart rate to return to normal as he surveyed the scene. The farmhouse showed no signs of life, other than the dim glow of what was probably an oil lamp. To his right, the door to the barn was slightly ajar. It was the obvious place to start.

Stepping gingerly around the cow pats and farmyard detritus, he tiptoed towards the barn, removing the safety catch of his revolver as he did so. He attempted to work out what was going on inside. Raised voices were rising towards a crescendo. Some kind of engine was spluttering asthmatically.

He slipped inside and took a moment to adjust to the gloom. The argument was continuing to rage between two men. Each of them was stood in a deep pit which housed the machinery. The task of sneaking up behind them was made easy

"You're taking too many ri…" yelled the younger one, as he felt the muzzle of the revolver, cold upon his neck.

"Don't even think about it old man," Freuntz snarled. He searched Guillaume for weapons. "Turn that thing off, then put both hands on top where I can see them."

The generator was slow to respond but eventually stopped. A piercing yelp from Olivier rent the air, his hands scorched by the red hot chassis.

"That will be the least of your worries if you don't shut it, old man." The self pitying whimpers meant the threat from Olivier was eliminated. Freuntz could concentrate on Guillaume, from where he knew instinctively any resistance might come.

"Now, you're going to climb out, ever so slowly, backwards, and then get on your knees, hands on your head…slowly… slowly, or your boyfriend will get it."

Guillaume obeyed as slowly as he dared, trying desperately to work out why his two look outs had been duped. Freuntz produced the hat and tossed it into the pit. It dawned on him.

"Old man, crawl over here…and I mean crawl. Don't even lift an eyebrow. No medals for bravery, here. Stop squealing while you are at it. Over here, quick! Take off his belt."

Still whimpering, Olivier did as he was told, and eventually managed to tie Guillaume to the printing press. Olivier was starting to sob. Once he had painstakingly removed his own belt, in a matter of seconds he was secured to the press as well.

"Now then gentlemen, we need to talk."

✵ ✵ ✵

Freuntz allowed a minute or two for the anger to dissipate, the baleful glances to cease. He began.

"I know a lot about you, and I could hand you over to my colleagues right now. They are experts in inflicting and prolonging pain. They will take you to places you can't even contemplate. Some people endure, sometimes for days. They break in the end, though. Old man, I think five minutes would be plenty for you, so think carefully about what I have to say. Remember, they are always looking to refine their skills-old flesh, new flesh it's all the same to them," he hissed in Guillaume's ear.

"They see themselves as artists," he continued, "but you wouldn't want to be their canvas. So, you see, right now I am the only friend you've got." Freuntz paused. He wanted to allow the gravity of their predicament to sink in.

"For reasons you don't need to know, I want to help you. First of all, they are closing in on you and your broadcasts. You are going to need someone to distract them. I can not only help you with that, but I can ensure that the two most fanatical are dealt with. If we are going to work together we need to establish some trust. I realise all this has come as a shock. But the question you need to ask is this-who holds all the cards here? Exchange of information always helps build up that trust, so who is going to go first? What about all this lot? It's a real hive of industry. Old man, you look the entrepreneurial type to me. Let's start with the cigarettes."

Freuntz swept an arm around the barn and let the question hang in the air. Still grimacing, Olivier sought approval from Guillaume, who nodded his assent.

"Before you start," Freuntz interrupted, "Why do you risk writing things down, and passing them in cigarettes?"

Taken aback by how much Freuntz obviously knew, Guillaume spat back,

"Old Raymond… too many punches… he would forget as soon as he got out of the door. Can't fault his bravery though. Survived two roof collapses as well, before they finally shut the mine."

"Anyhow, the cigarettes."

Clearly recognising that this was his field of expertise, Olivier launched into a description of his exploits in the Middle and Far East, before war broke out.

"They smoke all kinds out there. We have made cheap ones we flavour with all kinds of stuff-licquorice, cubeb-a kind of pepper. We've used flax to make them burn longer, cow dung to make them smell-and keep the Germans away. And urine, even urine. We've had to, or the good tobacco wouldn't have lasted this long."

He turned to look at Freuntz , who remained impassive.

"But the best ones are called Kretek. They have all kind of things in, and smell of cloves. People like the smell and the taste, but the funny thing is…some people use them during sex. It inhibits the swallowing reflex and makes them feel like they are choking. Can't see the appeal myself. Trade is trade though," he reflected, as phlegmatically as the pain in his hands permitted.

"So, on occasions, we make them three or four times the normal strength. Apparently they can make people pass out."

Freuntz looked at the pile of packets, waiting to be filled. The tub of tobacco and spices was almost empty. It didn't seem that there would be much more production in that area.

"What about these then?" Freuntz asked, pointing to the pile of notes by the edge of the pit.

"Same thing. We forge the coupons to get the petrol to run the generator, as well as barter with some of the other farmers. For the notes, the same idea, we can barter if we need to. This machine is a beauty. Swiss made, twenty years old, but as good as new. We got it here just before the Germans." Olivier and Guillaume exchanged the faintest of smiles, recollecting another near fatal encounter.

"For the money, it's virtually impossible to get the inks now… and the paper is virtually impossible to get, as well. We've tried our own, used flax. Just like the ancient Egyptians, but it makes the paper rough, unless you really knock it about."

Guillaume had now regained some measure of composure. He was desperate to move things forward, if there was to be any of the promised collaboration. Otherwise, it would be an endless homage to Olivier and his business acumen.

"You've obviously taken care of aunty. Did she have a message for us?"

Freuntz had forgotten about the woman in the ditch.

"Hmmm... Devant... 11... h..t..m..n. 11 is obviously the time the train leaves. Devant? Code for one of the tracks? Let me guess. Au dessus? A côté de? Derrière must be code for the other main lines… and Hartmann…" Freuntz allowed himself to recollect how many times he had heard the troops in Russia give thanks for the Hartmann Process. It toughened armour and vastly increased the load bearing capacity of steel.

"Part of Whuffy?" Guillaume continued, determined to exploit the slight shift in initiative now that he was asking some questions. "We know all about the dummy buildings and imitation tracks they have been so busy with, up north. Won't fool the British for ever. But why Whuffy?"

"Scarecrow. And what do scarecrows do? Pretend to be something they aren't." All three managed the briefest of smiles that the Germans were capable of whimsy.

Freuntz realised that he needed to find out about the radio, and how they transmitted and received messages. Sharing his own expertise could smooth progress, and start to inform his decisions about how he would help them.

"We can decode the messages. But they don't make much sense. You need to be straight here, because any broadcasts for longer than five minutes now, and they will have you. You don't know how desperate they are. The fate of the war in the West hinges on them finding you. You would be a real prize… make you feel good that, does it?"

"Must be something to do with Vergeltungswaffen then," Guillaume said with a grimace, his arms aching from their prolonged shackling to the press.

Once again Freuntz was shaken by how much they seemed to know, but was willing to let them go first.

"Revenge weapon, that's what it means," groaned Olivier, in even more distress from the prolonged ordeal. "We don't know what it does though."

Freuntz fell silent, weighing up the enormity of the decision he was about to make, the information he was about to divulge, and the momentous consequences his actions might have. For what seemed like an eternity he was silent, but then began to describe the pilotless rockets which had been developed, known as V 1s. They could be launched on London within weeks, could obliterate any planned invasion and not only that, an even faster, more deadly one was being tested in Germany, the V 2.

"They can out fly any plane. They are too fast to be shot down from the ground. Fifty, a hundred a night. They will be unstoppable if they launch them in any numbers. Unstoppable. So how are we going to do it?"

✫ ✫ ✫

Dusk was falling. Freuntz lifted a bedraggled Francoise from the ditch where he had left her. He mumbled an apology, retrieved her clogs and returned her coat. She re-mounted her bike, and wobbled off into the teeming drizzle.

Freuntz set off in the opposite direction, and reflected on how he could make full use of his discoveries. The talk in the courtyard now assumed greater significance. The smell of the cigarettes in the canteen could be explained. The bundles of banknotes in his inside pockets offered scope for exploitation.

He smiled to himself at the quality of their identity papers, almost as good as his own work.

The key, though, would be the radio broadcasts.

# Chapter Twenty Four

It was fortunate for Freuntz that Wolfgang had such trust in him that his absence for most of the day excited so little interest. Once back in the office, concentration proved difficult for Freuntz, as he ploughed his way through the mound of intercepts, directions from Berlin, and what were euphemistically described as 'witness statements'. A grisly familiarity with the means by which they were extracted meant that he paid them only cursory attention.

Wolfgang was already rubbing his temple; the desk bound drudgery of the day had already degraded his attention to detail. In its place, anticipation of the evening ahead grew. Freuntz had developed the capacity to concentrate on his own work, whilst filtering Wolfgang's rambling for nuggets of worthwhile information. Suddenly, he was paying rapt attention.

"As you know, we are getting closer, but they are getting smarter. That area out near the mines is perfect for them. But once you include the farms, lanes, old buildings and all the rest, it is like a needle in a haystack. It is still taking us more than five minutes to triangulate the transmissions. But once, once, we have the new equipment in a few weeks, we can nail them for good. Coming from Russia, though, so who knows when it will actually arrive?"

"The key thing, Freuntz, is to keep the lid on them for these next three or four weeks and the job is done. That's the key, the next four weeks." Exhausted by his succinct analysis, Wolfgang lapsed into silence. He resumed, in a tone Freuntz had rarely heard.

"The problem is, it is like squeezing a balloon, and if you squeeze one area the pressure grows somewhere else. Without a lot more troops it is going to be difficult. And where do we find them, Freuntz? Where?"

Freuntz responded with a resigned shrug, and returned to his paperwork. Silence didn't suit Wolfgang. He was soon onto another theme.

"Enjoy it with Marianne? She is unique isn't she?" he enquired in a tone which was half genuine enquiry, half admiration.

Freuntz didn't want to be interrupted. He nodded, and puffed out his cheeks.

"Hot wax. That is something. Where do they learn that stuff? I've never understood receiving pain, not by choice anyway. Now, inflicting it, that's something else." He realised he would get nowhere, and so summoned the ever willing Briedel. As he slowly put on his overcoat, he couldn't resist one last attempt to elicit some response from Freuntz.

"Third night running At 'The House of Pleasure," he leered. "That blonde is really special. She had to cut me free last night. Keeps a knife in the bedside cabinet, Makes sense I suppose, in that game. No doubt about it though, no doubt at all! The thrill, Freuntz, the thrill. Helpless…and a woman with a knife. Something to think about. Might have to create some kind of perm…. Ah, Phar, Café Gasquet for me and then it's over to you for the rest of the evening. You know where to find me. I know I am leaving things in good hands," he continued, in a tone he intended to be genuine, but came across as sarcasm. Briedel held the door open, and he was gone.

Freuntz looked anxiously at the clock. He simply had to reduce the mountain of paperwork, before leaving some time to compile his own file. Official stationery was essential. The real work would come later.

His first broadcast.

※ ※ ※

It always took time to assemble the radio. As they shivered in the dark of Martin Belvoir's barn, Guillaume and Olivier shared the same expression. Surprise. They hadn't trusted Freuntz to keep his side of the bargain. But there it had been, right on time as agreed - the horoscope and the fourteen letter phrase, amongst a torrent of meaningless verbiage. "Sagittarius- keep your chin up." They were now clear to broadcast a short, sharp, genuine message, exactly one hour later. Guillaume looked at his watch. Twelve minutes to go, and then they would have to head for the signal box. Painting the logs first would make it a tight schedule.

※ ※ ※

Didier Melchen tried his best not to tremble, although he had a ready made excuse. The clearing skies indicated that the temperature was dropping fast. The fact that his signal box was blacked out helped conceal his apprehension. Why was he doing it? Could he remember the instructions? What if things happened in different sequence? Where was Olivier?

Under the new regime, he now had three guards, one of whom was meant to be outside at all times. For ten days the orders had been followed meticulously, but now the monotonous routine was losing its appeal. The period when all three were inside was lengthening.

He desperately tried to remember which cigarettes he was meant to offer, those from the end or the middle? Olivier had spent more time grimacing than explaining, but Didier felt he had it. He would soon know. At ten o'clock precisely Hermann Greumann climbed the steps. Didier already had the coffee brewing.

"Could freeze a penguin's nuts off out there," Greumann grumbled. "Even colder for you Pluskal," he smirked, before flapping his arms dramatically. "Never mind, soon be twelve. We'll try to keep the fire in for you... won't we? Won't we, Axel?"

Determined to extract the maximum from the situation-anything to relieve the boredom-Axel gave a prolonged shrug of the shoulders and a knowing smirk in return.

"Jesus, this tastes like camel shit," Greumann spluttered, "And believe me I know what I am talking about. We used to complain about the flies in Libya, but Christ, what would I give to be surrounded by a swarm of those bastards. Better than frostbite."

"Anybody would think you were in Russia. Believe me, that is cold. Only people as dumb as the Ivans could put up with it. They wrote the book on cold, those…" retorted Pluskal.

As he was about to bore his two colleagues yet again, with stories they had heard a dozen times, the phone rang. Right on time, thought Didier. Predictability, routine, they had their good points. Greumann barked confirmation that all was quiet. On hearing that the train would leave right on time, he put the phone down, and prepared to resume his monologue.

Didier swallowed hard, and produced the cigarettes. In the half light it was difficult to see properly. But somehow, inside, he felt calm. He carefully pressed the bottom of the packet to make sure that the first two protruded.

"Takes me back to Benghazi, that smell." said Greumann. "All those camel jockeys smoked them. Did I ever tell…"

"Yes, you did, so shut up, for…"

Didier managed to offer the third one to Pluskal, and then produced the matches. All three inhaled deeply. Didier wondered whether he had given the right ones. He tried to avoid staring at them. Why were they not working? He didn't need to worry. The alluring aroma of the smoke meant all three inhaled even more deeply, determined to savour its seductive properties, before returning to their duties.

The first frenzied gasps came from Greumann, who collapsed in panic, clawing at his throat. Pluskal staggered a couple of steps. He too crumpled in a heap. The cramped, gloomy conditions added to their sense of disorientation. The grunts and gasps made it worse. As Axel stumbled over the prostrate Pluskal, his head hit the corner of the desk with such force that he was soon unconscious.

Crouching outside on the steps, Guillaume counted three muffled thumps. He flung open the door. Greumann was making a forlorn attempt to get to his feet, but to no avail. In an instant Guillaume had the chloroform soaked cloth over his mouth. He let him slide to the floor.

Following behind, Olivier, completely unaccustomed to such visceral close quarter combat, hesitated, unsure what he could see, indecision paralysing him. What had he been told to do? He was saved by Didier, who flopped on top of Pluskal, and stayed there. His immense girth choked the life out of the wheezing German. The clenched fists were limp in less than a minute

"Now, quick, one each," yelled Guillaume, as the three adjusted to the dark.

"This one's gone," hissed Didier.

"Quick, get it in his mouth," yelled Guillaume. He suffocated Greumann. He avoided the bulging eyes, white in the gloom.

Olivier could just about see the prostrate Axel, by the signal levers. Grunting and grimacing, he rolled him over. He forced the cloth into his mouth. He clamped his jaw shut with his foot. Within two minutes the last, guttering gasps had ceased. All that could be heard was the heavy breathing of the three assailants.

Olivier slumped to the floor, the enormity of what he had done, suddenly overwhelming him.

"No time! No time! The train leaves in five minutes. Quick, get the cloth out, the tablets in." In contrast to the whimpering Olivier, Didier was energised, and forced the tablets into the mouths of the three dead Germans. He sprinkled each with whisky, as instructed by Guillaume.

"Some in the coffee, quick! Spread one or two tablets on the floor. Come on! Come on, Olivier!"

Olivier realised he had no choice. He levered himself to his feet. He tried to focus in the gloom. The prospect of what else lay ahead filled him with dread. The phone rang. Guillaume looked at Didier. Didier shrugged and picked it up.

The voice at the other end meant nothing. He struggled in vain.

"Moment, moment…" spluttered Didier, desperate to stall his inquisitor.

Suddenly Olivier took the receiver from him, as Didier whispered the name of Greumann in his ear. He swallowed hard. He barked his responses in fluent German, interspersed with plenty of coughing and croaking. Tension made injecting the required level of authority difficult. He decided to listen. He began to relax.

The conversation was brief, but concluded with a demand for the signal sequence. Didier once again gave thanks for the predictability of the German mind. He mouthed the sequence-three green one yellow, three times over. Olivier put down the receiver, and slumped to the floor once more, his shirt soaked in sweat.

"You hero. Who would have thought it? I've finally found a use for you," said Guillaume, grinning in admiration. "Only one more thing for you, now. Shoot him. Straightforward after that performance, I would say. Here, it needs to be with one of our guns. Like he was trying to run away. Didier, don't forget. Take the red flag. And the lamp."

Didier and Olivier were about to head out into the gloom. Guillaume suddenly realised. "Hey, the main thing DiDi, the points. Christ, nearly forgot!"

With a grunt Didier forced down the pedal, clenched the lever in a meaty paw, and was rewarded with the sound of machinery clanking into place. At the same time, Guillaume was delving into his satchel for the luminous paint. Within seconds he was clambering onto the roof. He began to daub the roof with a manic intensity, Olivier and Didier disappeared down the track.

Olivier was trembling. He stumbled along the track, the uneven gravel gnawing at his legs, already weak from his ordeal.

"This is far enough." shouted Didier, "About twenty metres … and in the shoulder."

Olivier grunted his acknowledgement, and did his best to estimate twenty metres. It was agony to try to squeeze his blistered finger around the trigger. He took aim. He found it impossible to keep his arm still. He grasped his wrist with his other hand. Still it shook. In the distance he heard the steady chug of the approaching train. Despite the freezing weather, sweat was pouring into his eyes. He felt sure his heart would burst. It was now or never. With a deep breath, he summoned his last reserves of daring. He closed his eyes and fired. Didier collapsed with a piercing yelp.

Olivier remembered his orders, and headed straight back to the signal box. He was climbing the steps, as Guillaume lowered himself from the roof.

"Put the gun away," hissed Guillaume. "Now don't forget the signal sequence-three green, one amber, three times over. Last part. You can do this."

After a quick handshake and a nod of approval, Guillaume thrust the paint back into the satchel. He loped off down the track, gazing approvingly at the re-set points, where the track split to head north west or north east. He followed the north westerly track, towards the cutting through the woods.

The distant sound was louder now. The long gradient out of Veziers had been negotiated. The train was picking up speed. A shrill blast on the whistle indicated that it was approaching the signal box. Olivier had done his job.

As he entered the cutting, he smiled to himself. Hundreds of trees which had fringed the embankments on either side had been cut down to make attacks more difficult. Painting ten of them on either side of the tracks had been the hard part. Hard, but not impossible. His hip was aching and the journey of no more than six hundred yards had seemed to take for ever. The thundering noise from behind left him with little choice. He flung himself into the undergrowth, the earth shaking as the train clattered past. He counted at least ten of the low, flat wagons. An unexpected bounty.

The last wagon passed. He set about turning over the logs so that the luminous paint was visible. His hip ached more and more as he heaved each one over, the painted side uppermost. He mopped his brow. He cursed his hip. Eventually, it was done. He scrambled up the embankment and waited. He scanned the sky, listening for the low roar. It didn't take long.

✳ ✳ ✳

It was only the third time that Dieter Riedel had driven the train along this route. But he knew something was wrong. There wasn't a cutting so soon after the signal box, and neither was there a stretch of flat track, leading towards the bridge he could see ahead, as the track curved to the left. Neither had they crossed a river on the previous two trips. The implications began to sink in. It was already too late.

The luminous paint led them straight to the target. The RAF Typhoons swooped low, the fusillade of bombs and rockets ripping into the wagons. His decision to jump was fatally delayed, as he froze in panic. Ahead, the track erupted, before disappearing into a cloud of dense, white smoke. Behind, the grinding sound of wagons being derailed was overlaid with the sound of dozens of huge girders spilling onto the side of the track. A direct hit on the boiler obliterated him in an inferno of scalding steam and flying metal.

From the cutting, Guillaume glanced up. The sky began to take on a lilac tinge as the fires spread. He didn't have much time. Finally, the last of the logs was in its original position. He disappeared into the woods.

Alone, beyond the signal box, Didier finally bled to death, his femoral artery severed by Olivier's panic stricken marksmanship.

✳ ✳ ✳

Unusually for Freuntz, he had found it difficult to concentrate since returning to his office. The pile of routine paperwork had almost been dealt with, but his mind was torn. How had the attack gone? How could the latest events be added to the file? Colluding with a possible informer? On the night of such a vital consignment? Dereliction of duty? It was fertile ground. But then it came.

The low hubbub was shattered. The teleprinters began to clatter. Voices were raised, commands were shrieked, telephones rang. Freuntz felt a profound sense of satisfaction. He allowed a minute or so to elapse before he ventured onto the balcony. He was about to join the frenzy below, undecided whether to compound matters by a series of ambiguous commands. There was no ambiguity about the figure bounding up the stairs.

"Where is he? Where is he?" screamed Gerhard, his voice a mixture of derision and calculating accusation. "Tonight? Tonight? Who is supposed to be in charge? We can round them up if we move. We have it narrowed down. But it's a matter of minutes. And then they are gone."

As Briedel appeared behind him, Freuntz motioned with his eyebrows and left Gerhard to berate him furiously. Briedel was in no mood to listen. He summoned the determination to push Gerhard to one side. He bounded into the frantic melee below. With a deep breath, he assumed command.

Briedel's reaction stung, but Gerhard couldn't afford to show it. For all his fury, his place was to return to his desk and await orders from his superiors. He smoothed down his uniform. He smoothed his hair. But his impotence re-ignited his sense of wrong. He turned to fix Freuntz with a baleful glare.

"We are going to have to talk."

# Chapter Twenty Five

The first clap of thunder startled Nicole, but left Wolfgang in the same deep sleep he had been enjoying since she released him. She had made him wait before untying him. The ritual was the highlight of the whole performance. She had felt his groaning would never end. These recent encounters had meant that the knife served a purpose that was both practical and relatively innocent. Given the nature of some of her clients, it could serve a more pragmatic, not to say threatening, purpose. It would remain close to hand.

The sound of the raindrops against the window helped drown out his rhythmic breathing. Once she had wrapped the silk dressing gown around her, and allowed her head to clear, she lifted the advent calendar down before gazing at it longingly. The approach of Christmas both excited and saddened her.

It excited the part of her that still sentimentalised the event, even after four years of war. Indeed, it may have added to its emotional charge, the urge for a return to normality a natural and human reaction to the abnormal circumstances she and so many others were living through. But it also played to the melancholy facet of her personality, as it forced her to confront the fact that she had never had the 'normal', family centred celebrations familiar to so many. She couldn't wait to start opening it.

"I've been watching you." he whispered, as he slipped beside her. "Always a special time, and these just add to the excitement.

Or they did when I was growing up. No, I suppose they still do." he added, allowing his voice to trail away. She was surprised at this suggestion of genuine intimacy, in contrast to the perfunctory, often mundane, conversations they usually enjoyed.

"It's really beautiful. Did you make it yourself?" he continued, closely scrutinising the windows, delicately decorated on small squares of embossed paper. They all featured a series of traditional festive images, simple in origin, sophisticated in their artistry.

"You have some surprising depths. Never had you down as the sentimental type... all your own work though?"

Nicole nodded briefly in acknowledgement, before expanding on her designs and their symbolism. He paid dutiful attention, gently stroking her hair as she described the illustrations yet to be opened.

"No religion for me... but my mother made me go a few times with Aunty Mimi when I was little. Felt she was doing the right thing I suppose, because she was certainly no Christian, if you heard the things she used to say about people. I've been told she had a foul mouth, a really foul mouth, but I think there was something deep in her that hoped the stuff about sinners who repent being the most welcome. And there is definitely something magic about the night before...wondering if he would come."

To her surprise, he responded with his own story. "I had one too, more basic than yours though. No wonder, with my father. A real hard man, a miner...hard...hard. He thought if he showed his softer side normally, it meant he was weak. That would never do. No, behind my windows- verses, verses from the Bible. And I had to learn them. No chance. The more he beat me for not knowing them, the more I refused. Thought he could beat it into me. Not much of an argument for religion, is it?"

Determined to exploit this sudden vulnerability, Nicole pressed on.

"You will never guess what the last one is for, for Christmas Day?" He feigned deep thought, with the semblance of a knowing smile, so she decided to put him out of his misery.

"A rabbit. That's right, a rabbit. When I was four...our last Christmas..." Her voice began to waver, "My mother was convinced that having a pet would give me something to care for…maybe she had some kind of feeling … a premonition, is that the word? We wouldn't have another Christmas together. I'm sure she knew. When I burst into tears, she thought it was happiness and gratitude. But what did we sell in our butchers shop? Rabbits!"

The revelation was followed by an awkward pause. Wolfgang eventually responded.

"Similar for me. When was that? '23? Christ, things were bad. The present I remember, and it is easy to remember because I hardly got any, but these… a brand new pair of football boots… I mean new…even a stamp cost millions of marks back then. We had just started a team and he wanted me to be the best, no matter what it cost. And it did cost."

"On Christmas Eve, it started blowing a blizzard and we couldn't play any more…about 4-30…and as I came round the corner…the pawn shop van was there and they were about to drive off. I waited until they had gone, and when I went in, our living room was bare… not that we had much…. all that was left was two wooden chairs and this little table…bare flag floors. He had pawned the lot to buy them. When I got up on Christmas morning…"

By now, aware that these revelations were imposing an emotional toll, she slowly began to stroke the ridged scar tissue at the base of his skull.

"He had disappeared. But at half past nine he suddenly came in. He had a big branch of a pine tree which he had hacked off, and then he stuck it in the coal bucket. The smell of pines was just magical…and he sat on the chair and watched me open the parcel. I never really saw him happy…. but that was as close as it got…and you know what? It was absolutely bitter that day. We hardly had any coal in the coal bucket, and once we had burned the coal, he threw the 'Christmas Tree' onto the fire as well, and disappeared up to bed. It wasn't even noon."

Silence fell before a sudden outburst indicated that this period of reminiscence would be short lived. Now was the time to bring her knowledge about 'Alain' into play. Too late.

"Jews… they owned all the pawn shops those blood suck…"

His well-rehearsed rant was stopped dead in its tracks by a furious knocking on the door.

"It is Briedel. Come quick, we have them."

✣ ✣ ✣

As they approached the yards, Gerhard was torn. On the one hand there was a smug satisfaction that he had got the information as a result of his own endeavours. Information was power. It would enable him to patronise Wolfgang, but only up to a point. On the other hand, he was furious with himself. Not getting Uncle Charles in, as soon as he had heard about him, had proved to be a mistake. As was only going through the motions with Pierre Navanne. His instinct didn't usually let him down. On that crucial occasion it had.

He was already calculating how documentation on the two could be slanted to his own advantage. That would have to wait, though, until the third was suffering in custody. He had expected more from Uncle Charles, but the mere threat of more pain, only a little more, had produced the decisive result he craved.

He emphasised to Meyerling the importance of approaching as sedately as possible, so as not to advertise their intent. It was already too late. The fact that Charles was not in the canteen, as arranged, had alerted Raymond. He busied himself by the rubbish bins. He maintained a wide field of vision across the yards, whilst remaining out of sight himself.

He watched as the car pulled up. Four plain clothes men bounded up the steps. Two of them were familiar from their regular presence in the canteen. Once they were inside, Raymond headed for the main gate at a brisk pace. He briefly interspersed spells of shadow boxing, determined to maintain his image- nonchalant, idiosyncratic,

Freuntz was already at the gate. His seniority counted. He nodded to the troops on guard. Raymond strode past. The orders were to wait in the yard for Wolfgang, so that was what he intended to do. He saw Raymond head up the cobbled street. He pondered what was in the mind of the old man. How could he think he would escape?

As he watched, almost wistfully, four burly figures charged towards him. They were already panting, the pursuit hardly begun. They were about to pass through the gates. The familiar Mercedes screeched to a halt.

Freuntz was there in an instant. A furious row erupted on the pavement about who had seniority and what the tactics should be, Gerhard, determined not to be deprived of his triumph. The two stood chest to chest, eyes blazing, Gerhard the more calculating, Wolfgang the less coherent, more manic. Gerhard realised who had seniority, but was prepared to wait no longer. He gestured to his men and they resumed the chase,

As he saw Wolfgang's hand move towards his holster, Freuntz intervened.

"Quick, I know where he is headed, believe me. Those donkeys will never catch him at that speed. Come with me, there is a quicker way. I know where he is headed. To the bridge. Come on."

Still seething at the public challenge to his authority, Wolfgang slowly moved his hand away. After a blistering glance in the general direction of Gerhard, already slowing to a brisk walk, as the steep hill took its toll, he turned to set off after Freuntz. Freuntz was already making the mental calculations necessary for Raymond to at least prolong his freedom.

He realised that there was a limit to how long his deception could be maintained. A couple of deliberate wrong turnings were the most he could expect to get away with. They emerged onto the Rue de Lyons, the bridge silhouetted in the watery winter sun. Freuntz had to look twice. But there he was, already into his shadow boxing, his red beret perched proudly on his head.

Raymond then began a laboured attempt to mount the parapet. He was finding it difficult to lift his leg high enough. From the corner of his eye he spotted the four figures, coming down the slope towards him, desperately trying not to reveal their intentions by running full tilt. It was all the incentive he needed. With a final heave he was upright on the parapet. The four closed in on him.

The billowing clouds of white smoke, belched out by the approaching goods train, threatened to engulf him, Wolfgang took aim. Both shots whistled past Raymond, now balanced precariously on the parapet. He half turned to see where they had come from. The four were now running, shouting something he could not possibly hear. The thundering sound from the tracks below got louder.

Wolfgang took aim again. With a defiance which was poignant in its purpose, and beautiful in its execution, Raymond straightened up. He saluted elaborately. Then, with the grace of an acrobat, he launched himself into a perfect back somersault, disappearing into the clouds of smoke as the train emerged beneath the bridge.

Freuntz and Wolfgang dashed to the bridge as the smoke began to clear. Gerhard and Mayerling peered over the parapet as the last wagon disappeared slowly up the gradient. Raymond lay beside the tracks, his body contorted into a shape only made possible by the force with which his spine had been severed when he landed on the chimney of the train.

As they peered onto the track below, the folly of their rivalry registered first with Gerhard.

"We had him! We had him!" He was careful to keep his criticism general rather than specific, communal rather than personal.

"There's never more than three in a cell. Never! Only one knows the next cell, how to link up. He was the link in the three, he knew who was next, but now, now… We have the other two, we have them, but now…."

Fury was slowly being replaced by frustration for Gerhard. For Wolfgang the exertions of the pursuit, followed by the escape from his clutches of such a prized catch, now extracted its toll.

A piercing pain shot from his chest to the back of his skull. In an instant his florid complexion had become ashen. He collapsed limply to the ground.

With a callous indifference only righteous indignation or blind rage can produce, Gerhard and his three colleagues turned on their heels and headed back up the slope. Their response was noted by a distraught Briedel, as he began to administer first aid.

✽ ✽ ✽

For Nicole, looking through her box, her sole connection with her past, always produced one of two responses. She ran her fingers over the cards, their suggestion of what might have been, had circumstances been different, tantalising, yet depressing. The enigmatic nature of the messages fed a resentment which fuelled her defiant nature. On the other hand, it left her tearful with regret about the brevity of the relationship with her mother, precious moments whose rarity imbued an extra, more poignant potency. Even now, the box had a musky smell which intensified the longing.

Her conversation with Wolfgang had left her in a more positive mood, not only because of the pleasant surprise his reminiscences had provided. It indicated that her experience was not unique to her alone. Although he hadn't said anything directly, she surmised that his upbringing had been as fragmented and unhappy as hers.

Her mind was wandering, trying once again to fill in the gaps. She got out the letter from Aunty Mimi, buried as always beneath the other items, the only tangible links to her upbringing. She lingered on the Bordeaux post mark and fleetingly wondered if it was actually as exotic as she imagined it to be. She knew she shouldn't, but she was drawn inexorably towards the final two pages.

The death of her mother always reduced her to tears, but it was the account of the rape which incensed her. The mismatch of wealth and privilege, when combined with its brutal exhibition of contempt, left her cheeks drained of colour and her fists clenched in fury. The fact that the perpetrator had escaped scot free prised opened the emotional wounds even wider.

It was twenty minutes before she lifted her head from the table and a further five before she wiped her eyes.

✲ ✲ ✲

The three of them were hung from the signal gantry, under which the goods trains passed as they approached the gradient out of Veziers. Prior to being thrust outwards, as the noose tightened, his whimpering elicited only contempt for Charles from his captors. In contrast, the stoical demeanour which Pierre adopted suggested a withering contempt for them, and generated a grudging admiration for his defiance. Raymond simply dangled like a marionette, some of whose strings were broken.

All trains were halted, the workforce lined up along the tracks below. All were left alone with their thoughts, before shuffling back to work, accompanied by a chorus of shrieking whistles and hissing steam. As Gerhard watched the corpses twist in the wind, he was forced to suppress a thought which had appeared more frequently in recent weeks. This was a policy of diminishing returns.

More worryingly, he couldn't think of an alternative.

# Chapter Twenty Six

As had been predicted, the day had started with a light drizzle. But heavy rain was now sweeping the main street of Chemeny, the gusting wind adding to its unpredictable whims. For Heinrich Posner it confirmed the sense of remaining in the cabin of the requisitioned coal lorry, opposite the Café Lafayette. The café blended perfectly with the rest of the street, indeed the rest of the town. All life and colour had long since been leeched away by the privations of war time austerity.

He remembered the urgency with which Gerhard had emphasised that he must not be spotted, his stare fixed, his tone menacing. This was sure to be just as futile an exercise as the others. The wind moaned, the rain rattled the windscreen, he wondered how he could achieve anything of worth. Two days pounding the pavements in the rain didn't appeal at all. The office job back in Orleans had its attractions.

The raindrops which cascaded down the windscreen made visibility difficult. If Freuntz was a suspect, why did he sit so prominently, visible to all from road or pavement? After all, the only other customers were an elderly couple, both deep in their own thoughts, oblivious to each other. He could have sat anywhere.

He certainly lingered over lunch, and time was now dragging. Freuntz seemed determined to linger just as long over his newspaper. The only other customer was a burly figure, sat at right angles at the next table, also determined to linger over his lunch. The risk of revealing himself in attempt to get closer ensured that long range observation would suffice for now. Orders were orders. His predecessor, Volker Reissen, had disobeyed orders.

He was now battling the Partisans in Yugoslavia.

"Has the old man set up the account?" asked Freuntz, the paper obscuring his face. Guillaume nodded once, before adding, "He thinks your forgeries are as good as his."

"How is he holding up?"

Freuntz lowered the paper and knew that a pause in the conversation would follow. Guillaume gave a barely perceptible shake of the head, but his face provided the answer.

"Since Didier..." he responded as he raised the soup spoon to his mouth, "He is a risk. Guilt before...." He blew on his soup in exaggerated fashion. "But now... doesn't care. May have to cut him loose." Another pause, another sip of soup. "Loves the danger, the bank, impersonating a German officer." Another pause. "It's like a drug."

With the paper obscuring his face, Freuntz deftly removed the bundle of notes from his pocket and placed them by his plate. "Enough for two deposits. Wait for the date, though."

Guillaume bent even lower towards his bowl. With equal deftness he removed the flat, white boxes from his inside pocket. He placed them behind the sugar bowl. Freuntz arched his eyebrows.

"Valsamol?"

Another almost imperceptible nod of confirmation. "How much do you know?" Freuntz shrugged. Guillaume began to pull the bread apart. He had to prolong the time available to brief Freuntz.

"Stimulant. Very powerful. British. Convoy crews. Battle fatigue. Keeps you awake." Another sip of the soup. "Side effects though. Any characteristic, any. Magnifies them." A tear of the bread. "Brave? You'll fight the Russian army. Scared? You won't get out of bed. Suspicious? You'll argue with yourself in the mirror. Wary? Not trust your own mother. A few of your boys in Italy got hold of some. Fourteen of them shot dead. Three corporals. Just went berserk."Another pause.

"And one more thing. Some of them took three or four at once... made them ... more virile... go all night... and I mean all night. Officers tried to get them all in ... but no chance."

"The signal box?" Freuntz asked

Guillaume nodded in satisfaction. He reflected on the role the tablets had played in his efforts to deceive the Germans and obscure the course of events there.

"The British have dropped us others. They send us all kinds of stuff to try out. You would be surprised."

"These will do for now."

With that, Freuntz lifted the bundle of notes before replacing it in exactly the same place. The mime complete, he pulled on his trilby hat. As he squeezed past Guillaume, already calling for the proprietor, he swept the boxes into his pocket and headed out into the gathering storm.

In the cabin, Posner was wondering what he could possibly write. An uneventful lunch. Afterwards, the man sat by Freuntz was joined by a wiry figure who had almost been knocked over as he dashed across the road to escape the deluge. With his hat pulled low, it was impossible to identify his face. Was there a suggestion of a moustache? He couldn't be sure. He had seemed to take ages to regain his breath. But so what?

✵ ✵ ✵

The ache in Wolfgang's skull had dulled to some degree. But it had been replaced by something which nagged at an even more profound level. He had adjusted to the fact that his condition was terminal. His equanimity had surprised him, especially given the repeated disruption to the project. Who could he rely on? That was what had him sweating through the lonely hours before dawn broke.

The sheets itched. He yelled for the nurse. She scurried to his bedside. Commanding others. It was ingrained. He hadn't really needed the water. He resumed his contemplation. Gerhard and his cohorts were clearly not up to the task of seeing 'Whuffy' and the 'Revenge Weapon' through to completion. They probably thought the same about him. The ever loyal Briedel was just that- loyal. No chance of penetrating insights there. And Freuntz? The doubts were growing. He was to blame for the fiasco at the bridge. Why hadn't he stopped him firing those shots? He hadn't known the way, as he said he did. How would he know anyway?

He's losing his focus, Wolfgang strove to convince himself. Too keen on visits to Marianne. Diluting his loyalty and belief in the cause? He certainly seemed to be away from the office more than ever. Procedures and attention to detail, he did have his uses, but not for this one. No, if the project was to succeed, he would have to do it himself. That bit he could cope with. Wolfgang attempted to drag himself upright.

"Nurse!"

His needs attended to, he prepared to study the maps and weather forecasts. He forced himself to study them for the tenth time that day, but was soon losing interest. Freuntz entered the ward, accompanied by a doctor pleading forlornly that the patient should not be over burdened.

Freuntz removed his overcoat and concluded the pleasantries. Wolfgang seemed even more agitated than normal, a considerable feat given the copious amounts of medication he was being prescribed. He wasted no time

"They know nothing, nothing. I can't be kept in here. I feel much better than before I came in, so it has been like a rest home in one sense. But look at all this," at which he swept his arm towards the piles of documents which covered the floor and side table. "You know me, paper work." He gave a prolonged grimace. "That's why I need you. But they keep piling it on. And to make matters worse, I can't stay awake for any length of time, so when I wake up there is another pile. It makes my head ache, even more. Real shooting pains. And so it goes on. I've asked for something to keep me awake but they won't listen… say it's too risky. But they don't know what's at stake. If they don't sort it, I'm going to sign myself out."

Freuntz listened in his usual dutiful manner and waited for the frustration to evaporate. Eventually it did. Wolfgang then began the process of bringing him up to date with developments. He saved the most crucial information until last.

"New Year's Day. Can you believe it? New Year's Day? They've got to be ready to launch." He gripped the table. He was face to face with Freuntz. "New Year's Day? Can you fucking credit it?" He relaxed his grip and sank back in to the pillows. His breathing became more measured.

"A sacred mission. That is what it is. Oh yes. Sacred. And I have been charged with it. The preservation of The Reich. A life's work, the culmination. The mass destruction of London is imminent. Now we will change the mind set of the British. We will bring them to heel. That, or reduce them to rubble. Not before time. Now we'll see how keen the Americans are to land. Incinerated on the beaches. And all from a hundred miles away." Freuntz watched Wolfgang closely, studying his reaction. He nodded, and began his response slowly.

"That's why I'm here. To give Berlin a military perspective, not a medical one. You know what I mean, of course. Err on the side of daring. They- we- need you back… fully functioning… in charge… if we are going to see it through. Now, look at these."

Freuntz reached into his inside pocket and slipped the box of tablets beneath the documents. As Freuntz described their properties, he couldn't help but notice how Wolfgang's expression began to lighten. He described their origins, emphasised their benefits, but excluded any reference to their side effects.

The doctor reappeared, tapping his watch. Freuntz reassured Wolfgang, as plausibly as he could, that he would soon be back in the fray. He put on his overcoat and bade farewell.

Wolfgang could barely contain his impatience. But once the doctor disappeared, he swallowed two of the tablets and forced himself to look at the maps again. This was his strength, his specialism, even. His grasp of terrain and topography had enabled him to sum up tactical opportunities in an instant, on so many occasions in Russia. Promotion to the General Staff had been mooted. No substitute for walking the ground though, he accepted.

He didn't know whether he was imagining it or not, but studying the maps suddenly didn't seem so onerous. He forced himself to focus on the area north and east of Veziers, dominated as they were by the arteries of the war effort, the railway lines. It was no use, the tracks were well known to the RAF, that much was clear. He tipped the maps onto the floor and ripped open the buff envelopes. His heart began to sink. His mood swung. He began to doubt the potency of the tablets.

He gave the latest, more detailed maps a cursory glance. Pessimism threatened to overwhelm him. But suddenly, as if a blindfold had been removed, the possibilities began to reveal themselves. The mines had been shut for over ten years, but the network of cuttings, sidings and branch lines criss crossed the area, connecting the arteries, just like capillaries in the body, he reflected. And there it was. The answer.

Ten minutes of feverish calculation then ensued. The potency of the tablets confirmed in his mind, his mood brightened and the practicalities were assessed. He eventually allowed a smile to play across his lips as he flopped back on the pillows, elated not exhausted. It was imperative to walk the ground tomorrow.

After a couple of minutes, his pulse began to return to normal. He quickly swallowed another two tablets.

✼ ✼ ✼

Even though it was not yet mid-day, the clouds banking in the west were making it seem like dusk. Wolfgang could barely contain his glee. If the forecasts were correct, it would be one squall after another for the next two weeks. Perfect. Low cloud ceilings and swirling mist were manna from Heaven. Deterrence of air raids was even better than trying to shoot them down. His request for extra anti-aircraft batteries would be met only partially, he was certain. But even a few extra could inflict sufficient damage on the RAF, render more raids prohibitively expensive. The window of opportunity was priceless.

A forest of buddleias sprouted from the base of the middle of three towering slag heaps which loomed away to his right, their branches already bending in the wind. To his left, four rusting wagons, still full of shiny cobs of coal from the final shift, thirteen years earlier. They bore eloquent testimony to the mineral wealth which had underpinned the prosperity of the area for so long. Absent slates left the Bath House open to the elements, all its windows smashed. Towering above it all was the skeletal framework of the pit head winding gear, its huge wheels rotating impotently in the strengthening wind. He had the map in his mind. Just as he had hoped, things began to fall into place.

Beneath a mat of couch grass, ferns, and moss he could now see the outline ahead, the sleepers rotting but intact, the rails absent. He began to pace out the distance, just short of two hundred metres, he reckoned, if his estimate was right. His stride quickened in anticipation. There they were. Despite the abundant vegetation, the tracks could be seen to start again. Mottled, rusty, but clearly visible. Rusty- but intact.

He immediately began the calculations in his head. Two hundred metres or so, one rail twelve metres, ten sleepers for each pair. Two tons of gravel for ballast would be the maximum. Redeploy fifty forced labourers from Whuffy, six skilled men to supervise, one week maximum, he rapidly concluded. Especially if there were no air raids.

He couldn't resist a skip. Even this slight exertion took its toll and in no time at all he was panting, a stabbing pain shooting into the base of his skull. He loosened the top button of his greatcoat, slowed his pace and began to draw up his plans. Back to the office, nothing committed to paper and inform only those he felt needed to know. They could be counted on the fingers of one hand.

None of them in Veziers.

# Chapter Twenty Seven

The precise details of what had actually happened were hazy. Something about a relapse had been as much as Briedel, whose normally taciturn demeanour had bordered on the surly on this occasion, was willing to divulge. His eyes fixed firmly ahead, the journey had otherwise passed in silence. But for Nicole, his silence could not diminish the thrill of being chauffeur driven in a Mercedes. Even the sun was trying to break through after days of constant downpours.

Eventually, they turned off the road and into the drive. She was ready to be impressed. Once the avenue of lime trees came to an end, and the house was revealed in all its mellow sandstone finery, she was.

As soon as Briedel had slammed the car door behind her, with a derisory grunt, she was eager to take in her surroundings. It was plain that the mansion, as she thought of it, was undergoing a rapid transformation. Engineers were laying phone lines, new furniture was lined up at the bottom of the steps, and uniformed staff, both military and medical, were bustling in and out. Fresh paint was being liberally applied by a group of elderly men, obviously unfit for the physical rigours of the forced labour programmes.

Still unsure of why she was there, Nicole swallowed hard and repeated her motto, "Own it. Look like you belong." Once through the doors, she thrust back her shoulders, but forced herself not to stare too much. She searched for Wolfgang. Rooms off the ground floor were obviously due to become offices. Medical staff seemed to be confined to an annexe of some kind off to the left.

She was determined to maintain her façade of sophistication, as she lingered over the removal of her gloves, finger by finger. She surveyed the crowd. She could tell from the military uniforms that these facilities, whatever they were, would be confined to senior officers only. Unsure whether to park herself on the elegantly patterned chaise longue, she opted to wait by the biggest grandfather clock she had ever seen.

She was beginning to panic when, from behind her, a haze of perfume which she knew must be expensive, enveloped her. Three elegantly dressed women sashayed past. They homed in on their targets. They draped themselves around the officers, before disappearing upstairs

So that is how it is, she thought. She saw him descend the staircase. He brusquely elbowed three of his colleagues to one side, as he reached out to grab her arm. He immediately led her towards the staircase. Being glad to see her was one thing, but he had never been like this before. His eyes had a slightly dazed look to them, his face was flushed, his breathing rapid and shallow.

As he led her forcibly up the staircase, his garbled conversation was interspersed by rasping gasps. "Impressive isn't it. Better than the last one. Direct hit, two weeks ago… had only just left, ten minutes earlier."

The dust which covered the wooden floor indicated that the house had been empty for some time. The colour in the paintings which adorned the walls was faded. She had no time to develop her train of thought any further. He thrust her into the last room on the corridor, slammed the door behind her, and immediately began to paw at her clothes.

✵ ✵ ✵

At almost the same time, Olivier had concluded his latest performance at the Chemeny branch of La Banque du Nord. He could barely contain the relish with which he had embraced his new role.

Bruno Briedel. It had a ring to it.

※ ※ ※

By mid-afternoon he was finally asleep, his frantic performances having finally taken their toll. He was snoring deeply. Three times, he had been like a man possessed. That look though, that was what lingered in her memory. His eyes had bulged continuously since they had first embraced.

As she watched his chest rise and fall, she was finally able to reflect on the exchange of intimacy they had been able to manage, before their last manic session. It turned out that they had more in common than she could have imagined.

Nicole's revelations about her mother were based on Aunty Mimi's letter, a letter she knew off by heart. They had been delivered in a halting and tentative manner, a mixture of emotion and uncertainty about what his response might be. She hadn't needed to worry.

"Sounds like she was a whore as well."

Nicole had been temporarily puzzled by the "as well", but he had ploughed on. "She was blonde as well. She had a mouth on her and she put it about … she humiliated my father, humiliated him. He was simple. In his tastes I mean. No, he wasn't simple, like in stupid; he was shrewd in lots of ways. No, not stupid … but not bright in a school type way. Mining was all he was probably fit for, to be honest. The thing about miners, about miners above all, well apart from us in The S.S.… is loyalty. That was all he wanted, and what he didn't get from her. He was hard, but you know what, he treated her like a queen. He could have smashed her to a pulp any time he wanted, but he saw himself as a cut above that. That's not how a man, a real man, behaves. No, he would never hit a woman. She seemed to know this, and instead of counting her blessings, she hurt him even more, in a way she knew he couldn't deal with… with words. They hurt more than any punches. Scars on your mind last longer than any bruise or cut."

"No, the only way he ever seemed to be able to stop her– even if only for a few seconds- was when he was sneering at her about 'The Bastard'. He knew that hurt her, even if only a little. It was something to do with what had gone on when she was a teenager. The night she left, he repeated it over and over, but somehow she wasn't as bothered as before. She knew she had won. I mean a fucking nigger. That was the clincher. He went downhill fast after that."

"You know what, once you've seen a woman behave like that…" His eyes were finally beginning to droop, "it affects how you treat women as …"

Nicole replayed the conversation a couple of times. An opportunity was presenting itself. This time she would make her point about Alain more forcibly. That would have to wait, though. She stood briefly by the window, surveying the scene in the courtyard below, still the centre of frenzied activity as the light began to fade. She sighed deeply, as if prolonged inhalation would somehow make the refinement of these new surroundings a permanent part of her. Somewhere deep inside she believed she was destined to live like this on a permanent basis. Surely, this was what all the hardship was leading her towards?

All of the furniture was expensive, but old, she guessed- fifty years or more? The wallpaper was heavily embossed, but dull. The crumpled eiderdown had an exotic floral design, faded by the constant exposure to sunlight since the house was last inhabited.

The wardrobes smelt of mothballs, even before she opened the door. To her surprise, its contents were set out as if their owner was about to reappear at any moment. Ready, apart from the fact that they were covered in dust, and were even more dated than the furniture. Nevertheless, she reflected that not only had their owner been a man of some means, but he also possessed a meticulous concern for order. Three identical pairs of black shoes, six identical white shirts with wing collars, four identical, heavy woollen suits told the story of a life lived according to convention and respectability. A pillar of the community, no doubt.

She closed the door and pursed her lips, pondering her next move. The notion that she belonged in these exalted surroundings had aroused her curiosity. She resolved to investigate the two chests of drawers The smaller one contained little of note other than socks, gloves, scarves and several pairs of spectacles. Undeterred, she moved towards the larger chest, as Wolfgang began to snore in earnest.

To her delight, the first drawer was full of loose photographs, apparently unworthy of placing in an album. Landscapes, gardens and snaps of the house at various stages of construction, were heaped together with family group poses from as long ago as 1892.

Who were these people? Was one the owner of the suits? An age of elegance and formality, earnest expressions maintained at all costs- a different era altogether- seemed to be captured. As she let her imagination wander, she opened the drawer below, and to her delight there were more than a dozen photograph albums, each dated and labelled.

Proud parents, with first one, then two children, both boys, stared back from the pages. The one which stood out showed the proud father pointing to what was obviously an expensive saloon, in which the two boys were sat, hands on the steering wheel, their heads barely visible above the dashboard.

The next album had a more functional purpose, recording the development of the family business. Some were taken inside the factory, and captured the workforce in typically rigid poses, the nobility of labour epitomised in the quiet dignity of their expressions. Others showed the workers assembled for group photographs in the factory yard, the owner sat proudly in the centre of the front row, the date displayed in ornate print on a board between his feet.

She couldn't help but notice how few men there were in the photographs after 1914. She started to wonder where the factory might be, and whether it was still standing. After all, the house was.

She continued to linger over each, prolonging the tactile pleasure provided by the high quality paper. Suddenly, her attention was brought into sharp focus as she studied the group photographed in the yard in 1919. The old man wasn't there but a younger man was, a young man who, even all these years later, had the hangdog look which indicated he was much younger than the camera suggested. For a moment she felt a vicarious sadness. But only for a moment. As she flipped forward to find the photograph for 1921, there were now two figures in suits in the centre of the front row. Her curiosity was awakened.

The next photograph showed the two men from the centre of the photograph, shaking hands with employees who were retiring. Her eyes narrowed and her pulse began to race. The lop sided grin, the lustrous head of hair, parted slightly left of centre, the possibilities began to flood her mind. She stared out of the window briefly, before forcing herself to study the album once more. The competing emotions of dread, curiosity and fury threatened to overwhelm her. She gasped.

And there it was. The photograph showed an intricate wrought iron sign, which had obviously just been installed above the entry to the yard. The words 'Corporation Lafarge 1923', made an unmistakeable statement of entrepreneurial faith in the future. In the yard the employees were gathered, a mixture of the nonplussed and the exultant. In the foreground, exuding a conceit which resonated down the years, the elegantly dressed figure stood with his arms outstretched in triumph. The expensive suit, the moustache, the spats, and finally the cravat, all portrayed an image of affluence. But it was the rings- heavy, expensive, one per finger.

The affluence, or otherwise, of this self-satisfied figure from the past was of no concern to her. She let the album fall to the floor. She sat, shaking, on the edge of the bed. Her head spun, her face was ashen, her eyes reddened.

There was a fierce knock on the door.

"Come, it is time."

"Two minutes," she replied, desperately playing for time to regain her composure. She flung on her clothes, scribbled a hasty note to Wolfgang, and fled down the stairs.

The astonishment, which had turned into an incoherent fury as she dressed, was rapidly usurped by a forensic calculation of how the wrong could finally be avenged. The journey back to Veziers passed in complete silence, Briedel's simmering disdain palpable. She couldn't care less.

By the time he held the door open for her, all that remained were the fine details.

✵ ✵ ✵

Her opportunity came three nights later. A perfunctory performance for two of her regulars had induced a mood which matched the weather. As she descended the stairs, she was beginning to wonder if she would ever assuage her pain, a pain kept raw by constantly reacquainting herself with the contents of Aunt Mimi's letter.

Suddenly he was by the bar, a figure transformed from the self-abasing shell she had taken pity on so recently. The same suit, the same shirt and tie, but exuding an undeniable brio, a self-confidence bordering on arrogance. It was the arrogance which fuelled her desire. His shoulders were back, his jaw was jutting, and there was an unusual glint in his eye. His grin looked even more rakish than normal, indicating that he knew something nobody else was privy to.

She strode towards him, at the same instant as he started towards her. He was about to speak when she noticed Mayerling over his shoulder. She briefly indicated that he would have to wait.

"Where's your boss?" she whispered.

Mayerling pointed at his watch and replied, "He's already twenty minutes late."

"If he does arrive, send him up. I will have something special for him. Tell him to knock, the door will be locked."

She fixed her grin and returned. By now he was stroking his moustache, anticipating what lay ahead. He took her hand. She couldn't help but notice how flushed his complexion was. "Nicole, I have something for you, you won't be disappointed. No, not like last time."

"Alain, I have something for you also, and you won't be disappointed," she said breathlessly, laying extra emphasis on his name. Mysterious and alluring. He resisted the temptation to purr.

She led him up the stairs. The beads of sweat were starting to trickle down his forehead. She turned to glance at him. Just like a racehorse, sweating up before the big race, she thought. A stallion possibly, given the rabid energy he was exuding. She savoured what lay ahead.

Outside her door, she took his hand, tracing her other hand over the rings. In turn, he took her hand and traced it over his groin. He looked expectantly towards her. She knew she was supposed to be impressed. She obliged by pursing her lips. He began to sigh.

"New life Nicole, a new life."

Once inside, she took the initiative. She would prolong the parts she wanted to prolong, but not yet. He undressed with a frantic urgency, whilst she was more languid. The counterpoint of their desires added a delicious piquancy she wanted to prolong..

Having removed her dress, she extracted the two jade ribbons from her box and mimed provocatively what awaited him. This was an occasion for the special lingerie, she had resolved, and she disappeared into the bathroom to get changed. She licked her finger, and placed it on his lips.

His suit had been placed with immaculate care on the chair as usual, and the handkerchief was protruding prominently once again. The mixture of recklessness and routine would have intrigued her on other occasions. There was no mistaking his readiness to perform. He would have to wait. The process of placing a ring on each of her fingers was one to be undertaken with relish.

✣ ✣ ✣

Down below in the bar, Gerhard had arrived and was deep in conversation with Mayerling. Once he had removed his dripping overcoat he worked out the sequence of events. He sent Mayerling off to find Posner. He smoothed down his hair, composed himself, and began to walk purposefully up the stairs. Not too fast now, he told himself. This is one to savour.

He approached the top of the stairs. From behind him, footsteps, heavy ones. He turned. It was Wolfgang, jaw clenched, completely self-absorbed, his stare vacant. Gerhard was still slightly ahead. He speeded up and arrived at the door first, determined not to cede his place in the limelight.

At the same moment, Nicole emerged from the bathroom. She entwined the ribbons; she swayed her hips, purring. There would be little time for the magic to work. The argument escalated outside. Her carefully calibrated plan for revenge would be redundant if she didn't act.

As his eyes darted towards the door, Alain was equally aware that his own plans were in ruins. He was the focus of the argument outside, and his time was limited. Nicole's face was now contorted in fury. She dropped the ribbons, clenched her fists and moved towards him. The briefest expression of bemusement flashed across his face. In an instant he had decided.

He grabbed the handkerchief, and bit down heavily upon the tablets he had sewn into the corner. The door was thrust open as the two rivals burst through. Nicole turned briefly to take in what was going on. She turned to resume her assault, but then realised that she would be deprived of vengeance. His body was shaking violently, his eyes were bulging. He was already foaming at the mouth.

Against a background of shrieked expletives, his paroxysms became more violent. But Nicole was not to be denied. She climbed astride his shuddering body. She savoured the moment. She stared into his eyes. She raised her fist to deliver justice for her mother. From behind, a strong arm gripped her wrist. She screeched as she wriggled to break free, but still tried to catch his dying words, each preceded by "So sorry." 'Sophie', 'Didier', 'Guillaume'.

It was over, his foam flecked lips were already turning blue, and she was dragged away.

It was Wolfgang who had deprived her of her revenge. As he enveloped her in a huge hug, he poured out how much he had missed her, how he couldn't keep away, and that if he had his way they would be together on a permanent basis, once his duties permitted.

Gerhard was aghast at such public, emotional outbursts, even more so when they came from Wolfgang. He was obviously indifferent to the practicalities of the investigation which needed to be undertaken, oblivious to protocol. Routine must be followed. Another botched investigation he fumed. Another contribution for the file, he consoled himself.

He tried to shut out the sickening sounds of mutual reassurance, as Mayerling and Posner finally arrived. The smell of bitter almonds told him the cause of death. The box of tablets could be analysed later, and the bank notes could go in the safe. The question of his identity was quickly solved, as the papers were spread out on the dressing table.

✡ ✡ ✡

Anne-Marie Ducasse was not used to visitors to their remote farm house, especially visitors who banged on her door with such force in the middle of the night. The banging became more frenzied. Her arthritis rendered the descent of the stairs both laborious and painful. Eventually, she released the third of the locks. They burst in.

The bombardment of demands increased in volume as Anne-Marie was reduced to a cowering mute. The bombardment came to an abrupt end as Alain appeared at the top of the stairs, wondering what the fuss was about.

# Chapter Twenty Eight

"We need to have that talk"

The urgent tone left Freuntz little option other than to break off from his phone call, indicating to Gerhard to sit down with a gesture which bordered on the dismissive, irritated by the fact that he hadn't had the courtesy to knock.

After some icy pleasantries, Gerhard took up the running. Freuntz couldn't help but notice his wan complexion, and concluded that the nature of whatever they were about to discuss was preying on his mind.

"I think that you will agree with me that the situation we face is a critical one. Where is your boss?" Freuntz pondered before responding.

"We haven't seen him since the …the fiasco at the café, where he… uhm… blundered into something you had set up, would that be a fair description?" The grimace rendered words superfluous.

"He is running things from the Lafarge place, direct line to Berlin, any instructions to us by courier. There's been a real clamp down, as you know. Whatever he is doing, it worked first time."

"If anything has worked, I prefer to think it is in spite of him, not because of him."

"The train did get through though, three British planes shot down, and the visibility was so bad. They must be desperate, flying so low in these conditions. Sitting ducks."

"Makes you wonder how they knew, though."

Freuntz knew full well how they knew, and had been mortified by the failure of the raid.

"There have been too many mishaps, too many attacks. It can't have been luck. It looks co-ordinated. The Resistance, they don't have the numbers if you ask me, nor the calibre, looking at those we have managed to get our hands on. Old men, has beens, 'never will bes', yet so much disruption. No it can't be them. Not without some inside help."

Freuntz weighed up the thrust of Gerhard's argument, and realised it was time to plant the idea, and ideas were never more effectively planted than when the listener wanted to believe them.

"He hasn't been the same since Russia. He was always a hot head, always willing to take risks. After all, that's what made him so successful. What's changed now, though, is the lack of calculation, risk against reward. He is more erratic, more unpredictable. You can't read him. He seems to think he can deliver the Revenge Weapon project on his own. Anyone else- even his own staff- he sees as a hindrance now. This latest secrecy. In some ways it fits the pattern, that's if you can have a pattern of unpredictability."

"Well, at the café he looked unhinged if you ask me. Again, a useful front. Now, let's look at the evidence, just some of it. This for instance." Gerhard brandished the file on Uncle Charles, fully embellished only that morning. "Look at the date. Ages ago, but he did nothing. Worked in the yards... and even more significantly, related to the blonde at Café Gasquet ... and Jewish as well. That alone should be enough. Remember the courtyard when we had them all lined up? Who was he talking to? This Alain character, who it turns out isn't Alain at all. We do know he was involved in forgery, the black market and counterfeit money, though. And what about the old man at the bridge? Another operation compromised by his apparent zeal."

"What you are saying is that he is a... a traitor?" Freuntz asked as querulously as possible, delighted that Gerhard was responding, just as he had predicted.

"I don't think we can see things any other way. This erratic behaviour, certainly makes it look like he is desperate to do something. But think about it, if you want to conceal that you are the traitor, make it look like you are doing all you can to reveal the real one. Puts the spotlight somewhere else doesn't it? Perfect."

"You do realize, don't you, what a risk you are taking, saying things like this?" Freuntz asked, before adding, "I have to say I agree with you, though. New Year's Day is the deadline, and we haven't got long. He could put everything at risk, so close and yet so far. What better time for treason?"

"The woman is the key," Gerhard asserted. "He is obsessed with her, but after the other night, she might be susceptible to someone else in uniform After all, she seems to go for older men. What about tonight?"

"Why not just pull her in?" Freuntz asked. Desperate to avoid such an outcome, given what she might reveal about their meetings, and especially Uncle Charles, Gerhard had his response prepared. As he was about to explain his thinking, he lent forward, his chest just above the desk, both hands clutching at his midriff.

"Give me a minute... just a minute. Gall bladder I think. I will be fine." His contorted expression indicated otherwise, as the sweat began to trickle down his forehead. Freuntz was about to call for help, as he thrust a glass of water towards the stricken Gerhard. He had been right, though. After a couple of minutes the faintest tinge of pink returned to his cheeks, and he resumed.

"Two reasons. Firstly, the names she supposedly heard. There are twelve Guillaumes in Veziers, and we've hauled them all in. Only three kept in for further investigation, and that's mainly for appearances sake. It could easily be part of a deception to distract us. But secondly, I think we will get more out of her by indirect means. You will also get more out of it," he added, hoping that this bait would be irresistible. His attempts to portray the image of a sophisticated man of the world were forlorn. Nevertheless, Freuntz allowed him to conclude.

"I believe she is very good. What about tonight?"

✳ ✳ ✳

The slow swelling of badly sung carols lent a maudlin air to The Café Gasquet. The teeming rain outside had a depressing effect on the customers, a few of whom attempted to create some festive cheer as their clothing steamed in front of the roaring fire, the only cheerful element in the darkened bar.

Freuntz had taken a while to work out how he might play this, the only certainty being that anything he did find out would not be relayed to Gerhard. The accounts of Olivier's final moments had been confused, and he needed to press her on what had actually happened.

Once he beckoned her over, he wasted little time in making the running, introducing himself as Wolfgang's right hand man. She wondered briefly why she had not seen him in there before, but quickly concluded that finding out might make things more interesting.

Having listened to him explain how limited his opportunities were, given the pressure of events as well as the volume of work Wolfgang loaded on to him, she realised he might be easy to keep interested, and hence help her deliver for Gerhard. Offer some of her special services and keep him coming back for more. She was impressed by his approach- blunt, even brusque- in contrast to so many who were uneasy in her company, if they were honest. Payment guaranteed them her attention, even if it was time limited.

The preliminary sparring over, Freuntz decided to get to what was the nub of the issue, as far as he was concerned.

"There were some last words, I believe, and that, even amongst all the yelling and groaning, you heard what they were."

"Straight in. You don't waste time, do you? She paused. "Yes, three names, and sorry, sorry, sorry all the time. You couldn't tell clearly, but there was no doubt. One of them was my mother…"

Freuntz was taken aback. "Your mother, how did he know her?"

"It goes back a long time. Some day I might tell you."

"One was the man shot at the signal box, and he's dead. Was there another?"

"Slow down, slow down. Usually all these questions come later."

Freuntz gave a half smile, a tacit admission that he was pressing too hard.

"Now," she resumed, "Anything you like in particular?"

Freuntz thrust his wrists towards her in the manner of a convict waiting to be handcuffed. Her eyes widened slightly at the sight of the angry red weals, which suggested his activities were both recent- and intense.

"Why are we waiting, then?" she said with the husky voice which she had learnt to deploy to bring the preliminaries to a close.

Once upstairs she quickly had him stripped to the waist, but a change of pace always ensured she was in charge, she found. She was determined to prolong the process of tying him up. Eventually she had one wrist firmly in place. She was about to start on the second when he interrupted.

"No, no. Only one wrist for now, I need to be able to control the pace of things. And you as well. Both wrists later."

She adopted a look which implied approval of someone who knew what they wanted.

"Now, before we get down to it, what was the third name?"

She was slightly taken aback by his persistence, but saw it as part of his direct approach in all matters.

"It was Guillaume," she said with a sudden edge to her tone.

"Guillaume? Who do you think he meant?" he asked, as she started to unbuckle his belt. Lying back and enjoying it was certainly a pleasurable prospect, based on what he had seen so far, but he needed to be clear about what she knew. "I am told we have arrested all the Guillaumes in the area, and little or nothing of note has been discovered. Are you sure?"

"You can bet he isn't called Guillaume, officially at least, if it is the one I know, and I think it will be. Haven't seen him for years now. The so called Alain pretended to be a farm labourer of some kind, and so was this Guillaume, a real one though, or at least he was born on a farm, well out in the sticks. Thanks for letting me know though. It means I can get him sorted out by your colleagues tomorrow, and I want you to make it painful. And prolonged. Just how you like it as well, I can just tell," she sighed, running her lips slowly around his navel.

His upbringing had been devoid of the physical contact and tactile pleasure taken for granted in so many families, when parents cemented the bond with their children by playing, tugging and tickling. As her blonde hair brushed across his skin, the gentle sensation produced a perfect combination of anguish and delight. When combined with her appreciative moaning, she threatened to overwhelm him completely.

His belt was finally unfastened, but as his eyes closed and his muscles began to relax, the wailing of the air raid klaxon jolted him back to reality. She immediately tried to untie him, but as her frantic endeavours became more forceful, they also became less successful, her panic palpable. The wailing became louder, and her palms were sweating. Finally, she reached into the drawer in the bed side cabinet, produced the knife, and cut him free.

They dashed down the stairs. Nicole could settle another score by letting Gerhard know the whereabouts of the real Guillaume. She would relish the account of how he had suffered. Disappointingly, she hadn't had chance to find out more about Freuntz and his activities.

For Freuntz, there were two thoughts uppermost. Firstly, if she knew about Guillaume, then he himself might be implicated. Secondly, as the low crump of anti-aircraft fire began, off to the north, he prayed fervently that he had transmitted the message correctly.

✯ ✯ ✯

Condensation was already fogging the windows of the café. Posner took out his notebook, more in hope than expectation. Rain was sweeping the streets, blown by the strong, gusting wind which still showed no sign of abating. He wiped the window for the third time. The prospect of another fruitless day was already causing his spirits to sag.

Three figures were queuing outside the bank, holding their umbrellas like grim death. As Freuntz appeared, he thrust his papers at the first figure in the queue who dutifully shuffled backwards. Umbrella firmly clamped close to his head, he looked repeatedly at his watch, apparently impatient to conclude whatever business he had, as quickly as possible.

"What happened?" Guillaume hissed from behind.

Freuntz shook his head in bewilderment.

"Not only three more shot down, but two more crashed near the reservoir. Flying blind. All operations halted. Are you sure you read the message properly?"

"Checked it over and over," replied Freuntz, staring straight ahead, but realising he didn't need to keep his voice low, as the wind swirled.

"The British want me out. Need to re-form some cells. Christmas Eve. Space for you as well- if you want. Midnight, Three Poplars Field. They won't wait, though."

"Just as well, the blonde knows who you are. Keep away from the farm if you can."

The edge had gone from Guillaume's tone. He forced his mind back to practicalities, despite an image of a sunny day with Nicole briefly threatening to cloud his train of thought.

"How did you get the information in the first place?"

"Special courier. Only five to sign. I was last."

"How about the second one?"

"Same procedure, but only three. I was last again"

Guillaume frowned, "How do you know they all signed?"

Freuntz hadn't considered it, assuming that being asked to sign last signified his status. After a brief pause, Guillaume continued, "He isn't playing you is he, narrowing down the suspects? You need to make yourself scarce, too."

"Jesus," said Freuntz, as the implications sank in.

"The blonde has to go, before she can do any more damage. Look out for yourself though, she is obviously well connected. Protected as well? It all needs to be sorted by tomorrow at twelve. The barn will be set up as we talked about, and then I'll be at the plane by midnight. You do what you can with your side of things." He began to lower his umbrella in anticipation.

As the keys began to turn in the heavy locks, Freuntz realised he didn't have long to lay his mind at rest.

"How are they missing the trains?"

"Leave that with me." The pair disappeared into the bank, briefly conducting mundane transactions they could have completed at any time. In the café, Posner was already buttoning the collar of his raincoat, knowing deep down that he would learn nothing in the bank. He set off anyway. Half way across the road he saw Freuntz emerge, wrestle with his umbrella, and set off at a furious pace.

As Guillaume brushed past Posner in the entrance, he was already castigating himself for missing the blindingly obvious. They were using the complex of lines, sidings and cuttings around the mine to change routes to confound the efforts of the British.

✧ ✧ ✧

The decision was made. As Guillaume crouched in the undergrowth, his sodden clothing meant that he could delay no longer. He had to balance how quickly dusk would fall, and how much of the saturated slurry he could dig, before his hip made further progress impossible.

The perimeter fence had long since fallen into disrepair. He gingerly eased himself through a gap. His feet squelched in the mud. He crept slowly towards the middle of 'The Three Sisters', the three huge slag heaps which loomed forbiddingly against the darkening sky.

He went through the story Raymond had told him so many times, embellished in his own inimitable style, but without question a story of courage and resolve. The signal gantry Raymond had christened 'The Cross of St Agnes' remained, rusting but identifiable by its flaking red and white paint. The name had been given by Raymond and his fellow miners as they emerged into the daylight to end their ordeal, a reflection of their belief that their prayers had been answered.

Fifty paces, Raymond had said. Guillaume made allowances for the differences in stature. He would need forty. After thirty, he was at the foot of the slope. He made a rough and ready calculation and began to scramble up through the brambles. With a quick look back to check his bearings, he began to dig.

The tangle of vegetation which had flourished since the mine closed proved to be a help, not a hindrance. The mat of roots bound the soil together, and initially he was able to remove the earth in solid cubes. He stacked them with care to begin with. But as the pit deepened, his frustrations began to mount. His hip began to ache. Rain was pouring down his neck. As fast as he dug, the pit filled with water which was running down the slag heap in rivulets.

With complete darkness about to descend, Guillaume was ready to abandon the task as hopeless. His digging was becoming less rhythmic. Fatigue and frustration took hold, his cursing more vitriolic. Then, with one desperate, scything action, the tip of his spade stuck in something more solid than mud.

Intrigued, he carefully levered the spade free. He began to clear the mud. As he did so, his heart began to race. There it was, rotting but whole, the pit prop which supported the entry to the adit was intact, seventy five years after mining had first commenced. Even better, as he removed more mud, the cast iron plate which had blocked the entrance was there as well, rusting but solid.

He suddenly remembered the danger he was in. Immediately, he put down his spade. One spark and he would be blown to pieces. Carefully, he began to carve away at the rotting wood. Eventually, his knife plunged through into thin air. There it was. The rush of pungent gas almost overwhelmed him at the same time as his hopes soared. He quickly plugged the gap with mud.

Methane. The plan was still a possibility. With difficulty, he extricated himself from the pit. As he slithered to the foot of the slag heap, he gave silent thanks to Raymond for his bloody mindedness. But even more for his meticulous recollections.

The old warrior would be avenged.

# Chapter Twenty Nine

He ran his tongue along his lips once more. He could still taste her. Locked in his office, Freuntz had only been able to focus on the task in hand in sporadic bursts. The morning had changed everything. His sense of what was and was not important had been shattered for ever, and in so fundamental a fashion that he questioned whether he should continue at all.

In front of him lay the papers, which he had finally organised to produce a coherent series of accusations. Some were founded in fact. Others had been fabricated. They were damning, when considered in the round. The hours of forging and redrafting appeared to tell a compelling story. The accounts of fictitious witness statements, print outs of radio transcripts, bank statements, and logs of Wolfgang's whereabouts provided just some of the documentary underpinning. Freuntz was numb.

The fierce knock on the door interrupted his descent into self-pity. Mayerling was taken aback by Freuntz, when he finally opened the door. His cheeks were drained of colour, his eyes were red rimmed, and his responses hesitant. Mayerling was moved to ask if he was well, expecting little by way of response.

"No, no, I am fine, honestly, probably just the long hours.... same for all of us. Any news from the hospital?"

"Yes, just a check up, nothing major. He should be back by five."

"That is good... encouraging to know," Freuntz concluded. Mayerling handed over the documents and bade him a temporary farewell.

The phone call came at 2, by which time he was ready to play the final cards. The file would go by special courier to Berlin. As he made his way down to the car, he placed the evidence about Wolfgang in a sealed envelope on Gerhard's desk.

✳ ✳ ✳

Finally the rain had relented, but the mist which shrouded the low lying fields lent an ethereal quality to the journey to the Lafarge mansion. It left Freuntz alone with his ghosts and his conscience, always an uncomfortable experience.

Having presented his papers, he was left to wait in the hall downstairs. Determined efforts to engender some festive spirit were under way. A huge Christmas Tree had been lavishly decorated, beneath which a series of would be choristers performed their favourite carols.

Three quarters of an hour later, Wolfgang appeared at the top of the staircase, and summoned him with an imperious wave. Introductions were formal rather than friendly. The idea that the wait downstairs had been deliberately prolonged began to niggle Freuntz. Was the forced formality confirmation that he was a suspect, and that one false move would be fatal? Was his loyalty being questioned? He was almost past caring. Almost, but not quite.

Wolfgang provided a brisk summary of the current situation, but revealed nothing Freuntz hadn't been able to work out for himself. His tone was crisp, but tinged with an underlying edge of triumph that he, and he alone, had brought the project to fruition. If he could have preened himself he would have, thought Freuntz. He was determined to wait his turn. He began slowly and deliberately, aware that hubris made any bait he intended to present all the more tempting. It was now or never.

"You must be relieved, relieved and very proud." The massage of his ego had begun. "The 5 p.m. conference should be a triumph for you. Christmas Day, tomorrow. What a present to the German people. 'The Revenge Weapon' virtually in place. What an achievement... and in the spirit of presents, here is one from me." Freuntz spread the maps on the table, and piled the supporting documents by the side.

"The Resistance, if indeed it has been The Resistance, have been active, I don't need to tell you that, and quite successful in trying to make it look like it wasn't them. Suggests some level of sophistication. Impossible to pin their radio transmissions down as well, even though we have extra detection vans. Personally, I think we would have had them, had it not been for these new broadcasts... and from right in the middle of Veziers. As I said, quite sophisticated, but not so sophisticated as to be undetectable. Here is their weakness... and how we... you, can finally bring this situation to a final... and triumphant conclusion." Freuntz was staring right at Wolfgang. He knew he was ready to bite.

"The key is how they keep in touch before communicating with the British. Look at these." Freuntz passed a sheet with a number of dates and times on.

"Activity of some kind on all those nights. Now look at these." Freuntz passed a sheaf of radio transcripts with the dates underlined, across the table. Wolfgang's eyes began to narrow in concentration.

"They use all kinds of nonsense phrases, British phrases and slang, horoscopes, and as we will see, something they think we have no idea about... cricket. Lots of supposed meetings, dinner arrangements, and parties as well. But look at this one, for example. They always use Sagittarius and it's always a fourteen letter phrase, 'fair to middling' for example, 'better days soon' another. On their own they make no sense. But that is just it. They aren't messages of information, they are messages to the British that they will be broadcasting later. Have a look for yourself."

Wolfgang scanned the first three, but the prospect of one final triumph meant that his attention was focused on planning ahead, not reflective analysis.

"Now, this is where you have to admire them." Freuntz unrolled some large sheets of grease proof paper, each covered in initials, through which the map, covered in red circles, could be seen clearly. "It was this that proved the most troublesome. But is actually so simple- as with most codes- once you have the thinking behind it."

"How do you know all this?" Wolfgang asked, in a tone which bordered on reverence.

"It's all down to an English prisoner we captured on a trench raid, Major Faulkner. He tried to explain it to us... he was very cool under pressure. He explained what a pavilion was. See, that's the p. So then you have the sheets this way up. And the other key to understanding it is that you can bat right handed or left. That changes the fielding positions. So does which end you bowl from. But anyhow, let's look at one."

Wolfgang picked a message at random and Freuntz overlaid the sheets as instructed.

"P-Pavilion end... R-right hand... fsl-forward short leg. Wolfgang peered expectantly at the sheets, but was visibly disappointed when the red circles on the map were still clearly visible.

"Try another." Wolfgang obliged, but once again the circles were still visible.

"Now try one from a night when they attacked."

Wolfgang obliged in a grudging tone. Freuntz manipulated the sheets He gave a triumphant yell as Freuntz placed 'l l' on the sheets below. A red circle, the disused Leclerc factory, was obscured. "Long leg," Freuntz explained. He was completely ignored by the besotted Wolfgang. Two more successful demonstrations and Wolfgang was ecstatic, fists clenched, eyes staring, thumping Freuntz violently in the middle of his back in triumph.

Freuntz realised he needed to retain his composure amidst the euphoria. He allowed Wolfgang to let off a little more steam before presenting his prize evidence. He read out the latest intercept. There was a need for an urgent update. The air raids were failing. "Dining at 8-30, digestifs at 11" added a whimsical, mocking tone. He overlaid the sheets with meticulous care in order to build up the tension. As he laid the final sheet, the initials 'd.e.c.' - deep extra cover- obscured the Rochaux farm. Wolfgang began hopping from one leg to the other in glee.

He was already savouring his final triumph. He could wrap up the final meeting at 6. The train could look after itself, especially if the fog persisted. Even if it didn't, he would be there to ensure the 'celebrations' at the Rochaux farm went with a swing. As he peered into the swirling mist, he exhaled slowly, desperate for some recognition that he had discharged his responsibilities, and the burden would now be lifted from his shoulders. He was oblivious to the final congratulations Freuntz was proffering. Freuntz wished him well, and closed the door quietly behind him.

Wolfgang gestured to the courier in the courtyard below, his engine already revving, that his journey would not be necessary.

✯ ✯ ✯

The delay in completing all the check-ups had infuriated Gerhard, but as he settled behind the desk he was relishing the task ahead. His file on Wolfgang ran to twelve pages, closely argued, meticulously phrased, and compelling in its arguments. He took some time to open the envelope. But as he scanned the evidence which Freuntz had provided, he couldn't resist allowing a smile to play on his lips.

Uncovering the real identity of Guillaume justified his strategy of using Nicole, and the explanation of how the messages had been deciphered elicited a nod of approval. The hand written note from Freuntz read,

"Remember what you said about the best way to conceal a traitor is to make it look like you are trying to unmask them. Look overleaf." It boosted his self-regard even further. The original message about the meeting was there, along with its deciphering. Only one thing had been changed by Freuntz. The time of the meeting was set for 9. Clipped to it was a terse reply, also deciphered,

'White tie and tails?'

He scanned the file one last time, and checked that his revolver was loaded. As he began to put on his overcoat, Posner rushed in.

"The woman at The Café Gasquet, she is dead. Dead! Not sure when it happened. Stabbed! Face down in the bath."

For a moment Gerhard was taken aback. But only for a moment. He quickly realised that there was little which could be done, given the momentous events which lay ahead. She had played her part to perfection. The secrets of their relationship had died with her. What could be better? There was work to be done.

He scribbled a brusque note for Mayerling, outlining how the investigation should commence. He was in no mood to look at any further paperwork and waved the telex operator away. If he had scanned it, even briefly, he would have seen that the long sought information, wired from Germany, had profound implications for him. It began,

Wolfgang Priessler, Born Erlingauer, D.o.B.13 Dec, 1910, and continued,

Father: Heinrich Priessler, Born Cologne, D.o.B. 6 June, 1880. Occupation –Coal Miner.

Mother: Eva Priessler Maiden name –Carlsson. Born Wolfsburg, D.o.B. 7 April, 1881. Occupation–Clerk*.

✲ ✲ ✲

Freuntz realised there was nothing more to be done at the barn, other than wait. He pulled his collar up, blew on his hands and crouched behind the hay bales in the yard. The implications of what he had done made it impossible to ignore his past any longer. He was back at La Pigalle.

✲ ✲ ✲

"Come on sarge, plenty of time yet," Mandel slurred.

"Have another," added Groener.

The warmth of the alcohol and the warmth of the invitation had suppressed the alarm bells; here had been a chance to join the knowing banter, to pretend that he was like them, even though they-and he-knew he wasn't.

After an hour or so, Sophie had appeared. Lucky Heller, he had thought. Once she had slipped beside him, from the corner of his eye he had become aware of their barely concealed smirks, thought he heard their suggestive, half-finished sentences. The closeness, the aroma, her scent, and the complete absence of bells had led to a giddy intoxication which owed nothing to alcohol. He had been oblivious to the fact that his 'kinder' had now deserted the field, to watch events unfold.

Now, they were alone. She had known the buttons to push and the strings to pull. In no time he had begun to open up, albeit in his customary faltering manner. She had also known her role; to listen, to prompt and to suggest.

She led him upstairs. His head was swimming, the tumult below, receding. The suppressed groans and muffled grunts penetrated the flimsy walls. They had been the only accompaniment to his pounding heart.

Once inside, she had moved with a practised ease. Before he could summon up a response, he had been stripped to his army issue underwear, a mottled grey in contrast to his weatherbeaten face and milk white torso.

He had moved to speak, but she gently placed a finger on his lips. She gazed intently into his eyes. On removing her blouse, the prickle of tension at the back of his neck had dissipated, as quickly as it had surfaced. Before him had been a vision which was in complete contrast to the image he had built up in his mind. It was an image reliant solely on the relentless sexual badinage of The Musketeers.

No wrinkles, no sagging, no furrowed flab, or missing teeth. And above all, no underwear reminiscent of barrage balloons. It was underwear she had slaved so hard in her own time to create, intricately hand stitched, entirely from the fragments and scraps she had smuggled out of the mill.

He had been rendered inert, yet alive. The buttons on his underwear had provided limited resistance to her seamstress fingers. She couldn't take her eyes off the cross shaped scar tissue which disfigured his thigh. Beneath the flimsy counterpane, upon the threadbare sheets, the aroma of countless previous assignations had still lingered. But her earnest eye contact muffled the bells still further. His tense, fearful rigidity had been no match for the soothing sighs, the flickering touch and the seasoned skill with which she went about her business. The challenge of a client whose every response was governed by a stoic acceptance of all that life threw at him, had spurred her on.

The tension was finally evaporating. But the bells wouldn't be silenced. She continued to weave her tactile web, but the images flickered. His mother, Meinke and above all, The Musketeers. What would they make of him now? His breathing was deeper. The faces had been leering at his vulnerability, so long concealed. But now revealed. His eyes were closed. She was moaning. The images swirled, the strokes firmer, more rhythmic. The voices taunted. His groaning had become louder. The moment of release.

With a feral strength, for which she had been no match, he had flipped her over, raised her up, and with a few grunting thrusts, accompanied by a barely decipherable yelp, it was all over.

Almost immediately, the guilt, the fear, the years of repressed emotion had overwhelmed him. He had rolled away, sobbing uncontrollably as he begged for forgiveness.

She had cradled him in her arms and stroked his face until sleep came.

✳ ✳ ✳

His anguished indecision about whether to return upstairs with a farewell note had eventually been resolved. And only just in time. The muffled shrieks were being subdued by a half naked figure he realised was Mandel. Groener was on his knees, removing the last of her clothing. Heller was virtually naked. Fear, panic and lust had galvanised Freuntz.

The adrenaline surged. The instincts honed by years of trench warfare had asserted themselves, second nature to him, completely alien to them. A kidney punch felled Groener. A brutal forearm pole axed Mandel. Heller's combination of amazement and nakedness rendered him especially vulnerable to the venom with which Freuntz aimed his right foot.

"You fucking scum, fuck off out of here before I kill the three of you!"

But it was the instigator of the whole, shabby debacle, who had attracted his attention. Grabbing him by the windpipe, he had propped the hapless Heller against the table leg. As he was about to administer a potentially fatal kick to Heller's lolling jaw, the grubby, degenerate, nature of the whole episode drained the avenging aggression from Freuntz, just in time to save Heller's life. With a brutal heave, Heller was shuddering on the floor. Freuntz had pressed a half hearted foot to the back of his neck, thinking what might be. But deciding against it.

Chased back to Germany by the French, this fiasco, and to cap it all, rumours of an armistice. November 9$^{th}$, 1918. It had been a ghastly day.

# Chapter Thirty

Freuntz slumped against the bales, his head in his hands, his mind spinning.

Suddenly, the sound of a car, creeping forward some distance away, forced him to concentrate. The engine was switched off. The footsteps became louder. He pressed his lips into the bales so that his breath would not reveal his presence. Through the gap, it was clear that the figure, inching on tip toe towards the barn, was Wolfgang. The silence confirmed that he was alone. Freuntz had left the door ajar, deliberately. He watched. Wolfgang slid through.

The temptation to settle things with Wolfgang required a huge effort of self-denial. He stared at his watch and forced himself not to replay the day's events. Five…ten…twenty minutes. The cold was beginning to gnaw. The silence was broken by a second car, negotiating its way slowly up the frosty track. As before, the figure took careful, measured steps so as not to alert anyone to their presence. It was Gerhard, revolver in hand. He, too, slipped silently through the gap.

Once inside, it took Gerhard a moment to adjust to the gloom, illuminated by just two oil lamps. He had no doubt about who he would find.

"Hands up! Hands up! And don't turn round, or it will be finished right now. Heroics on the Russian Front won't help you now. Your choice."

Wolfgang was in the pit which had concealed the generator, the pit which contained the printing press partially revealed to the right. Bank notes, packets of cigarettes and bundles of blank paper were strewn amongst the straw, between the two pits. But it was what lay in the straw to the left which excited Gerhard the most. The radio.

"Oh this is sweet, so sweet. Caught in the act, and yes, this is the final act, your final act. Keep your hands up and your eyes forward."

Gerhard pressed the revolver against Wolfgang's neck and carefully removed his holster. The power, the fate of another resting on his whim, it produced the first tingle in his bladder.

"One of the elite … a traitor….it is too good to believe… too much… but, but, too shocking." There was a more calculating edge now. "Yes, truly shocking. The fate of Germany lay in your hands, but despite your supposed superiority you were not equal to the task. The fate of thousands, no millions, and you put it all at risk for a whore. Conveniently for you, probably too conveniently, she was found murdered earlier today. Can you see how this is beginning to look?" Gerhard emphasised his power by gently drawing his revolver across the nape of Wolfgang's neck.

"Yes, convenient. That is a perfect summary of the outcomes of your repeated blundering. No doubt your incompetence will be used at Staff Colleges of the future as a classic study in how not to do it. The old man at the bridge, we had them. Openly colluding with a black marketer, conveniently also dead as a result of your intervention. Enriching yourself at the expense of The Reich. And with forged money."

The torrent of accusations, the dire predicament he was now in, and in at the hands of an inferior, rendered Wolfgang speechless. Gerhard allowed a brief silence and then continued.

"Your henchman, Freuntz, told me about the money… about your ego…he even mentioned the tablets, prohibited for all German soldiers." The mixture of mockery and accusation convinced Wolfgang that enquiring about the circumstances of Nicole's death would invite yet more withering contempt. Still facing away from his captor, he slowly shook his head at the revelation of his betrayal by Freuntz, his mentor. A slow burning fury began to fuel the search for a response to the onslaught. The revelation about the codes had not only diffused his suspicions, but duped him so perfectly.

"Your authority, your power, the façade you have maintained to conceal the treachery you have committed, I am going to take the greatest pleasure in stripping it away, layer by layer… yes layer by layer, incident by incident, calamitous misjudgement by calamitous misjudgement …. Or was it misjudgement? Could it be carefully calculated treachery, more like? Yes… strip it away… and that's what you are going to do now. Strip."

Wolfgang was astounded by the command, mystified as to its purpose. He realised that although he was in no position to challenge it, it might offer the opportunity to turn the tables on his gloating captor. He gradually lowered his hands. He began to unbutton his jacket.

"The woman…dead you say?" he enquired in hushed tones. "Dead? You can't hang that one on me, you know full well. If anybody had a motive to see the back of her, well… who more than you?"

Wolfgang had grasped how desperate his predicament was. One wrong comment could be fatal. Equally, simply accepting the situation held out little promise of a favourable outcome. He risked a brief half turn. He recognised that the glazed stare and smirk of triumph on Gerhard's face meant that the adrenalin was pumping. However, the momentary interruption in his triumphal oratory suggested that his response had struck home. He dropped the jacket to the floor. He began to unbutton his shirt, blowing on his hands to prolong the process.

"As for Freuntz, never more than a loyal functionary. In the great scheme of things, organisation men… lapdogs… followers… procedures, they count for little. I could summon up a dozen of his type in twenty four hours." Wolfgang was now speaking in a measured and calm way. The thrust of the sentence carried extra menace. He needed to return to the area where Gerhard was most vulnerable.

"She spoke a lot about you… a lot. She told me about your times together… and what you got up to." He looked up at Gerhard. He was perspiring, despite the cold. Wolfgang allowed a knowing smile to linger on his lips. "Always made interesting listening."

Silence was now his ally, ridicule his weapon. Wolfgang knew that for Gerhard, the fact that she had spoken about his weaknesses, and that they were common knowledge, was a devastating blow to his self-esteem. He let the sentence linger as he removed his shirt.

"Of course, more realistically... what you didn't get up to."

For Gerhard, the dripping contempt, with its implied indictment of his capabilities, began to summon up long buried memories. His response was always the same when the blows rained down. It didn't matter whether they were verbal or physical. He felt his self confidence start to crumble. He was paralysed into inarticulacy. The familiar sensation grew stronger.

Here, though, was a chance to confront his demons, turn the situation to his advantage and deliver a humiliating blow of his own to his tormentor. His triumph would be total. Wolfgang was now stripped to the waist. He fumbled unconvincingly with his belt. He turned to face Gerhard. He slowly raised his eyes. Gerhard had dropped his trousers, and was naked from the waist down.

"Well, she was right," Wolfgang sneered. "No chance of much action from you. I mean look at..." To his amazement Gerhard responded,

"Go on, go on."

Unsure where the instructions might lead, and perplexed by the pleading tone in Gerhard's voice, the removal of the safety catch was all the encouragement he needed.

"You could have done with some of those tablets. I still have some. Night after night, I mean...and you paid her... call yourself a man?"

"Keep going...keep going..." The hoarse tone in is voice indicated that the insults were having the desired effect.

"Don't know how she managed to stay awake."

"Keep going... keep going..." Gerhard gasped, pleaded, begged. Gerhard pointed the gun right between Wolfgang's eyes. He closed them, dreading his final moment.

"No! No... don't stop, don't stop!"

The dam burst. Gerhard urinated all over Wolfgang. He gasped and groaned in the ecstasy of release.

As he crept into the barn, Briedel's emotions overwhelmed him. The sight of his lover, stripped to the waist, submissive to, and encouraged by, another semi-naked man whose anguished responses left little doubt as to what they were engaged in, was too much. He aimed straight at Gerhard and fired.

In the same instant, the first tongue of blue flame raced across the straw to ignite the petrol cans, buried beneath the straw in the corner. They erupted with a deafening roar. Gerhard slumped forward into the pit and onto a bewildered Wolfgang, who desperately tried to lever him aside. Too late. The next tongue of flame snaked towards the pit. It ignited the cans, concealed beneath the generator. The experimental petroleum, supplied by the British, exploded in an instant, a blue tongue of flame bathing the barn in a surreal half light.

Its gel like consistency was designed to adhere to flesh. And then incinerate it. All oxygen was sucked from the immediate surroundings. In the pit, the temperature briefly reached two thousand degrees.

The searing pain, as his skin scorched and flayed, could not be eased by the piercing shrieks. His paralysis doomed him to a lingering death amidst the inferno. Not unlike the death suffered by so many at the hands of the Blowtorch Battalion.

Gerhard's last memory was the overwhelming smell of cloves, as the tobacco stocks were incinerated. Christmas Day, the most miserable day of all.

✣ ✣ ✣

As he set off towards Three Poplars Field, Freuntz resisted the temptation to look back at the conflagration. He should really have expected Briedel. His arrival had provided an unexpected bonus.

He lengthened his stride.

✣ ✣ ✣

The brilliant moonlight meant that it didn't take Guillaume long to locate the adit once again. He laboriously scraped the mud away from the supporting beam. His dilemma had been whether simply to blow up the tracks at the earliest opportunity, or delay as long as possible so that the ensuing confusion would provide the ideal cover for his escape. He calculated how long it would take to get to Three Poplars Field, and opted to leave it as late as possible.

Once the beam was revealed, he painstakingly scooped away the rotting wood. His arm was aching. He didn't dare go faster. He combined the plastic explosive, the timers and the fuses. Their maximum time was five minutes. He prayed that Raymond had been right- that no seams ran any further west, the direction in which he would be fleeing.

He looked at his watch.10-36. He gave thanks for so much else he had learnt from Raymond since attending his first Communist Party meetings. The second of his burials beneath the rock falls had led to his miraculous escape via the adit. Guillaume packed the second pad of explosive against the framework.

The costs of mining in such an unstable area were becoming prohibitive, long before the Depression forced the closure in 1931. Raymond's miraculous escape had led to the adit being temporarily sealed. But when torrential rain caused a landslide from the slag heap, burying it under six feet of liquid mud, forty eight hours later, it seemed that nature had provided an effective- and cheap-solution. When the mine closed for good, later that year, it was but one of many tasks left unfinished.

He looked at his watch again.10-47. He began to force the final wad of explosive carefully against the beam. He set the fuses for 11, allowing himself five minutes to escape. He realised that he would be airborne very soon.

He carefully removed the mud with which he had packed the gap on his previous reconnaissance. He allowed himself a sigh of satisfaction. He inhaled the gas which was now beginning to escape. He wiped his hands, straightened up, and in a last tribute to Raymond, came rigidly to attention. He held his salute and mouthed silently,

"Vive La France."

As he scrambled down the bank, the shrill whistle in the distance indicated that the train was passing the signal box. His spine tingled. Should he alter the fuses to be certain to blow up the train as well? One final gesture. One final coup. One back for Raymond, Olivier, and all the others.

The rhythmic clatter of the train was becoming louder. He was uncharacteristically hesitant. He mopped his brow, came to a halt, and tried to impose some order on his thought processes. It was tempting, so tempting. But he knew where duty lay. He ducked through the gap in the perimeter fencing, and set off for the rendezvous.

✫ ✫ ✫

Pieter Hansen had first noticed the smell when the breeze finally dropped that afternoon. Brought up in the heart of The Ruhr, he was familiar with the hazards of coal mining. He knew what methane smelt like. He had first tried to contact Wolfgang at 6-30, only to be told that he had already left the conference. Two further attempts were to no avail. His final call to the yards in Veziers was dismissed contemptuously, in less than thirty seconds.

The first shaft, sunk in 1871 and capped off in 1912, lay between the tracks, right where Hansen was issuing his final commands, as the train trundled towards him. The train was slowing to negotiate the newly laid track. The ground was vibrating. He paused. His men awaited their next orders. He couldn't be sure if the vibrations were caused by the train. He received his answer. The rumbling reached a muffled crescendo. A huge tongue of orange flame erupted with a thunderous roar beside him.

A hailstorm of gravel, sleepers and fragments of track were blasted skywards. In rapid succession, four other huge eruptions; the remaining mine buildings starkly black against the leaping flames, the troops paralysed into fatal inactivity. The shock waves thrust them first one way then another.

Any attempt to react was rendered futile, as the train jumped the tracks and ploughed into the framework supporting the overhead conveyor belt. Eight tankers carrying the rocket fuel for the missiles were dragged against a heap of long abandoned machinery, and then a pile of rusting girders. The first four survived intact, but not the fifth. The fuel gushed. It ignited with a deafening blast, consuming the remaining tankers and wagons in one all encompassing, violet tinged fireball.

The aerodynamic perfection of the missiles was unrecognisable. All two hundred and ten were reduced to smouldering, mangled scrap. Equally unrecognisable were Hansen and twenty seven of his colleagues, identifiable only from their dental records.

✭ ✭ ✭

As he approached Three Poplars Field, Freuntz realised that his footprints were clearly visible against the hoar frost which was now covering the ground. He dropped into the drainage ditch. In a token effort at deception he waded thirty yards to his right, the icy water lapping around his thighs. He levered himself up the gently sloping embankment, squatted low in the brambles, and prepared to wait. Fatigue was beginning to catch up with him. He began to shiver visibly in his dripping clothes, his eyes repeatedly threatening to droop. The emotional turmoil of the day's events began to take its toll.

He hadn't realised he had fallen asleep, nor how long for. A slow rumble away to the right indicated that a plane was somewhere near. Immediately, the noise decreased. But as he rubbed his eyes and slapped his face in order to refocus his attention, he remembered that the plane would use the reservoir as a marker, before turning into its descent.

The noise began to increase. The fingers of mist now appearing, then disappearing, made it difficult to see across the field. Above the mist, the Three Poplars stood out clearly. The sky to the east had a faint orange tinge. He peered into the distance. The noise of the aircraft intensified. Suddenly, there it was, the 3-1 3-1 3-1 identification signal being flashed as confirmation. It must be Guillaume.

Feuntz knew better than to reveal himself too soon. The plane roared past, no more than twenty metres in front of him. He saw a shadowy figure emerge from beneath the poplars, crouching in anticipation. The plane, having turned at the far end of the field, taxied towards him, engines revving, desperate to be away.

It came briefly to a standstill. Guillaume ducked beneath the wings and clambered inside. The mist seemed somehow thicker, now. Any delay would make the take-off even more hazardous. Freuntz was about to straighten up.

Suddenly, away to his left, he spotted a figure wading laboriously through the water. With what seemed like a supreme physical effort the figure negotiated the embankment, paused to gather what seemed to be some last reserves of strength and began to stand upright, removing a revolver in the process. Briedel!

Freuntz began to scramble through the undergrowth the sound of his footsteps, obscured by the roaring engines. He was within ten metres. Briedel was swaying as if he might collapse at any moment. He required both hands to hold the gun steady. He fired into the gloom.

From the door of the plane, Guillaume, ignoring the shrieks from the pilot, resigned himself to escaping alone. Torn between reluctance and redemption, he aimed a three second burst of machine gun fire in retaliation. He slammed the door of the plane shut. The engines roared.

Freuntz felt the bullets rip his stomach open. He doubled up in agony, the strength draining from his legs. He toppled forwards. He rolled down the bank into the icy water, face down. The shock momentarily galvanised him into turning over, desperate to avoid drowning. With a huge effort he was half turned. From above, the lifeless body of Briedel toppled onto him, his uniform in tatters, one side of his face scorched, one eye sightless.

The weight pushed Freuntz beneath the water. He gasped in pain at the impact. His strength was ebbing fast. Briedel loomed above him, pinning him to bottom of the ditch. Their faces touched. He was staring at Freuntz in the same piercing, accusing manner as the children of Zhubrevno. Freuntz felt the water filing his lungs. The feeble gurgling slowed. The visceral human instinct to survive ebbed, replaced by the fatal acceptance that it was over, an acceptance of whatever fate awaited him.

He was back in the ditch on the road to St Valery, the body of Briedel, not Meinke, above him, the liquid not warm, but icy. This time there would be no reprieve. Nor did he deserve one.

His will finally broken, his body went limp.

# Chapter Thirty One

Perched precariously on the table, still sticky from celebrations the previous evening, she had fixed the last sprig of holly in place. The bar had been deserted, and hence too good an opportunity to miss. Nicole lifted the lid, and summoning up all her expertise had begun to tap out the tune to 'Silent Night', one finger at a time.

She was becoming slightly more tuneful when Freuntz appeared. He had waited for her to look up, not wanting to interrupt her endeavours.

"A hidden talent, mademoiselle, very impressive." She shrugged modestly in response and closed the lid.

"I have been sent to collect you. He wants you at the Lafarge place by noon. I think he sees you as a present to himself." Nicole looked at the clock and realised that it was not yet 9-45.

"I can see what you are thinking… a bit early. But I thought it would give us time to resume where we left off the other night." He thrust forward his hands in a gesture of supplication. "I will make it well worth your while, and that way three of us will get a present."

The determined, self-confident tone was there again, and given that her shift didn't start until six, why not?

He had followed her up the stairs, breathing camly, his gaze fixed straight ahead, her hips already swaying. She opened the door. Freuntz inhaled a combination of fragrances and aromas which seemed to capture the essence of Christmas perfectly. For a moment he had been tempted to waver, but Nicole's pragmatism helped him restore his resolve.

"How do you want it?"

"With the blindfold this time, but tie me up later... a special treat... it is Christmas."

A furious knock on the door had brought a sigh of frustration from Nicole, but after a brief conversation she turned to reassure him.

"This will only take five minutes, get yourself ready. No more than five minutes."

She had been as good as her word. She had feigned approval of his enthusiasm and the sight of his clothes strewn all over the floor. His muscular torso was still impressive, the first flecks of grey at his temples the only clue as to his age.

"Well, let's make a start," she had said, as she produced the velvet blindfold. He lay perfectly still, as she secured it with a vigour she knew he would appreciate. She briefly brushed against him, allowing the scent of her perfume to increase his sense of anticipation further. She took each of his hands, and instructed him to grasp the wrought iron bed frame.

"I expect you to be- instruct you to be- in that position when I return. I want to see your veins bulging." She had developed a taste for role play, and the dramatic element amused and excited her. The fact that it paid extra was simply a bonus. Once inside the bathroom, the decision was straightforward. A special occasion required her special underwear. She intended to make him wait.

To her surprise, when she re-emerged, he had obeyed her to the letter. Unseeing and inert, his body taut in anticipation, she traced the silken restraints along his outstretched arms, eliciting a prolonged sigh of appreciation. She knew to retain complete control of the tempo, and soon the low groans told her it was time begin the massage. She languidly rubbed her body against his chest, the lustrous silk exciting his senses, ensuring that her hair brushed against every part of his skin.

"Do not move... I don't want to have to use the wax." Freuntz inhaled the pungent smoke deeply, and mumbled acceptance as she wafted the candle beneath his nostrils. He was aware that she was changing position as he felt her astride him, her feet beside his ears, still only partially naked.

The pre-orgasmic moaning from beneath served only to encourage her. She was in control, a control she relished and was determined to exploit. He was her slave, and she could decide the pace. As well as the pain. The blindfold was secure. The knife was in position.

But as she lowered the sheet tentatively, she was astounded by the sight- red, angry and raised- which was revealed. He took her audible gasp as a sign of anticipation of what lay ahead, and an appreciation of the sight before her. She was about to lower her lips, but recoiled instead. There it was. The cross shaped scar which ran the length of his thigh.

"Pa.." she began, but her reaction had already told him that this was the time. He locked his calves behind her neck and felt for the knife. With a sweeping arc he thrust it upwards into her stomach.

"… pa"

Experience told him to twist the knife on the way out, and he plunged it in again, repeating the twist. Blood gushed onto the sheets. He forced her head down onto the mattress to silence her screams. He began to extricate himself from the tangle of limbs, his chest smeared with blood. Her breath was becoming shallower. He bent over her to deliver the final blow. The anguished gasps couldn't disguise the word she repeated, more feebly each time.

"Papa!"

He relaxed his grip on the knife. Blood rushed to his head and he collapsed against the bedside cabinet. He dug his thumbs into his temple, his stare transfixed. She raised her arm to point to the corner of the room.

"The box… the box…"

Her mouth was moving more feebly by the second, rendering her words inaudible. With one last, croaking, whisper she attempted to turn her head, her eyes already glazed. Her body was soon still, the room silent apart from his frenzied breathing. He stared, mouth gaping. He shook his head. Soon the sobbing began, the first time he had cried since childhood. It convulsed his body as the consequences of what he had done began to register.

He couldn't stop. He forced himself to look at her, face down on the bed, the sheets soaking up the blood. He was speechless, the sobbing slowly replaced by a silent shuddering. He couldn't touch the luxurious, blood drenched underwear, so tactile so recently. It was a haunting yet tangible link to the evening at La Pigalle, seared into his memory all those years before. He lent forward and buried his head in his hands.

After what seemed an age, Freuntz realised that he had to look in the box. He removed the lid. The tears resumed. The ribbons, the material Old Man Hoffmann had sourced for him, the hand drawn birthday cards still in their envelopes, which he had posted from different towns, the different handwriting styles, the embossed paper which had taken ages to save for. He shook his head, trying to imagine why he had gone to all that trouble. He opened another envelope. The scribbled farewell note from La Pigalle served only to reinforce what might have been, had circumstances conspired differently.

But it was the letter which Madame Chalroix had written to Nicole which he lingered over longest. He tried to assimilate the story of the daughter he never knew. The description of him was both detailed and complimentary, given the brevity of their encounter. It was clear that she had wanted Nicole to know as much as possible about him, and it could only have been recounted to her by Sophie, hence the description of his physical features in such detail, determined to fix a lasting image of him in Nicole's mind.

The tenderness of the description was overwhelming him. He looked around the room. He grabbed the threadbare towel. He turned her over. The blood was no longer flowing. He tried in desperation to wipe around the wounds. The wounds he had inflicted. He pressed gently. To his horror, the blood began to ooze again. The realisation that there was a semblance of life left, but a life he had extinguished, galvanised him. He pressed his lips to the widest gash. The taste was alluring. Still there was life. But not for long. The trickle stopped. He straightened up. He saw his reflection in the mirror. He wiped his mouth with the back of his hand, then licked it until the last smear was gone. He placed a gentle kiss on her lips.

He decided to place her in the bath, her expression serene, her blonde hair tousled. He lifted her gently, cradling her in his arms. He watched the bath fill. He cursed the speed with which the water trickled. As he lowered her, he took meticulous care to protect her head. He picked up the nail scissors and removed a lock of hair.

He realised that what he had done had required what he had despised in Wolfgang all along, a ferocious will. The devastating consequences of its unthinking application had predictably resulted in tragedy once again. He dressed slowly, eyes glazed, fixed on the lifeless body.

A long day stretched ahead. Momentarily, he doubted whether he would be able to see it through, whether he indeed did have the will. One last, lingering look at the bathtub reinforced his doubts.

Made in the USA
Charleston, SC
10 August 2012